D1713972

Approaches to
Teaching Tolstoy's
Anna Karenina

Approaches to Teaching
World Literature

Joseph Gibaldi, series editor

For a complete listing of titles,
see the last pages of this book.

Approaches to
Teaching Tolstoy's
Anna Karenina

Edited by

Liza Knapp

and

Amy Mandelker

The Modern Language Association of America
New York   2003

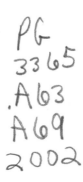

© 2003 by The Modern Language Association of America
All rights reserved
Printed in the United States of America

For information about obtaining permission to reprint material from
MLA book publications, send your request by mail (see address below),
e-mail (permissions@mla.org), or fax (646 458-0030).

Library of Congress Cataloging-in-Publication Data

Approaches to teaching Tolstoy's Anna Karenina / edited by Liza Knapp and Amy Mandelker.
    p.   cm. — (Approaches to teaching world literature, ISSN 1059-1133 ; 78)
            Includes bibliographical references and index.
        ISBN 0-87352-904-9 (cloth) — ISBN 0-87352-905-7 (pbk.)
1. Tolstoy, Leo, graf, 1828–1910. Anna Karenina. 2. Tolstoy, Leo, graf, 1828–1910—Study and
    teaching.   I. Knapp, Liza. II. Mandelker, Amy. III. Series.
        PG3365.A63 A69 2003   891.73'3—dc21   2002153212

Cover illustration of the paperback edition: *The Gare Saint-Lazare: Arrival of a Train* (1877), by
Claude Monet. Oil on canvas. Photo by David Matthews. © President and Fellows of Harvard
College. Courtesy of the Fogg Art Museum, Harvard University Art Museums, bequest from the
Collection of Maurice Wertheim, class of 1906.

Printed on recycled paper

Published by The Modern Language Association of America
26 Broadway, New York, New York 10004-1789
www.mla.org

CONTENTS

PREFACE TO THE SERIES

In *The Art of Teaching* Gilbert Highet wrote, "Bad teaching wastes a great deal of effort, and spoils many lives which might have been full of energy and happiness." All too many teachers have failed in their work, Highet argued, simply "because they have not thought about it." We hope that the Approaches to Teaching World Literature series, sponsored by the Modern Language Association's Publications Committee, will not only improve the craft—as well as the art—of teaching but also encourage serious and continuing discussion of the aims and methods of teaching literature.

The principal objective of the series is to collect within each volume different points of view on teaching a specific literary work, a literary tradition, or a writer widely taught at the undergraduate level. The preparation of each volume begins with a wide-ranging survey of instructors, thus enabling us to include in the volume the philosophies and approaches, thoughts and methods of scores of experienced teachers. The result is a sourcebook of material, information, and ideas on teaching the subject of the volume to undergraduates.

The series is intended to serve nonspecialists as well as specialists, inexperienced as well as experienced teachers, graduate students who wish to learn effective ways of teaching as well as senior professors who wish to compare their own approaches with the approaches of colleagues in other schools. Of course, no volume in the series can ever substitute for erudition, intelligence, creativity, and sensitivity in teaching. We hope merely that each book will point readers in useful directions; at most each will offer only a first step in the long journey to successful teaching.

Joseph Gibaldi
Series Editor

ACKNOWLEDGMENTS

This volume, comprising materials and articles on various teaching contexts and strategies for presenting *Anna Karenina* in the classroom, was prepared by soliciting responses to a questionnaire from faculty members at various institutions: universities, colleges, community colleges, and adult education programs. We thank our respondents for taking time from their schedules to write us at length about the challenges and rewards of teaching Tolstoy's novel. Their responses were extremely informative. Reading them, we were impressed by the wisdom, inspiration, and expertise that members of our field bring to the teaching of *Anna Karenina*. We consulted the questionnaire responses at various stages of preparing this manuscript. It is our hope that the respondents will feel as we do: that this volume expresses the collective wisdom of our field.

To the contributors we are grateful for their willingness to share with us opinions on all matters relating to teaching *Anna Karenina* and for the spirit they brought to this project. We benefited from suggestions made by the referees who evaluated our proposal, prospectus, and manuscript. Their judicious comments helped this book take shape.

We would like to pay tribute to our teachers from whom we learned about *Anna Karenina* and about the art of teaching: Robert Belknap, Richard Gustafson, Katharine O'Connor, Victor Terras, Thomas G. Winner. We are grateful to colleagues from our home institutions who have advised us during this process, in particular Clare Carroll and Hugh McLean.

Donna Orwin, the editor of *Tolstoy Studies Journal*, helped us in a number of ways. Our thanks go also to Natalya Kozyreva. We were fortunate to have the editorial assistance of Gabriel White and Aileen Paterson, with thanks to the Institute of Slavic, East European, and Eurasian Studies at the University of California, Berkeley, for support given for their work. At the MLA, we thank Michael Kandel for his excellent copyediting and for entering into the spirit of the volume; and we are most beholden to Joseph Gibaldi for his wise guidance from start to finish.

Finally, we would like to express gratitude to our students, who have made teaching *Anna Karenina* such a rewarding experience for us, especially those who took the graduate seminar Tolstoy and the West at Columbia University and the Graduate Center, City University of New York, and students in the undergraduate course Dostoevsky, Tolstoy, and the English Novel at the University of California, Berkeley. They have been an important part of this collective effort.

LK and AM

INTRODUCTION TO THE VOLUME

A Note on Citation and Transliteration

Following the choice of most faculty members who responded to our questionnaire, we use the Norton Critical Edition of *Anna Karenina* for all quotations from the novel, unless otherwise indicated. This version uses the translation by Louise Maude and Aylmer Maude, revised by George Gibian, and the edition contains a selection of critical materials. When citing, we have included, in addition to page numbers, the part number and chapter number so that those using other translations or the Russian original may locate passages easily.

We follow the Library of Congress system of transliteration from the Cyrillic alphabet, with the exception of common proper and geographic names, for which we follow convention and render them in the form that is likely to be most familiar to English-speaking readers. Thus we refer to Lev Tolstoi as Leo Tolstoy and to Moskva as Moscow. For the names of characters in *Anna Karenina*, unless otherwise noted, we follow the Maude translation found in the Norton Critical Edition.

Citations from Tolstoy's complete works in Russian are taken from the Jubilee Edition (*Polnoe sobranie*).

Teaching *Anna Karenina*

Amy Mandelker

When teaching *Anna Karenina*, most of us rejoice in the opportunity to quote Tolstoy's elegant claims for the autonomy of the literary work of art, given with reference to his "novel [*Anna Karenina*], the first I have written":[1]

> If I were to try to say in words everything that I intended to express in my novel, I would have to write the same novel I wrote over again from the beginning. (*Polnoe sobranie* 62: 269; my trans.; see *Anna Karenina* 750)

> People are needed for the criticism of art who can show the pointlessness of looking for ideas in a work of art and can instead steadfastly guide readers through that endless labyrinth of linkages which is the essence of art, and towards those laws that serve as the basis for those connections. (*Tolstoy's Letters* 1: 297; letter to Strakhov)

Russian literature professors have historically upheld Tolstoy's statement as the gold standard for the entire hermeneutic enterprise. Certainly, it is as precise a stimulus to close, attentive reading as could be desired by any *explicateur* or deconstructionist.

Similarly, Tolstoy's other famous pronouncement about the shape of his novel has initiated over a century of questing for the architectural ligature of his edifice: "I pride myself on the architecture [of *Anna Karenina*]—the arches are so joined that it is impossible even to notice the keystone" (*Polnoe sobranie* 62: 377; letter to Rachinsky; my trans.). Critics of structuralist-semiotic bent have cited Tolstoy's architectural metaphor as affirmation for the organicity and isomorphism of a layered, interconnected text. Readers of *Anna Karenina* are still searching for the "keystone" in the arch, with critical consensus (LeBlanc; Mandelker, *Framing*) tending to endorse Joan Grossman's view that the meeting of the protagonists of the double novel, Anna and Levin, constitutes that link. Teaching the poetics (the labyrinth of linkages) and structure (keystones and arches) of *Anna Karenina* thus receives extensive consideration in this volume.

As the twenty-first-century American college or university humanities classroom has emerged from poststructuralist, new-historicist, and cultural studies paradigms, Tolstoy's statements—although attenuated by a healthy skepticism for authorial intention and self-awareness—still suggest a valuable approach to teaching the nineteenth-century novel and *Anna Karenina* in particular. The radical nature of Tolstoy's defense of the novel qua novel—stridently liberated from the adornment of any thematic or ideological commentary—inclines our acceptance of the author's terms when we might otherwise resent the authoritative preemption of our approach to the literary work. However, we need no longer appeal to the demise of the author in order to secure our freedom to determine how and why we read or teach. Despite Tolstoy's directive not to read his novel ideologically, it is difficult to get away from the ideas in *Anna Karenina*. Those of us who teach the novel regularly find that it persistently detonates heated classroom debates of issues that continue to be topical: sex and sexuality, gender roles, social constriction of individual self-expression and fulfillment, social hypocrisy and cruelty, dysfunction in the family, the disorientation of modernity, and the industrialization and urbanization of culture. At the same time, teachers of literature will wish to take the opportunity to initiate their students into an appreciation of Tolstoy's virtuosity, even if the invitation is issued somewhat irritably by the suspect author himself. Liza Knapp's article in this volume, engaging directly the inner workings of the Tolstoyan labyrinth, is an exemplary and innovative model for how such initiation may work as a teaching strategy.

Classrooms that take up Tolstoy's challenge are rewarded by the perception of *Anna Karenina* as a literary experiment in novelistic form and structure. Indeed, critics have credited Tolstoy with literary innovations in "psychological prose" (Ginzburg) and inner or interior monologue (Cohn; Knapp, "Tue-la!"), while the Russian formalists worked out their famous theory of "estrangement" or "defamiliarization" primarily through reference to Tolstoyan prose (Shklovsky's "Art as Technique"). Tolstoy's implementation of symbolic detail and imagery is frequently cited as reason for removing him from the canon of realism and realigning him with modernism. Robert Louis Jackson's close reading of Tolstoyan detail in this volume offers a master class to teachers who wish to walk their students slowly and appreciatively through the novel's archways.

In addition to readings of detail and imagery, *Anna Karenina* has inspired a Bakhtinian, discourse-centered criticism. In a magisterial summation of Mikhail Bakhtin's theory of discourse in the novel, *Mikhail Bakhtin: Creation of a Prosaics*, Gary Saul Morson and Caryl Emerson cull examples from *Anna Karenina* to explicate their idea of prosaics and its implications for concepts of polyphony, genre, and discourse theory. In this volume, Emerson continues that task in her high-contrast study of Tolstoy versus Dostoevsky, reworking the traditional juxtaposition of Tolstoy, the monologic author, and Dostoevsky, the dialogic author. Julie Buckler takes up the Bakhtinian model of the novel as incorporating a plurality of genres to suggest a series of lenses for viewing Anna's demise: tragic, operatic, melodramatic, and farcical. Svetlana Evdokimova examines the unusual shape of the novel, with its out-of-kilter final section, eliminated by the publisher and published by Tolstoy separately. She suggests that the ending is an example of Tolstoy's continuing experimentation with extraliterary genres, concluding that Platonic dialogue caps *Anna Karenina* in the same way that the historical essay puts an end to *War and Peace*. Exploring the same problem from within the experience of the creative process, William Todd documents the installments in the serial publication of the novel to illustrate how marketplace pressures imposed on Tolstoy's artistic purposes in the shaping of the narrative.

At the time of Tolstoy's insistence on artistic design as the correct subject of literary criticism in general and of *Anna Karenina* in particular, Russian literary critics were formulating a didactic, utilitarian view of literature and the novel that Victor Terras (*Belinskij*) has compellingly chronicled as the armature for the subsequent modeling of Soviet socialist realist doctrine. While western Europe was producing criticism by the brothers Goncourt, Thomas Carlyle, John Ruskin, and Stéphane Mallarmé, Russian intellectuals were enduring an almost barbaric era of ideological demands on art that one isolated "art pour l'art" adherent termed "aesthetics as nightmare" (Moser). In particular, Nikolai Chernyshevsky, Vissarion Belinsky, Nikolai Dobroliubov, and Aleksander Pisarev demanded that literature reflect the social reality of its day, serve the utilitarian functions of instruction and enlightenment, and promote social change. In part, these views were a response to a historical situation of heavy censorship and conservative politics that forced many political debates into the pages of novels. Tolstoy's pronouncement against ideas in criticism is newly anarchic, and the politics of his novel are less strident, when contrasted to the contemporary dogmas of utilitarian aesthetics and didactic literary criticism. His novel seems less preachy when compared with Chernyshevsky's crudely ideological *roman à thèse*, *What Is to Be Done?* Because courses on the Russian novel generally require that the issues of a programmatic literary tradition enter into class discussions of *Anna Karenina*, many essays were commissioned for this volume that would offer guidance for teaching the ideas and cultural context.

Whether *Anna Karenina* is taught as the culminating refinement of the monstrous Russian novel—in the company of its European "loose and baggy" (James 113) counterparts—or as a thematic, artistic counterpoint to the sociocultural concerns it depicts, the rewards of including it in a course syllabus are considerable. It is therefore probably the most often taught nineteenth-century Russian novel in the American academy, despite the fact that it can be an abrasive work to teach. Students often respond negatively to what they sense is the author's hypermoralistic and manipulative destruction of a heroine whose transgressions, by contemporary standards, are nonexistent. The instructor must make an anthropological exertion to clarify the novel's sociohistorical context for an American audience. However, when *Anna Karenina* is taught in non-Russian courses where the syllabus is thematically or theoretically constructed, limitations of time may preclude any in-depth study of cultural context. For example, our survey respondents teach the novel in courses titled Adultery in the Novel; The Woman Question in Nineteenth-Century Literature; Sexuality in Literature; Sex, Death, and Narrative; Conflict and Peacemaking: A Study of Three Revolutions; and Indirect Free Discourse. The novel also works well in courses with a theoretical focus—for example, Russian Literature into Film; Theory of Narrative; Contexts of the Nineteenth-Century Novel: Gender, Narrative, and Nation; and *Roman Noir* and Nineteenth-Century Gothic.

The organizational and pedagogical problem most cited by survey respondents is the necessity to present specialized information in nonspecialized classes where the length of Tolstoy's novel already threatens to overtake class time.

Anna Karenina presents a greater technical challenge than novels with similar themes (such as Flaubert's *Madame Bovary*), in terms of translation, transliteration, and the peculiarities of Russian names, customs, religion, even a calendar out of sync with the West. Students encountering a Russian novel for the first time may also be intimidated as much by its sheer enormity as by its representation of an unfamiliar geography or by the strangeness of Russian names and honorifics. Knapp's introductory sections on names and setting provide a complete resource for explicating these issues with dispatch and ingenuity in the classroom.

Respondents to our survey were virtually unanimous in identifying the other main issue in teaching the novel as the difference in societal mores noted above. As one respondent observed, "It is particularly difficult for American students of the early twenty-first century to take 'adultery' seriously." The problem is compounded by the more general problem of teaching contexts; in the words of another respondent, "teaching Great Books just doesn't fly at Regional State Commuter College." Respondents commented as well that, while the eponymous heroine remains a compelling subject for classroom discussion, the character of Levin, who occupies equal novelistic turf, imports baggage that students frequently find cumbersome: the agricultural reforms, zemstvo politics, the sociopolitical ferment that followed the liberation of the serfs, the "accursed" questions debated by the Russian intelligentsia, and the existential and metaphysical questions that preoccupy Levin. Also disconcerting to many American undergraduates is the sensation of encountering an imposing didactic, moral authority. As one student commented after reading the final chapter of the novel, "I have never felt so manipulated in my life!"

Most instructors can turn these challenges into opportunities for generating discussion. In this volume, Tolstoy's moralistic and didactic tone is successfully disarmed through a variety of strategies. Donna Orwin and Gary Jahn both provide the context and biography of Tolstoy's philosophical, religious, and moral crises, exploring his persistent concerns with the mind-spirit-body division in his life and in *Anna Karenina*, as reflected in the novel's semiautobiographical protagonist, Levin. The often facile juxtaposition of Anna-adulteress-dead versus Levin–happily married–alive is thoroughly quizzed by Jahn's emphasis on Levin's psychological turmoil at the novel's end. Levin's conflicts in estate management and the general agrarian crisis in Russia are discussed as part of a course syllabus on conflict resolution by Mary Helen Kashuba and Manucher Dareshuri. The authors approach the problem of the industrialization of agriculture in a semi-Marxist manner, as *Anna Karenina* was in fact read by Vladimir Lenin and most subsequent Soviet criticism. Gary Saul Morson takes a different slant on the same topic of the reform bill, suggesting that Levin ultimately remains skeptical of any systematizing or schematic approach to life's problems.

The overpowering sense of moral authority and didacticism for which Tolstoy is famous is tackled through Kate Holland's close reading of the epigraph and related examples of authoritative discourse in the novel. Gina Kovarsky proposes classroom exercises to alert students to the textual mechanisms for Tolstoy's moral education of the reader. She uses the figure of Stiva as an example of Tolstoy's strategy for implicating the reader in the novel's moral conflicts, making it self-impeaching to assume a judgmental moral stance.

Whether the work of the novel is ultimately condemnatory of Anna and whether Tolstoy should be indicted as sexist is undoubtedly the issue most debated in the criticism. Anna's gender-specific predicament is explored in several articles that will be of particular value in courses relating to women's studies. Harriet Murav details the implications of civil and ecclesiastical divorce law for nineteenth-century Russian women in Anna's circumstances. Helena Goscilo surveys the novel's treatment of sexuality through the imagery of bodies, flesh, and gender roles. Judith Armstrong places *Anna Karenina* as a unique, Russian occurrence in the history of the European novel of adultery. These three essays taken together constitute a strong feminist critique of the novel. Gender concerns also inform David Sloane's discussion of Anna as reader and as author of her own romance in a Russian literary tradition of reading heroines. Both Armstrong and Buckler explore the type and tenor of Anna's role as hero or heroine.

Other theoretical approaches include the psychoanalytic analysis of dreams in the novel, used as a classroom exercise by Thomas Barran. Doing the dream work in class, students acquire simultaneously an understanding of Sigmund Freud's theories and the way in which Freudian psychoanalytic procedures of dream analysis parallel techniques in literary criticism, what Ken Frieden calls "Freud's dream of interpretation." Tracings of the novel's rich imagery, structure, and aesthetics can be found in this volume in the essays by Goscilo, Holland, Jackson, Knapp, Justin Weir, and Evdokimova. Innovative classroom techniques, such as mapping, journaling, and scavenger hunting are proposed by Mary Laurita, Jason Merrill, and Knapp. The use of supplementary materials, such as film versions or artworks, is discussed by both Andrea Lanoux and Weir. The passages concerning art in *Anna Karenina* offer Weir the opportunity to introduce the related issues of aesthetics and representation, as well as the uses of space and vision as novelistic device. Lanoux offers suggestions for screenings of film adaptations and considerations of novelistic form in contrast to cinematographic or stage treatments of the novel.

In addition to background information contained in Knapp's "Names" and "Setting," the "Materials" section provides the instructor with an overview of available translations and Russian editions, as well as a guide to definitive sources. To facilitate speedy reference, the essays in "Approaches" are grouped according to curricular contexts and teaching strategies. In "*Anna Karenina* in Tolstoy's Life, Thought, and Times," the authors discuss those biographical, sociohistorical, and philosophical events and issues that both influenced the creative composition of the novel and are debated by its characters: Tolstoy's midlife crisis and conversion (Jahn, Orwin), the sociopolitical reforms of the period and the plight of the peasantry as a challenge to the landowner (Morson, Kashuba and Dareshuri), the legal and social status of women and wives in Russia (Murav, Goscilo), and the pragmatics of reading the novel in installments (Todd). In "*Anna Karenina* in the Literary Traditions of Russia and the West," the articles focus on teaching the novel of adultery (Armstrong), novelistic genres (Buckler, Evdokimova), the Russian literary tradition of women's fiction (Sloane), and the Dostoevsky-Tolstoy comparison (Emerson). Finally, "Classroom Approaches to *Anna Karenina*" offers practical suggestions, pedagogical techniques, and master classes meant to bring the novel alive in a variety of learning environments and through a series of innovative readings in connection with other media.

Anna Karenina has a revered place in the college syllabus. Taught in the general curriculum most frequently with its sister works, Flaubert's *Madame Bovary*, Hardy's *Tess of the D'Urbervilles*, and Fontane's *Effi Briest*, the novel also occupies a pivotal position in the Russian literature sequence, where its enduring influence is apparent, most notably, in Anton Chekhov's series of "Anna" stories and in Andrei Belyi's masterpiece, *Petersburg*. Tolstoy continues to be championed as the great representative of the nineteenth-century novel and of his era, "as if George Eliot, Thackeray, Trollope and even John Stuart Mill had been rolled into one" (Gifford, *Tolstoy* 209). The amplitude of his virtuosity accommodates a welcome diversity of approaches to teaching *Anna Karenina*.

NOTE

[1]Although this remark appears confusing, Tolstoy did not consider *War and Peace,* written before *Anna Karenina,* a novel ("We Russians do not write novels in the European sense of the word" [Tolstoy, *Polnoe sobranie* 16: 7; my trans; see Tolstoy, War 1363 and 1366]). This view is not idiosyncratic but participates in the Russian novelistic tradition of formal experimentation. The first Russian novel, Aleksandr Pushkin's *Eugene Onegin*, is a novel in verse; Mikhail Lermontov's *Hero of Our Time* is a fragmentary collection of short narrative units; Nikolai Gogol's *Dead Souls* is subtitled a poem (the Russian, *poèma,* indicates an epic poem) although it is written in prose. Tolstoy's emphasis on the novelistic form of *Anna Karenina* is important for the critic and teacher to acknowledge, since, by overtly appealing to the European realist novelistic tradition, Tolstoy announces his intention to engage its signal themes and metaphysical debates.

The Names

Liza Knapp

Tolstoy's Onomastics and the Latent Meaning of Names

Leo Tolstoy assigned names to the many characters of *Anna Karenina* with great care, apparently with the aim of making them overtly realistic and covertly meaningful. In some cases, he came up with the right names early on, but in others he tried out different names in the drafts before fixing on the right one. For example, according to the testimony of his wife (Tolstaia 855), his eventual decision to name his heroine Anna instead of other names he considered (Tatyana-Tanya, Anastasya-Nana) was influenced in part by the fact that Anna had been the name of a neighbor's mistress who committed suicide by throwing herself under a train in a fit of jealousy and despair in 1872. Tolstoy's heroine was named after this real Anna, whose corpse Tolstoy saw shortly after the suicide. Some of the peasants in *Anna Karenina*, such as Agafya (Agatha) Mikhaylovna, were given the names of real peasants on Tolstoy's estate.[1] One of the more ridiculous-sounding names in the novel, Tyutkin, the coiffeur who appears in Anna's inner monologue just before her suicide, was actually the name of Tolstoy's tailor at one time. That Tolstoy worked in a fair number of names that were lifted from the world he inhabited or that were slight alterations of actual names (Shcherbatsky, Oblonsky) helped make the realm of his novel lifelike.

But the aura of realism surrounding the names of *Anna Karenina* does not keep them from also having symbolic meanings. For the most part, especially with major characters, Tolstoy mutes this effect, stopping short of the more Dickensian creations of, for example, Nikolai Gogol and Fyodor Dostoevsky.[2] It may be helpful to students familiar with the English literary tradition to know that what Tolstoy does with the symbolism of names in *Anna Karenina* is similar to what George Eliot does in *Middlemarch,* where names signify but gently, by open-ended hints that come and go, so that Dorothea may be a "gift of God" and also a dodo bird, and the book ends leaving us pondering the meaning of it all.

Tolstoy's names usually do not seem to be overtly symbolic. The idea that a name, and especially an ordinary one, may prove meaningful is consistent with overarching patterns in his fiction. As John Bayley put it, for Tolstoy "what matters is to recognize the truth that is under one's nose" (198). Richard Gustafson has shown that the everyday reality Tolstoy envisions is deeply emblematic and allegorical and capable of revealing spiritual and moral truth. And, as Gary Saul Morson has argued, the truths discovered in Tolstoy's works tend to be found in the prosaic world of daily life, where they are "camouflaged," "hidden in plain view" (*Hidden* 270, 5). Thus, it should not be surprising that the names of Tolstoy's characters often have latent significance.

Anna Karenina was written in the aftermath of Tolstoy's period of intense study of Greek texts in the original, when Tolstoy was still under the influence of Greek thought and philology. The Greek etymologies of commonly used Russian names made it possible to conceal the truth (express it in Greek) while keeping it in plain view, under one's nose. A number of the peasants have typical peasant names that seem to reveal something about their role in the novel: Levin's coachman Philip (from the Greek for "lover of horses") truly loves horses; the peasant Fyodor (the Russian version of Theodore [used in the Maude translation], meaning "gift of God") proves to be a godsend to Levin by telling him about the peasant Platon (Plato in the Maude translation) who lives for God and remembers the soul—this Plato represents the essence of the Greek philosopher Plato's wisdom, as does the Plato Pierre meets in *War and Peace*; and Agafya (Agatha), Levin's peasant nanny, is indeed the embodiment of goodness (her name comes from the Greek word for "good"), and the truth that Levin learns in his eventual epiphany about the peasant Platon was something that Agafya had been communicating to him all along. In these cases, the peasants' names contain some truth about who they are.

The same may be said of the seven major characters of the novel. Kitty's real name, the Russian Ekaterina (Catherine in the Maude translation), stems from the Greek word for "pure" or "unsullied." This attribute is certainly an important facet of how she is perceived. Levin's first name of Konstantin (Constantine) evokes constancy, and, despite what he reveals in his bachelor diary, he promises to be a faithful husband and a steady provider. Alexey, the shared first name of both Karenin and Vronsky, comes from the verb "to defend," and both these men, whose professional lives are devoted to the defense of the Russian Empire, are put on the defensive in their struggle over honor and Anna, with many expecting them to defend this honor in a duel. The name Stepan (Stephen), from the Greek for "crown," fits the ever popular Stiva. The name Anna has a Hebrew root, meaning "grace," a quality that describes her. The name Darya (Dolly's full name) means "gift," with connotations of divine provenance. Because these important characters are complex and evolve in the course of the novel, their names hint at truth about them in an indirect way.

In *Anna Karenina* Tolstoy returns to the issues discussed in Plato's dialogue, the *Cratylus*. There, in what becomes a general debate about the nature of language, Socrates and others argue about names and name giving. Does a name teach or reveal some truth about the essence or nature of the person who bears it? Or, on the contrary, are names arbitrary matters of convention or chance? Although this dialogue has been hard for scholars to interpret, Socrates gets the last word, as usual. He admits to the appeal of the idea that names reveal some truth about those who bear them but forces his interlocutors to recognize the limitations of this idea. The ultimate effect is to create a sense of questioning about the matter at hand. Tolstoy approached the names and naming process in *Anna Karenina* in much the same spirit. He creates a desire for names to be meaningful and, at the same time, a wariness about the process. The *Cratylus* should be considered along with the *Symposium* as a subtext for *Anna Karenina*. As both Donna Orwin and Svetlana Evdokimova argue in this volume, Tolstoy appropriated not just Platonic content but also the dialogue form, so that we are left with a sense of open-ended questioning, where the last word may be persuasive but is not presented as a final answer.

When Tolstoy gives a character a meaningful name, it should not be assumed that he is giving pat answers about identity or using the etymology of a character's name to tell that character's story. Rather, he is raising questions, along the lines of those raised in the *Cratylus*. Is the purity of Ekaterina—Kitty—a divine blessing she is born with? Is it an ideal she freely aspires to? Is it a fate she is doomed to live out? Is it a limit that keeps her in check? Is it a personality trait that comes into play on a daily basis? Is it a quality that can be effaced under certain circumstances or if her will fails? Is she being teased? Or is it an aura that has been arbitrarily associated with her and hides a fact that Anna alone sees—that Kitty is no purer than the rest of us, because "she too wants bon-bons and dirty ice-cream" (688; pt. 7, ch. 30)? Is it a red herring? Do the negative associations that some names contain spell a character's doom? Can they ever be lived down?

These questions figure prominently in regard to the last name Karenin. This name is one that Tolstoy made to order for *Anna Karenina*. He formed it by adding a typical Russian suffix for last names to the Homeric Greek word for "head." The name is apt. Karenin, Anna's civil servant husband with the ears Anna finds so unpleasant, does indeed seem to approach life cerebrally (Christian 179). He lacks heart and soul, except when he is temporarily filled with the Christian spirit of forgiveness as Anna is about to die after giving birth to Annie. In Karenin, Tolstoy presents us with a head just waiting to have horns put on it. Tolstoy came up with the right name for a cuckolded husband.

It may seem that what Tolstoy does in naming Karenin is akin to what Flaubert did with Charles Bovary, whose very name suggests that his destiny is to be cuckolded. (For discussion of the significance of the name of Charles Bovary, see Culler; Tanner 236–54.) In the opening scene of *Madame Bovary*, Flaubert laboriously draws attention to the significance of his hero's name by staging a scene in which the young Charles is asked by a teacher to say his name, proves unable to articulate it, is forced to repeat it. One effect of this scene is to draw attention to this name, which may seem unremarkable enough at first, and to suggest that it reveals in a prophetic way some truth about its bearer. In the name Charles Bovary, especially as Charles pronounces it—"Charbovari"—in the opening scene, echoes of the word *charivari* have been found, as well as all the bovine associations, which conspire in Flaubert's novel to make it seem only natural that Emma would go elsewhere to satisfy her more equine desires. If Flaubert seems to make the name Charles Bovary into a cruel joke, a charivari (i.e., the ritual cacophonous serenade of newlyweds, especially after a marriage that is thought to be inappropriate and doomed to failure) played on its bearer, what Tolstoy does in naming Karenin is more subtle. No particular attention is drawn to the name itself. To Tolstoy's Russian contemporaries, the name may have posed an enigma because of its oddness. The Greek root of the name is well hidden. When apprised of the meaning latent in the name, a reader is likely to see a correspondence between it and Karenin's identity or fate. But the exact nature of the correspondence is left mysterious. The reader has to interpret it.

The most overtly significant act performed by Tolstoy in naming the characters of *Anna Karenina* is usually seen as his assigning the name of Levin to the character who in many ways recalls Tolstoy himself (see Jahn, this volume). This last name has the same root as Tolstoy's first name, Lev (meaning "lion"). As it appears in Russian print, there is an ambiguity about its pronunciation: either Levin (the first vowel *yě*) or Lyovin (the first vowel *yō*) is conceivable. There has been some disagreement about which pronunciation should be used. Those who favor Lyovin, Nabokov among them, argue that it is likely that this pronunciation is what Tolstoy intended because he himself, following folkways, pronounced his first name Lyov rather than the more usual Lev.[3] (His nickname was also Lyova.) Thus, the pronunciation Lyovin makes the character sound more like Tolstoy's fictional alter ego. Also cited as a rationale for assuming that Tolstoy intended his hero's name to be pronounced Lyovin rather than Levin is that Levin is how the Jewish family name (with Levi as its root) is also pronounced. But in a recent study, Alexis Klimov questions both the arguments and the assumptions that have led many to pronounce the name Lyovin and cites evidence to support pronouncing the name Levin. He suggests that the Lyovin pronunciation "has been preferred mainly for its ethnically unproblematic nature" (109). Klimov closes with the testimony of Tolstoy's daughter, Alexandra, who in her eighties told Klimov that at home the members of the Tolstoy family always said, "Levin."

However it is pronounced, the name on the pages of the novel clearly evokes the author and gives this character an added dimension. But it is important to remember that Levin cannot be equated with Lev Tolstoy. In assigning meaningful names to his characters—whether Levin, Karenin, or Kitty—Tolstoy was hinting at correspondences between the bearer of the name and the meaning hidden in the name, not at a linear equation between the two.

The Russian System of Names and Tolstoy's Practice

The respondents to our questionnaire report that their students are often bewildered not simply by the multitude of different characters they meet in *Anna Karenina* but also by the variety of different name forms, appearing alone or in combinations, that Tolstoy uses to refer to a single character. For example, students have to get used to the fact that Levin, Kostya, and Konstantin (Constantine in the Maude translation) Dmitrich are the same person and that each of these names has a different effect. Indeed, the intricacies of the Russian system of names have been considered such a stumbling block to modern English-speaking readers that one translator, Joel Carmichael, decided to make things easy for his reader by getting rid of the patronymics and instituting a uniform system of referring to characters (869).

We think, however, that students are quite capable of mastering the Russian naming system. We recommend that instructors not only familiarize students with the Russian naming system and general nineteenth-century customs for using these names but also encourage them to watch how Tolstoy modulates names to create varying degrees of intimacy and detachment. Paying careful attention to the names in *Anna Karenina* has the benefit of encouraging close reading and also will help students keep the characters straight. The infinitesimally subtle effects have a cumulative impact. Exploration of the names combines naturally with discussion of transcendent issues, such as identity, destiny, gender, and family.

A Russian's name has three basic elements: the first name, the patronymic, and the family name. The patronymic is formed by adding a suffix to the father's first name; thus, Alexandrovich is the patronymic for a son of Alexander, Alexandrovna the patronymic for Alexander's daughter. Family names also have different forms in Russian depending on whether they refer to a man or a woman; thus Karenin is a male member of the Karenin family, Karenina a female one. In translations of *Anna Karenina,* however, the masculine form of family names is often used for both genders (e.g., Oblonsky is used for both Stiva and Dolly), with an exception usually being made for Karenina, where the feminine form has been retained for Anna in the title and throughout the novel.

In Russian, a person who is addressed with the formal second-person pronoun *vy* is usually also addressed by the combination of first name (in its full form) and patronymic: Stepan Arkadyevich, Darya Alexandrovna. A person who is addressed with the informal pronoun *ty* is usually also addressed by the first name alone, and then it is often likely to be not the full form of the name but a nickname or diminutive. The most neutral Russian nicknames are formed by contracting the first name: Konstantin (Constantine) becomes Kostya, Ekaterina (Catherine) becomes Katya. By adding more suffixes, variants of these nicknames may be formed that connote greater intimacy, familiarity, or derogation: Katya may become Katenka, Katiusha, Katka.

In referring to a person, a speaker or narrator can use any of a range of name forms: the first name (with or without patronymic) and surname—Alexey (Kirillovich) Vronsky—to make a complete reference, for example, when a person is first introduced or when there is ambiguity; the surname alone—Vronsky—to refer to someone in a detached, impersonal way, as a public figure; the first name and patronymic—Alexey Kirillovich—to refer to someone as a person one might address formally; the first name alone—Alexey—to refer to someone in a neutral but more personal and private way; the nickname—Alyosha—to refer to the person informally (e.g., Vronsky's mother refers to Vronsky as Alyosha when she tells Koznyshev what has become of him since Anna's death). In folk culture, a person can be addressed or referred to by the patronymic alone, which at times indicates respect in addition to familiarity; thus the peasant Platon is called just Fokanych in part 8.

Titles may also figure in the name system. A number of the upper-class families in the novel have inherited titles (e.g., prince or countess), which are institutionalized and part of the social structure. When these titles are used in the novel, they highlight social status. For example, when Tolstoy uses the title "princess" as he begins his narrative of Kitty's success as a debutante ("Princess Kitty Shcherbatskaya was eighteen, and this was her first season" [39; pt.1, ch. 12]), he draws the reader's attention to the fact that, by birthright, she is a princess. Titles of a very different nature are sometimes used for peasants: a peasant may be called uncle or grandfather where no familial relationship exists, the title signifying the community's respect for this person.

A Russian writer can make use of this rich array of names and titles to show different types of relationships (social, familial, emotional) with various degrees of intimacy and detachment. In *Anna Karenina*, Tolstoy takes full advantage of these opportunities. The name forms characters use for one another often reveal a great deal. As Gina Kovarsky shows in this volume, the third-person narrator's choices of name forms often signal the point of view. (A distinctive feature of the narration of *Anna Karenina* is how Tolstoy shifts from one character's point of view to another's, showing himself to be a virtuoso practitioner of free indirect speech and other related techniques.)

Different characters have different profiles in terms of the names used for them. Thus, some are nicknamed more than others (e.g., Kitty). Factors such as age, gender, marital status, and social position affect the choices of names, but personality and other circumstances, including the narrator's attitude toward the character, also play a role. Patterns are established for reference or address to a certain character. Deviations from these patterns signal special circumstances.

The Names of the Novel in Context

Introducing Prince Stepan Arkadyevich Oblonsky, Also Known as Stiva

The best place to begin to explain to students how the Russian naming system works is the opening sentence of the third paragraph of the novel. Having told us in a general fashion that things are a mess at the Oblonskys' because of the wife's response to the husband's affair with the French governess, Tolstoy introduces us to the adulterous husband: "Prince Stephen Arkadyevich Oblonsky—Stiva, as he was called in society—woke up" (1; pt. 1, ch. 1). (The Maude translation uses Stephen instead of Stepan.) Tolstoy gives the full nomenclature:

Oblonsky's title of prince, his first name, his patronymic, his surname, and also his nickname, Stiva.

Since the patronymic is a special feature of Russian names, which foreigners often find cumbersome or confusing, it deserves particular attention. Both on a symbolic and a functional level, the patronymic reinforces patrimony and family identity: Russians not only inherit their father's last name, but they also have his first name embedded in their patronymic. Further, the shared patronymic links siblings; that a woman retains her patronymic when she marries signals her continued bond to her family of origin. Thus the family bond between Prince Stepan *Arkadyevich* Oblonsky and his sister Anna *Arkadyevna* Karenina is embodied in their patronymics, even though she has shed her maiden name and title of princess.

Of course, the various components of the naming system, including patronymics, were part of the conventions of Russian life and taken for granted by Tolstoy's Russian contemporaries. Still, at times, because of how Tolstoy draws attention to names at various points, even the Russian reader who takes Russian names for granted is forced to ponder names in a new way. Tolstoy applies the device Viktor Shklovsky calls defamiliarization (*ostranenie*)—his technique of making perception less automatic and transcending convention and habit—to names, thereby forcing us to cease seeing them simply as labels (*O teorii* 12–17). In *Anna Karenina,* where paternity, marriage, the bonds between siblings, and relatedness in all forms play such a critical role, it is natural to expect names to be charged with special significance, because they are, in essence, a verbal expression of relatedness.

Oblonsky's title of prince may create some false expectations for students not familiar with this feature of the Russian social structure. In *Anna Karenina,* as students learn, being a princess or count does not necessarily mean having riches, power, prestige, and the protection of a strong family tradition. The Oblonsky family is a case in point. That the late Prince Arkady Oblonsky knew important people helped his son Stiva achieve his position in society. Yet when we meet Prince Stepan Arkadyevich Oblonsky (Stiva), he has squandered what he had and is now forced to sell off part of his wife's dowry. Although born a princess, his sister Anna Arkadyevna was left in quite a vulnerable state when she was orphaned. She had to be expediently married off to Karenin by her aunt. That she was Princess Oblonskaya may have given her a certain cachet in eyes of the titleless Karenin, but she had little left of her patrimony other than her name.

In *Anna Karenina,* as in *War and Peace,* Tolstoy often grants to families strong identities: genes matter. In general, he presents the Oblonsky family as having a congenital predisposition to dysfunctionality, although it manifests itself differently in brother and sister. In contrast, Tolstoy has endowed the Shcherbatskys, the birth family of Oblonsky's wife, Darya Alexandrovna (known as Dolly), with a strong instinct for familial self-preservation, which allows them to sustain the family even when one of them couples with an Oblonsky.

As the novel begins, Dolly is contemplating desperate measures (leaving her husband) and has abandoned her familial duties. As a result, the children are running wild and not being properly fed. But, by the end of the fourth chapter, the Shcherbatsky nature bred into Darya Alexandrovna wins out: she emerges from her room to set her family in order, her first act being to make sure that milk has been ordered.

Meanwhile her husband is out in the world, disseminating the charm that is also part of the Oblonsky heritage. He exudes his individual version of this Oblonsky charm in his role as Stiva. The way that Tolstoy initially presents this nickname, as if as an afterthought but clearly marking the importance of this information ("Prince Stephen Arkadyevich Oblonsky—Stiva, as he was called in society—woke up"), suggests that being Stiva in society is a central feature of this man's identity. Subsequent chapters show how Stiva's easy familiarity with others manifests itself, in a way that is especially striking in contrast to his old friend Levin.

In the Russian cultural context, Oblonsky's choice of Stiva as a nickname is significant. Instead of the traditional Russian shorter form of his given name, Styopa, he uses a Russian appropriation of the English Steve. English nicknames are also affected by several other characters in *Anna Karenina,* but these are more obviously English-sounding: Dolly, Kitty, Betsy, Annie. (When the novel is read in Russian, these women's nicknames in Cyrillic form jar the Russian text because of their foreign, nondeclining endings.)

The English nicknames are part of an English current that runs through the novel: the Shcherbatsky sisters are associated in Levin's mind with the English fairy tale "The Three Bears"; their mother wonders whether she should let her daughter choose a husband as English girls now do; Anna reads an English novel about English happiness on the train; Vronsky has an English horse trainer; Dolly has replaced her French governess with an English one; Vronsky's estate boasts many English innovations—even Annie has baby equipment imported from England; the program music that has such a bad effect on Levin is based on an English text (Shakespeare's *King Lear*).[4] This English influence may be more benign than the French influence, which is an obviously sinister force in the novel—from the French governess of the opening page to the French-speaking peasant of Anna's recurring nightmare who haunts her at her death. Yet, all the English elements, from Stiva's nickname on throughout the novel, no less than the French elements represent a foreign force that is threatening Russian life. As a brief look at Russian history shows, national identity has always been a vexed issue for the Russian nobility, which has a long history of ambivalently appropriating the trappings of European culture.

Missing Names as an Indicator of Familial and Social Oddities

After the formal introduction to Prince Stepan Arkadyevich Oblonsky, Tolstoy becomes much more casual in presenting his characters. From here on, readers usually must piece together the full set of onomastic coordinates of a given character from information scattered throughout the text. Often information is incomplete. This incompleteness is to be expected with characters who figure only in a minor or incidental way. Sometimes, omissions reflect certain social realities. For example, that Tolstoy does not mention most of the family names of the recently emancipated peasants in the novel reflects the social reality of their lives, which are so markedly different from that of the gentry families. But sometimes he does mention the family name of peasants, most notably when they have managed to make a go of a family farm by using the labor of different generations and both genders. These peasants have begun to build a sense of patrimony and family enterprise that was impossible under serfdom.

Kitty's friend Varenka is a character for whom the names used and omitted tell a great deal.[5] When Kitty first observes her in Soden, she notes that Mme Stahl always calls her Varenka and that everyone else calls her Mlle Varenka. The neutral nickname of the first name Varvara would be Varya; Varenka implies greater familiarity or diminished social status. Kitty can tell that her friend is neither Mme Stahl's relative nor a paid companion or servant. She eventually learns the mystery of their relationship: when the recently divorced Mme Stahl gave birth and the infant died, her relatives secretly replaced the dead baby with the newborn baby of a cook. (Tolstoy is drawing on his own family lore.) Eventually Mme Stahl found out that the child was not her daughter, but she kept on bringing her up, especially because the child's relatives had died. That Varenka's family name is never mentioned is telling. Her family affiliation is left blank. Furthermore, that she was christened Varvara (from the Greek for "stranger" or "alien") fits her as one who does not belong to a family, whether Mme Stahl's or anyone else's. Yet all are on familiar terms with her; she is Varenka to them. In Soden, people call her Mlle Varenka out of respect for her dignity and sisterly concern as she nurses the poor and sick, but this honorific also enforces her status as a single woman.

Varenka is called by her full given name and patronymic in a significant moment. In the mushroom-picking scene in part 6, Levin's half brother, Koznyshev, refers to her as Varvara Andreevna when he is about to propose to her—when she seems on the verge of also acquiring a family name, that of Koznyshev. But it is evidently her fate to go through life without the name of either father or husband. Koznyshev fails to propose, and she reverts back to being plain Varenka, nobody's daughter and nobody's wife but a sister to all. As Amy Mandelker has argued, in "escap[ing] from the marriage plot," Varenka sets a precedent for the future heroines of Tolstoy's postconversion works, who are "idealized single wom[e]n" (*Framing* 163–78).[6]

Tolstoy also uses names in a pointed way when referring to the flirtatious and happy-go-lucky Vasya Veslovsky, who is banished unceremoniously from Levin's estate and welcomed at Vronsky's in part 7. His family name comes from a root that means merriment (see Orwin, this volume). Also telling is that he is known so widely by the very familiar name of Vasenka (a more neutral nickname from his given name Vasily would be Vasya). That he is Vasenka so much of the time to so many different people suggests that there is something indiscriminate and unnatural in his intimacy. Whereas it is the agape Varenka projects that makes her Varenka to everybody, Vasenka exudes a facile form of eros. But, since one of the lessons of *Anna Karenina* is that both agape and eros are best expressed in a discriminate, measured way in a familial context, Tolstoy shows the limits of both Vasenka and Varenka.[7] Both these figures challenge the "limits of the familial realm" that Tolstoy cultivates so assiduously in *Anna Karenina* (Goscilo, this volume).

The Destiny of Names: From Kitty to Katya

In contrast to her friend Varenka, Princess Ekaterina (Catherine) Alexandrovna Shcherbatskaya, known as Kitty and destined to be Levin's wife, is securely fixed in a family and social set. Her father, unlike the rest of her family and friends (and even the narrator), does not call her Kitty but rather uses a purely Russian pet name, Katenka, which suggests that he sees things in her that others miss. This nickname symbolizes the special bond that Kitty shares with her father and also intimates that she has the right stuff to become the mother of Levin's children. Levin may have been initially attracted to her in the fairy-tale guise of Kitty, who along with Dolly and Nathalie was one of the Three Bears, but ultimately he comes to love her even more by other names.

In church during her wedding—with God as her witness—Kitty is Ekaterina or, more precisely, "the servant of God Ekaterina" (411; pt. 5, ch. 4). And it is Ekaterina (Catherine) who marries Konstantin (Constantine). When these two first names are paired in this fashion, during the sacrament of marriage, all the differences between Kitty and Levin disappear, and they become under these special and sacred circumstances momentarily (or eternally?) equal. In contrast, the default or unmarked designations Tolstoy uses for them—Kitty for Ekaterina, Levin for Konstantin—have the effect of ratifying the inequalities between them that are determined by age, gender, sexual experience, education, and authorial attitude. On the level of onomastics, this union of purity (Ekaterina) and constancy (Konstantin) promises to be a match made in heaven.

Another significant moment in Kitty's life that heralds a profound inner change is, likewise, marked by the fact she is not called Kitty. At the deathbed of her brother-in-law, Nikolay (Nicholas) Levin, she shows that, like the peasant Agafya Mikhaylovna, she has both a spiritual and practical knowledge of what to do in the face of death. Ministering to her suffering brother-in-law, she puts into action the sisterly love that went awry with non–family members on foreign soil, when she imitated Varenka and tried to nurse the artist Petrov in Soden. (For other aspects of Kitty's failure in Soden, see Morson, this volume.) Problems arose in Soden because of the sexual charm that Kitty so naturally exuded: Petrov was smitten, and his wife became jealous. But these problems do not arise now. From his deathbed, Nikolay begins calling Kitty Katya and speaks to Levin of "your Katya" (450; pt. 5, ch. 18). Levin is moved by the new, unkittenish side of his wife that is revealed as she cares for his dying brother.

From this point on, in moments when he feels a spiritual poignancy in his relations with Kitty, Levin will use his brother's name for her, Katya. That Kitty's pregnancy is announced at Nikolay's deathbed further heightens the significance of her new name. As she becomes the matriarch of the Levin family, whose survival depends on her womb, it is fitting that she has been given a new and Russian name by a dying member of the family. When, a few months later, Levin says to Kitty, "Katya, it is not good for you to be standing," and gives her a "significant look" (501; pt. 6, ch. 1), he is using this name and this look to remind her of her special status as bearer of a little Levin. (When Kitty is Katya to Levin, the focus is either on her soul or her womb.) In the moments when she is Katya, Levin gets a glimpse of her true—Russian—self, which is otherwise hidden beneath the persona of Kitty, with her *broderie anglaise* and other worldly concerns.

The Constraints of a Name: Anna Karenina

If Kitty's repertory of names reflects what Tolstoy presents as her healthy human relationships and family life, Anna Karenina's fate may be sealed in her name. Perhaps this sealing is the significance of the title of the novel. The heroine is addressed and referred to primarily as Anna, Anna Arkadyevna, or Anne (when Vronsky speaks about her in French), but not by nicknames. For a short name like Anna a nickname may not seem as necessary as for a longer name like Ekaterina, but in the Russian context nicknames may be used simply to connote familiarity, fondness, and intimacy. Many an Anna is fondly known as Anya. But such naming never happens with Anna Karenina. Although it may be imprudent to speculate too much about her lack of pet name, the lack fits with the profound sense of loneliness and isolation from human relations that engulfs and eventually destroys her. In Tolstoy's conception of his heroine, isolation played a crucial role. His wife records him remarking that "Anna is deprived of the joys of being occupied with this feminine aspect of life, because she is alone, all the women have rejected her and she has no one with whom to talk about everything that makes up the ordinary, purely feminine round of occupations" (qtd. in Turner, *Companion* 48).

Anna's adulterous love for Vronsky has the effect of straining all her familial and social relations. In a revealing moment, where Tolstoy uses names to make his point, Vronsky is trying to convince his brother's wife, Varya, to show some compassion for Anna, after he and Anna have returned from Italy to Petersburg. During this conversation, Varya explains to Vronsky that she cannot see "Anna Arkadyevna [. . .] and so rehabilitate her in society," because it would be too compromising and dangerous. ("Please understand that I *cannot* do it! I have daughters growing up, and I must move in society, for my husband's sake.") During this conversation, she insistently uses the formal Anna Arkadyevna, to which Tolstoy draws attention when he notes that she says it with "peculiar precision" (481; pt. 5, ch. 28). By enunciating the formal name in this way (instead of using just Anna), Vronsky's sister-in-law seeks to keep Anna at a distance, far from her family circle and social group. By contrast (and contrasts of this sort are an important feature of Tolstoy's poetics), Anna's sister-in-law, Dolly, hesitates about what name to use in referring to Vronsky when she converses with Anna during her visit to Vozdvizhenskoe in part 6: "Dolly did not know what to call him. She did not like to call him either 'the Count' or 'Alexey Kirilich.' " Anna helps her by simply saying, "Alexey" (576; ch. 23). Although Dolly's response is quite different from Varya's, it still shows that she, too, is unsettled by the situation.

The crisis of identity that Anna Karenina undergoes seems to be internalized in her name. Anna "is surrounded by doubles of herself: her servant, Annushka, her daughter, Annie, and her adopted daughter, Hannah" (Mandelker, *Framing* 158). Anna's last name causes problems of its own. On the most obvious level, much of the drama of her part of the novel relates to the fact that she suffers from being Karenina. To the surprise of many students reading the novel today, for Anna Karenina to become Anna Vronskaya was, given the divorce and child custody laws, not such an easy task (see Murav, this volume). There are also internal obstacles to her becoming Anna Vronskaya. She gives voice to these in her inner monologue before the suicide. For better or worse, Anna has decided that she cannot bear the social censure or her children's questions about "her two husbands" (691; pt. 7, ch. 30), which she would have to live with even if the divorce were granted, she married Vronsky, and Karenin gave her custody of Seryozha (Serezha in the Maude translation). She does not see the prospect of being Anna Vronskaya as a solution. In her poignant last moments, she returns in memory to her girlhood, when she was Anna Oblonskaya, with dreams of happiness ahead of her. Thus, although it may seem reductive to see Anna's drama as a struggle over her last name, it is worth pointing out to students that the title of this novel has important reverberations.

Anna Karenina was written in the midst of heated debates in Russia and abroad about adultery, marriage, and family life (see Eikhenbaum, *Tolstoi in the Seventies*; Mandelker, *Framing*; Stenbock-Fermor on this subject). The drafts of the novel make direct reference to the polemics between Alexandre Dumas's reactionary solution to the question of what is to be done when a wife commits adultery ("Tue-la!" ["Kill her!"]) and Emile de Girardin's liberal suggestion that many of the problems caused in family life because of adultery could be eliminated if women were granted more sexual freedom and if children always took their mother's name (Stenbock-Fermor 94–95). This simple solution would eliminate the issue of illegitimacy, for all children born would be legitimate. Against the background of this debate, the question of Anna's last name and that of her children takes on additional significance.

The Nightmare of the Two Alexeys: Karenin versus Vronsky

Anna's onomastic confusion is intensified by the fact that Vronsky has the same first name as Karenin. That there are two Alexeys in her life becomes the stuff of her repeated nightmares (pt. 2, ch. 11). It causes problems for the reader as well. When the name Alexey appears, the reader has to figure out from the context or the patronymic which Alexey is being named. When the two are referred to in close proximity to each other, Tolstoy often invokes a complementarity, so that one (usually Vronsky) is referred to by last name and the other by first name and patronymic (usually Alexey Alexandrovich, who is Karenin). In her inner monologue just before her suicide, as she is attempting to find a way out of the nightmare of the two Alexeys that she has lived with for some time, Anna refers to Karenin as Alexey Alexandrovich and Vronsky as Vronsky or Count Vronsky. Perhaps because she is in the position of having to distinguish between them in her mind (they cannot both be simply Alexey; they cannot both be her husband, because this is the stuff of nightmares), she is forced to distance them both.

Names are also a vexed subject for Vronsky. As Dolly learns when she visits Anna and Vronsky in part 6, he is disturbed by the fact that his daughter "has no name," that is, that her family name is Karenin. Furthermore, unless Anna gets a divorce and she and Vronsky marry, any future children born to them will also be Karenins. Vronsky tells Dolly, "Some day a son may be born, my son, and he will by law be a Karenin, and not heir either to my name or my property, and however happy we may be in our family life, and whatever children we may have, there will be no legal bond between them and me" (568; pt. 6, ch. 22). Vronsky is thus denied the traditional paternal privilege of giving his name to his children.

The New Generation: Anna Alexeyevna Karenina and Dmitry Konstantinovich Levin

Sydney Schultze notes that the first names of the daughter born to Anna Karenina and the son born to Konstantin Levin "reflect the parents' personalities. Anna's child is named after her, showing Anna's preoccupation with herself. Levin's child Dmitry, known by the nickname Mitya, is named after Levin's father, showing his respect for family and for tradition" (169n18). Students will be able to deduce that little Dmitry is his grandfather's namesake if they recall that Levin's patronymic is Dmitrich. Schultze's juxtaposition of these two children can be developed further, especially if one considers their full names.

These names reflect the children's opposing family circumstances. As a name, Dmitry Konstantinovich Levin is the fullest possible expression of Levin's overwhelming desire to perpetuate his paternal line—on the level of onomastics, it is Levin's dream come true. With this male heir, patrimony is secure.[8] By contrast, little Anna's name betrays her confused identity and her precarious familial status as the daughter of an adulteress. Little Anna bears the last name not of her natural father, whom she resembles so strongly, but of her legal father, Karenin. Thus, as a second Anna Karenina,[9] she is marked as her mother's child, despite or because of her mother's neglect of her. Her patronymic, Alexeyevna, perpetuates her mother's nightmare of the two Alexeys, referring perversely to either or both of her fathers; it is unclear whether this indeterminacy is a curse or a blessing.

As the novel ends, it is clear that Dmitry Konstantinovich Levin has in abundance what Annie lacked at Vozdvizhenskoe in her state-of-the-art nursery with its staff of foreign nurses who struck Dolly as being substandard. As Dolly notes, Anna herself seemed almost like a stranger there. Quite significant for Tolstoy is that Kitty, little Mitya's mother, breastfeeds him herself, while "touching his cheek with her lips" and whispering "only be like your father, only be like him!" (711; pt. 8, ch.7). With his mother's milk, he is being indoctrinated with the message that is encoded in his father's name (Segal 102). Little Anna Karenina, however, has clearly been sent very mixed and disturbing messages about who she is.

All along Levin has been convinced that life will have meaning for him only if he marries and perpetuates the Levin name. He is sure even while the baby is still in Kitty's womb that it will be a boy. Still, his emotional ties to his newborn son are initially more tenuous than he expected. Whereas Kitty communes with her baby in deeply spiritual ways, especially while breastfeeding him, Levin at first feels no bond to his child other than that of the father's name. Kitty and Levin both begin to worry about his apparent lack of feelings for his son. As *Anna Karenina* closes, however, there are signs that Levin's love for his son is beginning to develop and that patrimony will triumph (738; pt. 8, ch. 18).

The novel ends on what for the Levin family has been a very momentous day: early in the day, little Dmitry showed signs that he recognized "his own people," and in the evening, during his bath, Kitty and Agafya Mikhaylovna offer Levin final proof of this milestone in an "experiment" that demonstrates that Mitya "had that day obviously and undoubtedly begun to recognize all his own people": the child coos to his mother but frowns at the cook (737; pt. 8, ch. 18). Since it takes place during his bath, the experiment evokes a christening ceremony: he is being initiated as a member of the Levin clan. He is learning what it means to be Dmitry Konstantinovich Levin.

Some readers have been doubtful about how this scene, close to the end of *Anna Karenina*, celebrates the Levin family. Notable among them is Dostoevsky, who reacted rabidly against what he perceived as the self-absorption of Levin in his family while children elsewhere were suffering. (Dostoevsky imagines Levin saying to himself, "we've given the boy a bath and he's begun to recognize me; what do I care what goes on over there in another hemisphere?" [*Diary* 2: 1099].) To be sure, Dostoevsky's attack on Levin, expressed in passionate, warmongering harangues in *A Writer's Diary*, is motivated by his outrage at Levin's refusal to support the Serbian campaign (see the following section, "Setting," this volume). Bayley also draws attention to this bath scene. He observes that there is something contrived, "deliberative," and ultimately not very convincing about this Tolstoyan celebration of family, where Tolstoy gives the family "the last word [. . .] for the last time" (198).[10] Gina Kovarsky (this volume) argues that the scene is disturbing because it symbolically enforces the exclusion of Anna Karenina from the human family.

Whereas baby Mitya's bath becomes, as Dostoevsky remarked, "a veritable event," the young Anna Karenina (known as Annie) is neglected in part 8, except for a brief mention. At the train station, Koznyshev hears from Vronsky's mother that Karenin came after Anna's death and asked the desperate Vronsky for little Annie. Vronsky later regrets having let "a stranger" take his child but feels that he cannot go back on his word (705; pt. 8, ch. 4). (His code of honor prevails over his paternal feelings.) The child, in fact, already bears the family name of this stranger. Karenin's request to take Annie may have been motivated by a selfish desire for revenge on Vronsky and a legalistic need to exert his parental rights. Yet it is also quite possible that Karenin felt a bond with this child, beyond that of name (Segal 137–39). After all, he was the one who saw to it that she did not go hungry in the difficult period after her birth. The threesome, Anna and the two Alexeys, who were brought together after little Anna's birth by a rush of Christian love and forgiveness, come together again as Karenin cares for little Anna, who so strongly resembles her natural father and who is her mother's namesake. It may even be that Karenin, like Silas Marner, will be redeemed through his love and care for a child who is not his biological daughter. But it is also possible that Karenin will ultimately succumb to the "coarse power" that destroyed his compassion in the period after Annie's birth (382; pt. 4, ch. 19). Will little Anna Karenina's life continue in misery, like Berthe Bovary's? Or will it take a triumphant turn, like Pearl Prynne's? As Judith Armstrong, Helena Goscilo, and Svetlana Evdokimova all show in this volume, *Anna Karenina* diverges in significant ways from the European novel of adultery. One consequence of this divergence is that Tolstoy neglects little Anna Karenina and tells us instead about Dmitry Konstantinovich Levin.

NOTES

I am grateful to Amy Mandelker and Hugh McLean for their very helpful suggestions for improvements to this section.

[1]In this discussion of the meanings and associations of the names Tolstoy gave to his characters, I have often substituted a form of the name that is closer to the Russian original than the one used in the Maude translation found in the Norton Critical Edition. In these cases, the anglicized form used by the Maude translation is given in parentheses afterward. For comments on the drawbacks of the forms of the names used in the Maude translation, see the discussion of English translations in "Materials" in this volume.

[2]In Gogol's *Dead Souls,* we find "Chichikov," a name that evokes sneezing. The name of the hero of "The Overcoat," Akaky Akakievich, has strong scatological associations while meaning "innocent" (Maguire, "Legacy" 25). This type of meaningful name reflects the way in which Gogol uses satire to hint at a higher spiritual truth. For discussion of Gogol's onomastics, see Yermakov; Maguire, "Legacy." Dostoevsky's onomastics are treated at length in Passage. His character names often seem to signal attention to their meaning: Raskolnikov ("split"), Marmeladov ("marmalade"), Myshkin ("mouse").

Dostoevsky's reliance on symbolic names is a feature of his style, which often is called "fantastic realism."

[3]The final *v* in either case would be pronounced as an *f*.

[4]On English touches and influence, see Armstrong, this volume; Mandelker, *Framing* 64–67.

[5]Tolstoy's penchant for hiding meaning in characters' names is expressed in the drafts where the figure who eventually metamorphosed into Varenka first appears as Miss Flora Sulivant, the daughter of an English pastor (Zhdanov 165–67). The first name Flora recalls the name Florence, which even by itself was enough to make the public think of Florence Nightingale, who had already become an emblematic figure in debates on the woman question. In Sulivant, Tolstoy was clearly trying to approximate English surnames such as Sullivan, but that this name sounds like the Russian word *solovey* ("nightingale") suggests that he was indeed thinking of Florence Nightingale. Nightingale's life and work served as an alternative model for women, because as a nurse in Crimea and social reformer back home she did good works outside the family context. As Mandelker has noted, Varenka "is a heroine of the Florence Nightingale type, the Lady with the Lamp rather than the Angel in the House or the fallen woman out of the house" (*Framing* 56).

[6]See Grenier on Varenka's status as someone "whose field of activity is not confined to a single family" (101; see 100–04).

[7]It may come as a surprise when Oblonsky in part 8 announces that Veslovsky has got married. But that Veslovsky has, like Vronsky, gone off with the volunteers to fight in the Serbian campaign makes it clear that he has not settled down to become a family man.

[8]Levin's insistent attempts to secure patrimony may reflect his anxiety on this score: little is said in the novel either about Levin's father or about Levin's mother's first husband (Koznyshev's father). The money and land apparently belong to her rather than to her husbands.

[9]Tanner notes that the title *Madame Bovary* "does not refer unequivocally to Emma, since there are three Madame Bovarys in the book" (236), the two in addition to Emma being Charles's mother and his first wife. Likewise, the title *Anna Karenina* may refer to both mother and daughter.

[10]Although readers often find that Tolstoy's vision of the family sours in *Anna Karenina* (or after it), Anna Hruska demonstrates that from his early works on, Tolstoy showed a profound ambivalence about the family, the institution he is often seen as celebrating.

The Setting

Liza Knapp

Time and Space in Anna Karenina

As Vladimir Nabokov has shown in his *Lectures on Russian Literature*, time and space are brought together in unusual ways in *Anna Karenina*. The action of the novel lasts four and a half years and moves back and forth between various locations in Russia and western Europe, as it follows the lives of its seven major characters (Anna, Karenin, Vronsky, Levin, Kitty, Dolly and Stiva Oblonsky). Nabokov developed a precise timetable for the novel, which even pinpoints the opening to Friday, 11 February 1872, at eight o'clock in the morning (190).

The narrative of *Anna Karenina* depends on what Nabokov has called a constant "shuttling" back and forth of the action from place to place (148). Often the narration simply cuts from one place to another as it shifts from one grouping of characters to another. For example, part 5, chapter 6 ends with Kitty and Levin's wedding in Moscow, and the next chapter opens in Italy with Anna and Vronsky on their "honeymoon." Those who read *Anna Karenina* in installments when it first came out would not have been so struck by this abrupt change of place, because the transition coincides with a break between installments. (For more on the effects of reading the novel in installments, see Todd, this volume.) At other times, the narrator follows a given character as she or he travels from one setting to another. For example, Tolstoy uses this device when Anna returns by train from Moscow to Petersburg at the end of part 1 and when Dolly travels from Pokrovskoe, Levin's estate, to Vozdvizhenskoe, Vronsky's estate, in part 6. (In the Maude translation, these estates names have been shortened to Pokrovsk and Vozdvizhensk.)

Locales: Russia and Beyond

Most of the events described in *Anna Karenina* occur in the two Russian capital cities of Moscow and Petersburg and their environs or else on one of a handful of family estates, which all happen to be located in the same area of Russia. For Tolstoy, these were the important locales for gentry life. The action of the novel also at certain points crosses Russia's borders, which is consistent with the fact that travel to western Europe was an integral part of Russian gentry life: Kitty's parents take the ailing Kitty to a German spa to recover; a depressed Levin takes an aimless trip to western Europe; Vronsky and Anna "honeymoon" in Italy. The high-ranking servant of state Karenin and the officer Vronsky each at different points contemplate travel to the far reaches of the Russian Empire on matters of state business, although neither trip ever takes place (because of Anna). As the novel ends, Vronsky has joined the volunteers who travel to defend their "brother Slavs" in the Balkans from Turkish attack (698; pt. 8, ch. 1; 700; pt. 8, ch. 2). In the novel, this venture appears in an unfavorable light: for Vronsky it offers a convenient means of carrying out his death wish. In general, in *Anna Karenina* all these trips away from the heartland of Russia, whether to Germany, Italy, or Serbia, are presented by Tolstoy as acts of desperation: they are what you do when you are sick, depressed, or need to flee. Tolstoy's Russians abroad fail to find meaningful activity: what they do amounts to playacting, whether it is Kitty's attempt to imitate Varenka or Vronsky's posing as an artist. Here, as in the novels of Dostoevsky, the true heroes and heroines return to Russia anxious to begin or resume "real life," which is impossible on foreign soil.

Moscow versus Petersburg, according to Tolstoy

By showing different Russian settings—Saint Petersburg, Moscow, and the country estates—*Anna Karenina* acquaints its readers with some of the forms that Russian gentry life could take in Tolstoy's time. Tolstoy's personal tastes are clear in the novel. He presents the more European city Saint Petersburg in a light less favorable than that of the traditional Russian city Moscow, and he shows his preference for traditional life on the patrimonial estate. His bias, however, can introduce students to some of the important features of the Russian historical and cultural context.

The opposition of Moscow and Petersburg, which Tolstoy manipulates in *Anna Karenina*, has figured prominently in Russian thinking about cultural identity. In a favorite paradigm that reflects cultural attitudes, Saint Petersburg is considered the head of Russia and Moscow its heart. Before Petersburg existed, Moscow had been not just the political capital but also the spiritual center of Russia. It was exalted in legend as the third Rome. Whereas the city of Moscow grew spontaneously, Saint Petersburg was a planned, contrived, and therefore artificial city. It was created by an act of will by Peter the Great, to be, in a phrase Pushkin made famous in "The Bronze Horseman," Russia's "window on Europe" (see "Mednyi vsadnik" 274). European know-how was imported to plan the new capital, but the physical labor was performed by Russian people, many of whom perished in the process. Beginning with Pushkin's "Bronze Horseman," Russian literature has perpetuated the myth of Petersburg as a city where the pursuit of happiness is thwarted by forces over which human beings have no control.

In Tolstoy's novel, residents of Saint Petersburg lead an artificial life, where service to the tsarist regime, slavish devotion to the court, and the pursuit of idle pleasures and thrills (e.g., croquet and steeplechases) take precedence over family life. The family life of the Karenins, even before Anna's ill-fated trip to Moscow, strikes Dolly as unnatural. Adultery seems to be part of the fabric of Petersburg life. By contrast, Moscow is depicted in *Anna Karenina*, as it was in *War and Peace*, as a place that is more homey and more conducive to family life. Tolstoy establishes this contrast very well in part 7, chapter 20, where he describes Oblonsky's delight in visiting Petersburg. Oblonsky, a serial adulterer who has trouble remembering his wife and children and who has squandered his children's patrimony, finds the atmosphere of the city a relief after being in the bosom of his family in Moscow. He is convinced that in Petersburg people "lived, really *lived*, instead of vegetating as in Moscow" (659; pt.7, ch. 20). He enumerates the advantages of Petersburg life: men are not tied to one woman (Oblonsky calls to mind a certain Prince Chechensky, who spoke to him with impunity about keeping two families, a legitimate and an illegitimate one), children do not take over their parents' lives, careers are easily made, and people live far beyond their means and accumulate enormous debts (658–60).

Whereas Petersburg is clearly the seat of political power, Tolstoy's Moscow has more of an intellectual life. Even so, his depiction of this life is not flattering: Koznyshev and his learned friends in Moscow lack the hands-on understanding of Levin and show the hubris of cerebral men that Tolstoy so despised. Tolstoy also suggests that religious life in Moscow follows tradition, for better or worse. This feature manifests itself when Levin reluctantly goes to confession before his wedding and when the wedding ceremony takes on more meaning for him than he expected. In Petersburg, in contrast, whatever piety is depicted becomes tainted by the falsity that Tolstoy associates with this city: Karenin's friend, Countess Lydia Ivanovna, embodies a self-serving and perverted piety that eventually prevails over Karenin's heartfelt Christian feelings at the time of Anna's illness. Through details of this sort, Tolstoy constantly privileges the more traditional and more Russian Moscow at the expense of modern, cosmopolitan, and westernized Petersburg. He builds on the generally accepted opposition of the two cities in Russian cultural mythology but elaborates on that opposition in a manner that reflects his own anxieties and convictions.

Russian Country Estate: Cultural Context

Anna Karenina, like the novels of Turgenev or the dramas of Chekhov, is a prime source of information about life on the Russian country estate, a setting that played an important role in Russian history before the revolution and that has captured the popular imagination. Although the focus in *Anna Karenina* is on Levin's estate, Pokrovskoe, which appears in all parts except the seventh, Tolstoy depicts life on other estates as well. These include Dolly's Ergushevo (pt. 3, chs. 8–10), Sviyazhsky's estate (pt. 3, chs. 26–28), and Vronsky's Vozdvizhenskoe (pt. 6, chs. 17–25). Tolstoy has designed the geography of his fictional realm so that these estates are, by Russian standards, in close proximity. Visitors can travel by carriage from one to the other in less than a day (in part 6, Dolly leaves Levin's estate before daybreak and arrives at Vronsky's estate with plenty of time to spare before dinner at seven; Levin's estate is only some twenty miles from Ergushevo). As the owners of property in the same area, Levin, Vronsky, Oblonsky, and Sviyazhsky all come together during the provincial elections described at the end of part 6 (chs. 26–31).

As Priscilla Roosevelt and other cultural historians have argued, estate life became especially important to members of the Russian gentry because on the estates they owned and managed they felt an autonomy and power that was lacking in other settings. The country estate was often regarded as a refuge from state control and as an opportunity for creative activity that was both personally and socially meaningful. The emancipation of the serfs, which took place by imperial decree in 1861, altered the traditional structure of estate life. Set in the mid-seventies, *Anna Karenina* gives readers a sense of the new financial, social, and moral concerns that faced the landed gentry in the aftermath of the abolition of serfdom. Although many landowners embraced the emancipation of the serfs for moral reasons (Levin is passionate in this regard: he declares that "we wanted to throw off a yoke that was oppressing us all—all good men" [223–24; pt. 3, ch.3]), it deprived landowners of their free labor force and diminished their land holdings, since serfs were allotted land that had once belonged to their masters. As *Anna Karenina* shows, Russian landowners were challenged to find new ways of continuing to run their estates and new ways of interacting with the peasants, who, although free, faced enormous hardship. (Although the peasants received land when they were emancipated, they had to make redemption payments to the government, which had compensated their former owners when the emancipation took place. Since the land the peasants were allotted was often insufficient for survival, they were forced to work as day laborers for the landowners, or even to migrate to the city in search of work.) Opportunities for civic involvement by the landowners presented themselves as a result of the creation of the zemstvo, a form of local self-government that was introduced in part to provide services for the emancipated peasants (Pipes 265). Levin resists becoming involved in zemstvo activities. He claims to have no interest in serving on a jury where the peasant Alyoshka is on trial for stealing a ham and no interest in discussing the number of cesspool cleaners necessary in the area (223–24; pt. 3, ch.3). For an activity to be meaningful to Levin, he needs to feel that it affects him in a personal way.

By showing multiple estates, Tolstoy gives his readers a sense of the landowners' common problems as well as of the individual solutions. Thus he shows Levin, Sviyazhsky, and Vronsky each trying in his own way to do the right thing for the peasants. But once Tolstoy starts to analyze the issues, there are no satisfactory solutions. Sviyazhsky can afford to behave in a liberal fashion, wasting his money on the peasants and innovations, because he is childless and has no heirs to think of. Levin is not at all convinced that Sviyazhsky's progressive reforms do any good for the peasants. Vronsky's philanthropy is shown to be the desperate, empty attempt of an alienated man to leave a public legacy for himself: he builds a swank hospital for the peasants but neglects some of their more basic needs, such as a maternity ward. Levin, as a paterfamilias in the making, must find a way of assuaging his social conscience while preserving his patrimony.

Interpreting Estate Life

The descriptions in *Anna Karenina* of the various estates and how they are run provide insights into social and political issues of the day, but they also contain important clues about the personal lives of the inhabitants of these estates. The brief descriptions of the state of affairs at Ergushevo (236–48; pt. 3, chs. 7–10) offer telling evidence of Oblonsky's failings as a husband and father. When Dolly and the children arrive, they find that things are a mess, despite his efforts to prepare the estate for them. Oblonsky had made some cosmetic repairs but failed to think about practical matters, leaving Dolly with a leaky roof and not enough food for the children. Dolly, as a true Tolstoyan materfamilias, enlists the peasants' help and finds ways of protecting and providing for her children. Eventually, however, she and her children end up spending their summers at Pokrovskoe, where they depend on the loving-kindness of her sister and brother-in-law. Early in the novel Oblonsky sells woods that were part of Dolly's dowry, and later in the novel he begs Dolly to sell Ergushevo as well (711; pt. 8, ch. 7). In the Tolstoyan scheme, that Oblonsky neglects and ultimately squanders his family's patrimony is emblematic of his adulterous nature.

While life at Ergushevo in an almost parodic way reflects the Oblonsky family dynamic, Tolstoy's evocation of life at Pokrovskoe is more complex. Tolstoy scholars often point out that Levin's beloved Pokrovskoe resembles Tolstoy's family estate of Yasnaya Polyana, to which he had a deep-rooted attachment. Tolstoy's choice of the name Pokrovskoe seems natural. This was a popular name for country estates; his sister and his wife's family each owned property with this name. *Pokrovskoe* (from the root *pokrov*, meaning "protection, sanctuary") evokes specifically the idea of protection granted by the Mother of God to the Russian people. The Russian Orthodox feast of the Pokrov, which occurs in October, traditionally, according to folkways, marks the time when cows are mated.[1] Both the religious and the folk associations of the festival of the Pokrov fit perfectly with the realm that Levin creates for himself. When he first returns to Pokrovskoe in part 1, after Kitty refuses his offer of marriage, he devotes himself to the breeding of his prize cow, Pava. But he continues to dream of perpetuating the world of his parents by marrying and producing children of his own. His estate has the aura of a safe haven that protects family life, both bovine and human.

Pokrovskoe is depicted in detail throughout the novel, but what it represents becomes most obvious in part 6 when it appears in juxtaposition to Vozdvizhenskoe, where Vronsky and Anna have set up housekeeping. (Tolstoy employs his characteristic device of using the contrast between two similar but opposed things to reveal the true nature of each.) The telling differences provide material for class discussion; they reveal a great deal about Tolstoyan values and about how Tolstoy embeds these values in his seemingly realistic, prosaic novel (see Knapp, "Estates").

Tolstoy creates various revealing oppositions by means of analogous details regarding the life at both estates. For example, the communal activities at Pokrovskoe, jam making and mushroom picking, involve different generations and result in the preservation of goods for family consumption. In contrast, at Vozdvizhenskoe, as the visitor Dolly is appalled to find, the grown-ups amuse themselves playing children's games, with no utilitarian purpose. Life at Vozdvizhenskoe is presented as being very untraditional, unnatural, and un-Russian. Anna refers to the collection of people, which includes an architect and doctor, as "une petite cour" (562; pt. 6, ch. 19; "a little court"). At Pokrovskoe, everyone is family. Vronsky, unlike Levin, has no attachment to the land or the people and simply spends his money on his manor house and the hospital that lacks a maternity ward.

Much of *Anna Karenina* points to the superiority of Pokrovskoe and the family values it embodies. The novel ends with Levin, Kitty, their baby boy, and members of their extended family (including Koznyshev, the Shcherbatskys, the Oblonskys) all gathered at Pokrovskoe, while Vronsky and other misfits set off to fight in the Serbian conflict. Levin professes an isolationist skepticism about this whole venture. Using a type of argument that is characteristic of Tolstoy, he denies feeling any greater sense of kinship for his so-called brother Slavs than he does for the Turks that Russians such as Vronsky are getting ready to kill in the name of Slavic brotherhood. Most of what matters to Levin is at Pokrovskoe, and he likes it that way. He occupies himself with family duties, with managing his estate, with interactions with the peasants, and with his new passion, beekeeping. Although the affairs and concerns of the outside world still touch Pokrovskoe (especially when visitors arrive from the outside world), the estate has the feel of a separate kingdom.

Travel in Anna Karenina

In *Anna Karenina*, travel plays a determining role in the plot and in the narrative structure: both depend on Tolstoy's heroes' and heroines' moving from place to place and coming into contact with one another in different combinations. In this regard, the contrast with another multiplot novel is instructive. *Middlemarch*, like *Anna Karenina*, weaves together different plot lines, but it depends on a geographic constant—Middlemarch—to achieve this effect. George Eliot sets out to show that in provincial England of an earlier time people's lives willy-nilly intersected in prosaically dramatic ways by virtue of the fact that they all resided in proximity of one another. Middlemarchers do leave Middlemarch, of course. (For example, Dorothea and Casaubon travel to Italy on their honeymoon, where Dorothea has a fateful encounter with Will Ladislaw. And in the "Finale" we learn that both the Lydgates and the Ladislaws have left Middlemarch.) But by and large the town of Middlemarch provides the novel with its structure. Tolstoy uses a different method for weaving together his multiple plots: as a host of characters travel from place to place, their journeys entangle their lives in a different kind of intricate web.

The Effect of the Railroad on Russian Life and in Tolstoy's Novel

The mobility that is so essential to the structure of the novel on the formal level, moving the plots along and allowing them to intersect, reflects changes in the fabric of life that were greatly disturbing to Tolstoy as he wrote *Anna Karenina*. Greater mobility resulted from industrialization, from the changes to the patriarchal structure and to the pastoral ideal of Russian life. Both the symbol and agent of this new mobility was the railroad. Without the railroad this novel could not have taken shape. It infiltrates the plot and form of *Anna Karenina* even more than it does Dickens's *Dombey and Son* or Dostoevsky's *The Idiot*, other novels that expressed the age's anxiety about the railroad.

Tolstoy explores in multiple ways the changes wrought by the railroad on Russian life. The role of the railroad in *Anna Karenina* has been the subject of much excellent discussion.[2] Trains allow the heroes and heroines of the novel to come together and move apart, for better or worse. They make it possible for Anna to leave her son in Petersburg and rush to the aid of her brother and his family early in the novel. Whereas in the past the trip between Moscow and Petersburg by horse-drawn carriage would have taken no less than four days and four nights, the railroad, which opened between the cities in 1851, shortened the journey to twenty-two hours or less (Baehr 92). By the time of *Anna Karenina*, although the Trans-Siberian railroad was still a dream, trains already reached some distant provinces of the Russian Empire. When Karenin sets off on his mission to survey the status of the subjugated peoples of the Russian Empire, in a grand gesture he decides to travel by railroad and returns to the government the substantial sum of money allotted him to pay for twelve horses all the way to his destination. He makes it as far as Moscow, where he dines with the Oblonskys and then receives a telegram summoning him to the dying Anna's side. Here, again, the plot takes the form it does because modern inventions, such as the telegraph and railroad, have made it possible to cover great distances quickly, thus effectively altering the rhythm of life by changing relations to time and space.

Like the stagecoach of earlier times, the railroad provides opportunities for chance encounters with acquaintances and strangers, but in what is presented as a more frenzied way. *Anna Karenina* is full of such encounters, both on platforms and in train compartments. Levin ends up in Karenin's train compartment as they both travel to Moscow in part 4; in part 1, Anna and Vronsky's mother travel together to Moscow; later in part 1, Vronsky rides the same train as Anna back to Petersburg, where, as they emerge at the station, he meets Karenin and, watching Anna, determines that there is no passion between this husband and wife; in part 7, just before committing suicide, Anna is affected by the French conversation about the role of reason in human life she overhears in her train compartment. Instructors may want to remind students, for whom the idea of train travel may evoke rows of passengers all facing in the same direction, that these railroad encounters in *Anna Karenina*—like others described in nineteenth-century Russian literature, including Tolstoy's "The Kreutzer Sonata"—all occur in small compartments that, like those still in use in Europe, brought travelers into more intimate face-to-face contact with one another. Nabokov's diagrams of the seating arrangement of Anna's traveling companions are reproduced in his *Lectures*. In *Anna Karenina*, as in *The Idiot*, which opens with the chance meeting of Rogozhin, Myshkin, and others in a train compartment, the railroad has the effect of generating plots by mixing together people whose lives would not have intersected so fatefully without it (Bethea). Chance encounters in train compartments or at train stations in these railroad-generated novels have an aura of the fatalistic rather than of the providential.

Tolstoy points to other indirect effects of the railroad on aspects of life. When Levin and Kitty are summoned to the deathbed of Nicholas Levin, they find him in a hotel that depresses them "after their fresh home life." What is ultimately objectionable is the "modern, self-satisfied railway-induced state of bustle." Thus the railroad is to blame for this depressing atmosphere, which hits them so hard because it "was quite irreconcilable with what was awaiting them," that is, the death of Nicholas (445; pt. 5, ch. 17). Although Kitty is so intent on nursing Nicholas that she does not seem bothered by this atmosphere, Levin takes note of the ways in which the "railway-induced bustle" enters into this solemn event in the Levin family. Kitty meets strangers in the corridors as she goes from Nicholas's room to her own to get more pillows. When she summons the waiter to the room to help do things like change the dying man's shirt, the waiter has to interrupt his work in the dining room where he is serving a meal to some engineers. Although the railroad is only an indirect presence at the death of Nicholas, in what Tolstoy called the "labyrinth of linkages" of *Anna Karenina*, where parts of the novel are mysteriously linked because of a shared idea or image (*Polnoe sobranie* 62: 269; letter to Strakhov, 23 Apr. 1876), this death is linked to Anna's, in which the railroad plays a direct role.

Tolstoy makes it clear that the railroad has infiltrated all layers of Russian life. Children have even replaced the traditional game of horsey with a more dangerous variant that mimics train travel (Baehr 89). *Anna Karenina* also includes explicit discussion about the railroad and its effect on Russian patriarchal life. Railroad magnates are presented as selfish capitalists who have no regard for the rest of humanity. (To make the point, Tolstoy calls one Malthus.) By the end of the novel, Stiva (Prince Oblonsky, whose ancestors date back to Rurik) is working for the "Membership of the Committee of the Joint Agency

of the Mutual Credit Balance of Southern Railways and Banking Houses."
Oblonsky's entry into the capitalist world marks a break with the traditions of
his ancestors, who served only the state (651–54; pt. 7, ch. 17).

In *Anna Karenina*, Tolstoy appropriates the myth of the railroad that had
been developed by other Russian writers. In Nikolai Nekrasov's poem "The
Railroad" (1864; in Russian, "Zheleznaia doroga"), a young patrician riding the
railroad is haunted by the ghosts of poor workers who perished while building
the railroad for the rich and powerful. In the Russian cultural context, the railroad and the city of Petersburg are linked, because both were produced in a
top-down attempt to modernize and westernize Russia. Both were popularly
seen as forces that violated all that was sacred and traditional to the Russian
folk (Baehr 90).

The Railroad Age in French and English Novels

Instructors may want to inform their non-Russian-speaking students that the
Russian term for railroad, *zheleznaia doroga*, literally means "iron road." (The
Russian term imitates the German *Eisenbahn* and the French *chemin de fer*.)
This piece of information proves helpful in interpreting the nightmare that
Anna and Vronsky share, because iron figures in the words and actions of the
sinister francophone peasant (see Barran, this volume, for an interpretation of
this dream.) As Tony Tanner has noted, iron is an ominous presence in the network of symbolism of Flaubert's *Madame Bovary*, another novel of adultery to
which *Anna Karenina* can be compared in the classroom (316–20). In
Flaubert's novel, as in Tolstoy's, iron is associated with the railroad, among
other things. The presence of the railroad, which is so thoroughly a part of
Anna Karenina, was only beginning to haunt the realm of *Madame Bovary*, set
in an earlier time and in a different world. Emma still travels to her trysts by
horse-drawn coach, yet railroad construction causes a deafening and ominous
racket in Rouen, which already has railroad links to Paris. Flaubert's and Tolstoy's attitudes to the railroad have common elements.[3]

Instructors who teach *Anna Karenina* in conjunction with English novels will
find that Tolstoy gives a Russian point of view on the very issues relating to the
railroad that Dickens drew attention to in his fiction and articles. Tolstoy uses
the railroad in *Anna Karenina* in ways that recall what Dickens does in *Dombey
and Son*, where there is a death by train, a number of scenes in the vicinity of
trains and stations, and a number of questions raised in direct and indirect ways
about the effect of the railroad on human life. This shared concern with the
railroad is only one aspect of the relation between these two novels (see Mandelker, *Framing*).

George Eliot's *Middlemarch*, a favorite novel of Tolstoy's and one that is often
taught in the same courses as *Anna Karenina*, also presents a vision of the railroad that may fruitfully be compared to Tolstoy's. *Middlemarch* only hints at
the damaging impact of the railroad on modern life—by necessity, since it de-

picts an earlier world in which the railroad is being constructed. As Middle-marchers debate the pros and cons of this new force that is taking over neigh-boring farmland, Eliot allows multiple opinions to be heard, some outrageous and some sensible. In the hands of Tolstoy, misgivings such as those presented in *Middlemarch* become a full-fledged nightmare. This nightmare reaches its log-ical and apocalyptic culmination after *Anna Karenina*, in "The Kreutzer Sonata."

Horse-Drawn Conveyances

Tolstoy himself had a personal aversion to train travel, the result of a concate-nation of philosophical, political, and even physiological factors. It appears to have made him sick. In a famous letter written to Turgenev, he remarked that "the railroad has the same relationship to travel as a brothel does to love: just as convenient but just as inhumanly mechanical and murderously monotonous" (letter of 9 Apr. 1857, qtd. in Baehr 88). In this same letter, Tolstoy describes how uplifting it was for him after a train ride to switch to a horse-drawn vehi-cle. In typical fashion, he does not simply state his personal preferences, he jus-tifies them on moral grounds.

Levin has a similar response when he travels home from Moscow early in the novel after Kitty has refused to marry him and after his depressing visit to his brother Nicholas. In the train he converses with his fellow passengers "about politics and the new railway," but he feels "oppressed, just as in Moscow, by the confusion of the views expressed, by discontent with himself and a vague sense of shame." (This dynamic, in mild form here, becomes catastrophic in "The Kreutzer Sonata.") But these feelings change as soon as he is met at the station by his peasants, who have come to meet him in their horse-drawn sledge: "Levin felt that the confusion was beginning to clear away and his shame and self-dissatisfaction to pass" (84; pt. 1, ch. 26).

Travel by horse-drawn conveyances figures prominently in both the rural and the city life depicted in *Anna Karenina*. Many important scenes are associ-ated with cart and carriage rides. For example, after a night spent in a haystack musing about peasant life, Levin has all but concluded that he must abandon his gentry life, marry a peasant, and live a simple life of toil, when he suddenly catches sight of Kitty in a passing carriage, en route to Dolly's estate. The sight of her face makes it clear to him that he loves Kitty and that this love must pre-vail over his dreams of peasant life. Although there is nothing extraordinary about Levin's catching sight of Kitty in this locale (Dolly's estate is close by, and he even has been told that Kitty is planning a visit), it is still quite a coinci-dence that he should happen to see her at what he feels is a moment of deci-sion in his life. Here Tolstoy presents a chance encounter that is providential in nature, in contrast to the fateful meetings that occur between Anna and Vron-sky in the vicinity of the railroad. Yet these events, both the providential and the fateful, create a sense of anxiety about the fabric of human life and the role of chance in it.

Anna's memorable inner monologue occurs as she rides through Moscow in a carriage (see Knapp, "Tue-la!"). She reacts simultaneously to what she observes as the carriage moves through the city streets and to what is going on inside her. The outer and inner worlds interact to make her search for meaning particularly poignant. At one point, she recalls traveling to the Troitsa Monastery when she was seventeen, and she latches on to the fact that there was as yet no railroad—she traveled by horse and carriage.[4] Anna at this point returns to her former innocent self, for whom happiness still seemed possible. Although these memories occur in an inner monologue that is full of apparently illogical and random associations, the train of thought is quite clear: the railroad and all it represents have destroyed the young girl who made pilgrimages by horse-drawn carriage to the monastery. That purity has been lost.

Although Anna is clearly distraught throughout her carriage ride—to Dolly's, back home, to the train station—and although she expresses a great deal of animosity to the human race in general and to Vronsky in particular, she still has moments of hope and love while she is in the horse-drawn carriage. Her resolve to kill herself seems to take hold of her when she is on the train and in the station. Remembering the death that occurred at the train station when she first met Vronsky, driven by things she overhears on the train, and eventually by her vision of the iron-wielding peasant from her dreams, she commits suicide by jumping under the moving train. Her last moments are filled with religious feelings that date from an era before the railroad (she makes the sign of the cross, remembers her childhood and girlhood, begs God for forgiveness), but she is overcome by the train.

NOTES

I am grateful to Amy Mandelker and Hugh McLean for very helpful suggestions on this section.

[1] I am grateful to Gregory Freidin for pointing this out.

[2] Robert Louis Jackson's article (this volume) analyzes Anna's railroad journey back to Petersburg at the end of part 1. For a comprehensive discussion of the railroad in Russian literature, see Baehr; for a discussion of Tolstoy's vision of the railroad, especially in Anna Karenina, see Al'tman; Jahn; Schultze; Stenboch-Fermor. Bethea's discussion of the railroad in The Idiot also includes Anna Karenina (77–79).

[3] See Julian Barnes's information and speculation on Flaubert's response to the railroad.

[4] Tolstoy's contemporaries would have been aware that this particular railroad line was the subject of much debate and that church authorities objected to the idea of pilgrims arriving at the monastery in railroad cars (Baehr 88).

Part One

MATERIALS

Russian Editions and English Translations

Liza Knapp

Russian Editions

In 2000, the Tolstoy Group of the World Literature Institute at the Russian Academy of Sciences in Moscow began publication of what promises to be the definitive scholarly edition of Tolstoy's complete works, in a hundred volumes. It is hard to predict when the volumes containing *Anna Karenina* and related material will appear. This new edition of Tolstoy's works will replace the one in ninety volumes known as the Jubilee Edition (1928–58), which is the edition most often referred to in scholarly discussions. The essays in this volume cite the Jubilee Edition (Tolstoy, *Polnoe sobranie*) when they refer to Tolstoy's letters and other works.

Tolstoy began concentrated work in March of 1873 on the novel that became *Anna Karenina*. Large portions of the drafts appear in volume 20 of the Jubilee Edition. Excellent work on the metamorphosis of these drafts has been done by N. K. Gudzii, V. A. Zhdanov, and others. The drafts show Tolstoy's creative laboratory much as Dostoevsky's do, although they have not received as much attention. Logistics may play a role here: there are more of them, and even in Russian they are not as widely available as Dostoevsky's drafts. Extensive portions of the drafts of *Anna Karenina* have not been published in English translation (as have the notebooks for Dostoevsky's novels), but C. J. G. Turner (*Karenina Companion*) offers an excellent survey and discussion of them in English.

The early publication history of *Anna Karenina*, from its initial appearance in installments (1875–77) through its first appearance in book form in 1878, is discussed in detail in William Todd's essay in this volume.

The numerous Russian editions of *Anna Karenina* currently available do not all follow the same text of the novel, although variations are slight. In 1970, a new edition of *Anna Karenina* was published by Zhdanov and E. E. Zaidenshnur. In preparing this text, the editors sought to purge from it many small changes that had been introduced at different stages by the various people who participated in the copying, editing, and printing of the novel. Some of these changes were made close to home, by Tolstoy's wife and by his friend Nikolai Strakhov, who helped Tolstoy prepare the novel for publication. It has been suggested that Strakhov was given leeway to make certain corrections on his own in part because Tolstoy did not want to be bothered with some of the details. However, Strakhov reported that when he did consult with Tolstoy about some specific changes, Tolstoy would insist on his version and rebuff Strakhov's requests, even for changes that seemed innocuous to Strakhov. This experience led Strakhov to the conclusion that every word in *Anna Karenina* mattered to

Tolstoy no less than every word in a poem matters to its poet (Turner, *Karenina Companion* 53–54).

Those who edited Tolstoy in his lifetime sought, whether consciously or not, to pretty things up and to soften some of the idiosyncrasies of his prose, such as his tendencies for repetition and for referring to a given character by different forms of the character's name. These idiosyncrasies were thought to be confusing to the reader and even a sign of unevenness or sloppiness. Readers of the post-1970 Russian versions of *Anna Karenina*, which more closely reflect the way Tolstoy originally wanted *Anna Karenina* to be, may feel that they are getting a more unadulterated Tolstoyan literary style. There is currently a greater appreciation of certain elements of Tolstoy's prose that were found irksome by some of his contemporaries.

To appreciate the differences in the texts of *Anna Karenina* and what they reveal about Tolstoy's style and the sensibility of those who edited him, it is necessary to track the changes closely. This exercise is excellent for graduate students and others who can freely read the original, because it makes them more aware of the characteristic features of Tolstoy's style.

In his *Karenina Companion*, Turner offers an excellent discussion of these newer editions of *Anna Karenina*, as well as a list in English of the most significant of the variants. The revised Edmonds translation and the new Pevear and Volokhonsky translation make use of the more recent, "purer" Russian text of *Anna Karenina* (Edmonds is the most consistent in this regard), whereas the other translations follow earlier editions.

English Translations

A significant majority of respondents to our survey report using the Norton Critical Edition, which contains the Maude translation, revised by George Gibian. (For that reason and not because of a preference for the translation itself, this edition is being used for citation in this volume.) *Anna Karenina* exists in a number of fine English translations, though none of them is definitive or has unassailable advantages as a translation. Aside from the larger questions of how the translation reads in English and how it captures the spirit and the specifics of Tolstoy's original, a number of other issues figure into the decision about which English *Anna Karenina* to assign to students. Among these are: Does the instructor want an edition with a critical apparatus or explanatory notes? Does the instructor want a modern translation or one that reflects a sensibility of an earlier era? Is there a particular feature that the instructor is likely to focus on (e.g., cultural context or Tolstoy's style)?

A number of articles offer expert opinion on translations of *Anna Karenina*. Henry Gifford's essay "On Translating Tolstoy," which borrows its title from Matthew Arnold's classic essay "On Translating Homer," does a masterful job of setting forth some of the general issues that arise in rendering Tolstoy in English. Gifford examines the particulars of different translations of various works by Tolstoy, including the Garnett, Maude, and Edmonds translations of *Anna Karenina*. In "Problems in the English Translations of *Anna Karenina*," Richard Sheldon closely compares different translations of key scenes in the novel (the famous opening sentence, Anna at the ball, the seduction scene, Anna's suicide). Since these scenes are ones that instructors are likely to focus on in class, his article is an excellent source for instructors preparing to teach the novel. Sheldon's analysis of the translations draws attention to important features of Tolstoy's style while also offering a sense of the difficulties translators of *Anna Karenina* have faced. Zoja Pavlovskis-Petit's entry on *Anna Karenina* in the *Encyclopedia of Literary Translation into English* characterizes the translations of *Anna Karenina* from early ones to recent ones. Turner's article "The Maude Translation" gives a detailed discussion of the discrepancies between different versions of the Maude translation and the Russian original. In his recent "Which English *Anna*?" Hugh McLean provides an extremely informative evaluation of five available translations, including the new one by Richard Pevear and Larissa Volokhonsky. He compares different translations of a critical sample of passages. The article does more than answer the question (Which English *Anna*?); it also provides insight into the mysteries of Tolstoy's style.

I discuss the relevant features of five translations below. Included are the four that were mentioned more frequently by respondents to our survey as well as the translation by Pevear and Volokhonsky, which was published after our survey was complete. The translations are treated in the order in which they were originally published. Often they were revised and corrected when reissued. For this reason, it makes sense only to use the latest editions; my comments are addressed to these.

Constance Garnett's Translation, Revised by Leonard J. Kent and Nina Berberova

Constance Garnett, who provided the English-speaking world with masterful translations of so many Russian classics, also did an early translation of *Anna Karenina* (1901). Her translation has been thoughtfully revised and carefully corrected by Leonard J. Kent and Nina Berberova. While eliminating Garnett's notorious bowdlerisms, they preserved all the features that have attracted readers to her translations over the years. Garnett's fans praise her literary sensibility and find in her works a genius and inspiration that set her apart. A number of our respondents voiced a general preference for translations (like this one or the Maude) done closer to the period of the original text, on the grounds that these use a style, diction, and lexicon that is likely to be a closer English equivalent of Tolstoy's late-nineteenth-century Russian. It is true that some features of this prose may appear quaint or alien to our modern students, but they are likely to encounter the same problem when they read novels written in English in the nineteenth century.

Vladimir Nabokov peppered his brilliant and very informative discussion of

Anna Karenina in his *Lectures on Russian Literature* with negative comments about Garnett's translation of *Anna Karenina*, which may have deterred some of his readers from using her translation. This is unfortunate. It is important to note that Nabokov was using an earlier, uncorrected edition of the translation. Furthermore, his criticism of Garnett's translation reflects his own taste as a translator. His remarks suggest that he is likely to have been fully satisfied only with his own translation or one he closely supervised. (He envisioned such a project.)

The revised Garnett does an excellent job of reproducing the atmosphere of nineteenth-century Russia in a straightforward, unapologetic mode, while offering modern non-Russian readers the assistance they need. It resists the temptation to make Russian names sound too English. This edition has a ten-page section of commentary, which excerpts important critical statements about the novel, by Tolstoy, Dostoevsky, Thomas Mann, Nabokov, and others. It includes part of Tolstoy's letter where he speaks of *Anna Karenina* as a "labyrinth of linkages" (*Polnoe sobranie* 62: 269). This excerpt is more complete than that found in the Norton edition, which omits an important part. The revised Garnett edition has some very brief, informative notes and translations of French phrases at the bottom of the relevant pages. It reproduces the Russian table of ranks for military, civil and state service. One small drawback is that it lacks a list of major characters.

Louise Maude and Aylmer Maude's Translation, Revised by George Gibian

The Maude translation (1918) has much to recommend it. Louise Maude and Aylmer Maude knew Tolstoy personally and had a clear grasp of his patterns of thought. Having lived in Russia, they were familiar with many features of the world that Tolstoy was evoking in his novel. That they embarked on translating his works with his blessing makes their translation something of a sentimental favorite for Tolstoy enthusiasts. Respondents to our survey praised the Maude translation for being generally quite faithful to Tolstoy's original, as well as for using a "late Victorian diction" that seems appropriate to Tolstoy. But, among those who have closely compared the two period translations, the Maude and the Garnett, the consensus seems to be that the Maude translation is somewhat less satisfying in subtle ways. Gifford suggests that the Maudes lack the "creative sense of language" necessary "to make the ideal translation" ("On Translating" 22).

Turner has examined discrepancies between the Russian text of *Anna Karenina* and the Maude translation ("Maude Translation"), which is used not only in the Norton Critical Edition but also in the World's Classics Series published by Oxford University Press. He notes that even though a number of errors have been corrected in the recent edition of the Norton, there is still a need for further systematic correction.

In places the revised Maude translation in the Norton edition fails to capture

the right nuance of Tolstoy's Russian. One instance occurs in the scene just before Anna commits suicide. We are told in the translation that as Anna makes
the sign of the cross, this gesture "called up a whole series of girlish and childish memories" (695; pt. 7, ch. 31). The choice of "girlish" (for *devicheskie*) and
"childish" (for *detskie*) is not ideal, given that these English words can have pe-
jorative connotations (of something trivial or juvenile). Rather, the memories of
her earlier, more innocent, life are sacred. Because of its etymological root, the
Russian word *devicheskie* has nuances of "virginal" or "maidenly." These connotations, subliminally present in the Russian word, come to the surface in the
sexually charged context of Tolstoy's novel: on some level Tolstoy is suggesting
that the oversexed Anna is returning to a virginal state. Perhaps it would be too
much to attempt to bring these nuances out in the English translation. The
Kent-Berberova revision of the Garnett and Pevear and Volokhonsky translate
this passage, respectively, as "a whole series of memories of her childhood and
girlhood" (867) and "a whole series of memories from childhood and girlhood"
(768). This more neutral wording is better than "childish" and "girlish," which
steer readers in the wrong direction.

In rendering Russian names, the Maudes persistently anglicize them, so that
Agafya becomes Agatha, Platon Plato, Ekaterina Catherine, Konstantin Constantine, Stepan Stephen, and so forth. This policy has the effect of making
these names seem less foreign to English-speaking readers, but it blurs the important distinction in the novel between the Russian given names and nicknames and the English nicknames that are often used for certain characters. If
all the first names are anglicized to start with, then the anglicized nicknames
that Tolstoy used and that are marked in the Russian text as anglicisms, such as
Annie and Dolly, do not stand out as they should. When Kitty is called "Katya"
by Levin's dying brother, the Maudes translate the Russian Katya as "Kate"
(450; pt. 5, ch. 18), whereas the context very specifically requires a Russian
nickname, not another English one. (The Maudes may have reasoned that in
the context of English culture, Kate reproduces some of the same associations
that Katya has in Russian culture and that the nickname Kate has a feel that is
quite distinct from the nickname Kitty. But for Tolstoy ethnicity also was a
major factor in what distinguishes Katya from Kitty.) The nickname of Anna's
son by Karenin appears in the Maude translation as "Serezha" rather than the
more usual "Seryozha," a form that gives readers a better sense of how it should
be pronounced. In this translation the estates of Levin and Vronsky become
Pokrovsk and Vozdvizhensk, with the Russian endings lopped off.

The second Norton edition of the Maude translation includes a critical apparatus that many have found invaluable. (There have been substantial changes in
it since the first edition [1970].) Included are lists of principal characters and
Russian terms; an informative, brief chronology of Tolstoy's long and productive life; and a select bibliography of critical works in English. Throughout the
text are brief, informative footnotes explaining various literary and cultural references, identifying historical and literary personages, translating French phrases,

and so forth. The "Background and Sources" section contains a brief publication history as well as a selection of very short excerpts, mostly from letters and diaries. In these excerpts are some of the most important statements made by Tolstoy and others about the composition of the novel. The "Criticism" section, a hundred pages, contains an excellent selection, ranging in time from Dostoevsky's judgments on the novel in his *A Writer's Diary* to recent responses from North American, British, and Russian critics and scholars. Many of these pieces have been taken from longer works.

Because the Norton edition is so widely used on college campuses, some of the critical views expressed in it may have begun to affect the way students are responding to *Anna Karenina*. More specifically, what is known in Tolstoy studies as an anti-Anna stance has gained greater currency. (Gary Saul Morson's "Anna Karenina's Omens," which presents a cogent and eloquent argument "against" Anna, is now in the Norton edition.) Instructors note that their students show less patience with (and less sympathy for) Anna than they did in the past.

The critical apparatus that accompanies the Maude translation has clearly played an important role in making the Norton the popular choice for teaching. It currently costs roughly twice as much as the Garnett Modern Library edition.

Rosemary Edmonds's Translation

After the Russian version was published that sought to rid the text of *Anna Karenina* of editorial intrusions, Edmonds systematically revised her 1954 translation so that it would conform to the text of *Anna Karenina* that many scholars consider more authentic. Most of these changes are minor, and even their cumulative effect does not alter the novel in a significant way. Still, some of the variants from the "purer" version highlight intriguing features of Tolstoy's style. For example, in part 4, chapter 18, after Karenin and Vronsky have come together at Anna's sickbed in a scene of great intensity, the narrator follows Vronsky as he leaves the Karenin house and conveys Vronsky's thoughts to the reader, making it clear that Vronsky is surprised that he and Karenin appear to have reversed roles, with Karenin now having the upper hand. Tolstoy had written, "The husband, the deceived [or betrayed] husband, who had [. . .]" (in Russian, see *Anna Karenina* [Zhdanov and Zaidenshnur] 351). At some point in the editing process, the first mention of the husband—before the qualification is added—was eliminated so that the sentence was more straightforward and read, "The deceived husband, who had [. . .]." Scholarly Russian editions from the 1970s on, however, reinstated the original repetition. (Tolstoy is actually known for this kind of repetition, which both translators and editors have been tempted to eliminate.) This repetition creates an effect. It suggests the disordered state of Vronsky's thinking as he leaves the Karenins' house after a wrenching scene, as well as his perception of Karenin as a stock character—"the deceived husband." But now Vronsky finds this deceived husband acting in a surprising way. Tolstoy's original version dynamically reproduces Vronsky's wrestling with his conception of Karenin. Examples like this show that Tolstoy was, like his French and English counterparts, deftly experimenting with narrative point of view.

Of all the translations discussed here, Edmonds's is the only one to preserve this repetition: "the husband, the deceived husband" (440). (The Pevear and Volokhonsky translation incorporated many of the revisions of the Russian text made in the 1970s but not this one [415].) But even as the Edmonds translation seeks to be true to Tolstoy's intentions by reinstating his original phrasing in certain spots, some readers may find that it ends up straying further than necessary from the original in other areas. For example, Edmonds takes liberties with the names and does not always remain true to Tolstoy's usage. This edition lacks notes, which students often rely on for explanation of some of the historical and cultural data. No translation is provided for French phrases.

Joel Carmichael's Translation

The Carmichael edition has received high praise for what one of our respondents called its "combination of simplicity, vibrancy, and emotional depth." Sheldon finds this translation to be the "most supple in its English and most true to Tolstoy's style" of all the translations he considered (259). (The Pevear and Volokhonsky translation was not available at the time.) Joel Carmichael shows particular acuity in his ability to render Tolstoyan repetition in an inspired way. He does an excellent job of capturing the dynamism of Tolstoy's Russian. He has provided a readable *Anna Karenina* designed especially for the modern North American reader. It was characterized by one of our respondents as "not ponderous."

Carmichael has introduced a standardized system for naming characters. He thus does away both with the intricacies of the Russian system of names (forms such as the patronymic) and with Tolstoy's manipulation of this system to achieve different effects. His decision here is surprising, since on the whole he shows great sensitivity to Tolstoy's artistic techniques and a talent for rendering them.

This edition lacks explanatory notes. French phrases have mostly been translated into English. The bibliography of works on Tolstoy reflects an eclectic choice and is seriously out of date, listing no works published after 1978. The edition is compact but physically inconvenient for students because of the extremely narrow margins on all sides.

Richard Pevear and Larissa Volokhonsky's Translation

The new translation of *Anna Karenina* by Pevear and Volokhonsky is likely to become a popular choice for use in the classroom, especially now that it is available in paperback. It has a number of features that instructors often look for. There is a very informative list of major characters and a "Suggestions for Further Reading" section. The explanatory endnotes are excellent; they draw on the commentaries to Russian editions as well as on Nabokov's notes about the novel. French phrases are translated in footnotes.

The translation itself shows the same strengths that have drawn readers to Pevear and Volokhonsky's translations of Dostoevsky. Pevear and Volokhonsky have been credited with being able to reproduce verbal depths that other English translations of Russian classics failed to render. Whereas previous translators of *Anna Karenina* were governed by a more Victorian literary sensibility (Maude, Garnett) or by an inspired sense of the cadences of prose in English (Garnett, Carmichael), Pevear and Volokhonsky attempt to bring English-language readers as close as possible to the experience of reading *Anna Karenina* in the original. They consciously try to maintain distinctive features of Tolstoy's style that have often been muted or lost in translation. They reproduce, to the extent possible, the peculiarities of Tolstoy's syntax and his repetitions. Thus, in many ways, they have produced a very faithful translation. Readers familiar with Tolstoy's Russian text are likely to feel quite at home in this translation, although readers who are not familiar with the original may find this translation harder to read than others.

Because Pevear and Volokhonsky go far in their attempt to convey to the English-language reader the layers of Tolstoy's meaning and the links of various sorts that hold the novel together, they take more risks in interpreting Tolstoy's intent. Naturally, problems will arise when attempts are made to translate wordplays and to convey some of the subtle, hidden, and elusive meanings of words. If these are not translated, the effect is lost; if they are translated, infelicities can result that detract from the translation. This dilemma, of course, is one that arises constantly in translation.

Below, I examine in some detail a passage where Pevear and Volokhonsky render an effect that other translators either overlooked or deemed untranslatable. My purpose is not to weigh the pros and the cons of what Pevear and Volokhonsky have done here but rather to illustrate some of the mind-boggling complexities of the Russian text of *Anna Karenina* and the concomitant difficulties that come into play in translating it.

In Anna's inner monologue just before her suicide, as she rides her carriage through Moscow, she intersperses response to her inner life with comments on what she sees through the carriage window: passersby and shop signs. When she sees a sign that says, "Tyutkin, *coiffeur*," she is amused and says, "*Je me fais coiffer par* Tyutkin" and, smiling, makes a mental note to tell Vronsky that. "But at the same moment she remembered that she now had no one to tell anything funny to" (761). Her response to this random sign thus quite poignantly brings home to her what she sees as the truth about her ultimate isolation.

Pevear and Volokhonsky render the Russian surname Tiut'kin (transliterated as Tyutkin in some translations) as "Twitkin" (761). By altering the first syllable slightly, they have made an English equivalent that sounds silly and at the same time evokes something of the same lexical realm as the Russian. The Russian

surname Tiut'kin was formed according to regular patterns for forming surnames, from a root that is a colloquial or baby-talk term for a dog or pup. As
Nabokov points out (225), Prince Shcherbatsky tells his wife, whom he is chid-
ing for her aggressive matchmaking, that she should simply invite all the
"tiut'ki" ("pups") of Moscow (pt. 1; ch. 15). Tolstoy even draws attention to the
prince's use of this term by putting it in italics and then explaining in parentheses that "so the prince called all the young men of Moscow" (55). Kitty's father,
like Dolly and unlike Kitty's mother, knows in his heart that Kitty will not marry
any of these "tiut'ki" or Vronsky, because she is destined to marry Levin, the antithesis of Muscovite "tiut'ki."

The term suggests a fatuous and foppish quality (Turner, *Karenina Companion* 133). In this regard, Pevear and Volokhonsky's "twit" may seem apt, although
anachronistic because this word did not come into usage in this colloquial sense
until the mid-twentieth century, according to the *Shorter Oxford English
Dictionary*. Aside from this minor quibble, does "twit" capture the essence of
Tolstoy's Russian term? The Garnett translation uses "young bucks" (69); the
Maude translation uses the more literal "young puppies" (51); and Carmichael
uses "whippersnappers" (58), which of the three has the most verve. But none
of these connects to the later Tyutkin of Anna's inner monologue.

In their translation, Pevear and Volokhonsky signal the link between the
"puppies" disparaged early in the novel by Kitty's father and the coiffeur who
figures in Anna's thoughts before her death, by translating the first as "twits"
and the second as "Twitkin." What links the twits of Moscow and the ridicu-
lousness of being coiffed by Twitkin? Both signify the inane, futile existence of
the world that has engulfed Anna, a world to which Kitty herself belonged
when her mother was trying to marry her off. Kitty's father made his ironic remark about the *tiut'ki* of Moscow when he was trying to make his wife see that
there was something sexually degrading about her matchmaking for Kitty.
Although Anna is struck by the odd mix of the ridiculous Russian name coupled
with the French vocation of coiffeur (Nabokov 186), her observation comes at a
point in her inner monologue when she sees a sordid sexuality pervading all
human relations. The coiffeur Tyutkin is a part of this realm.

Translating *Anna Karenina* is a daunting task. Every word matters. Pevear
and Volokhonsky are the only translators to attempt to convey to the reader the
hidden meaning of the Russian name Tyutkin. Twitkin is an efficient and clever
equivalent for the Russian, but is this macaronic last name with its English root
not too bizarre at what is a very poignant moment in the narrative? Might it not
distract the reader from Anna's inner monologue? By translating the joke, they
may have gone too far; yet if they had not translated it, the reader would not
have known that there is something humorous about the meaning as well as
about the sound of Tyutkin. Furthermore, the reader would never have been
able to make the connection between the coiffeur in part 7 and the twits (pups,
whippersnappers) in part 1. These are the choices the translator faces.

A third alternative might have been an explanatory note, although given the labyrinthine nature of this particular novel, it is easy to envision notes of this sort taking up as much space as the novel itself. In fact, many instructors and *Anna Karenina* lovers dream of just such an annotated *Anna Karenina*, one that could serve as a guidebook for Tolstoy's "labyrinth of linkages."

Recommended Readings
for Instructors and Students

Amy Mandelker and Liza Knapp

The sources mentioned here are limited to works available in English. Our recommendations represent the consensus of the survey respondents, who provided lists of references and secondary reading they found useful in teaching *Anna Karenina*. Further suggestions specific to individual topics are provided in the volume's essays.

Russia in General

A useful general reference work for Russian literature is Victor Terras's *Handbook of Russian Literature* with wide-ranging entries on Russian literature and culture. Ronald Hingley's *Russian Writers and Society* gives an overview of Russian literature and its vexed context. We recommend the essays in the recent *Cambridge Companion to the Classic Russian Novel* (Jones and Miller). D. S. Mirsky's *History of Russian Literature* and Terras's *History of Russian Literature*, often assigned in survey courses, both combine detailed information with excellent commentary.

Priscilla Roosevelt's illustrated *Life on the Russian Country Estate* provides background on daily life in nineteenth-century rural Russian society.

Tolstoy

The critical work most frequently cited by questionnaire respondents is Richard Gustafson's *Leo Tolstoy, Resident and Stranger*, a synoptic reading of all of Tolstoy's oeuvre; it has yet to be superseded as the definitive study of Tolstoy's prose. Its publication inspired an era of revisionist Tolstoy studies deriving from signal concepts, for example, emblematic realism and the delineated segment. Gustafson suggests an interpretation of *Anna Karenina* profoundly integrated with Tolstoy's persistent artistic, spiritual, and philosophic concerns. Other general monographs on Tolstoy are John Bayley's *Tolstoy and the Novel*, Richard F. Christian's *Tolstoy: A Critical Introduction*, Henry Gifford's *Tolstoy*, Donna Orwin's *Tolstoy's Art and Thought*, Rimvydas Silbajoris's *Tolstoy's Aesthetics and His Art*, and Edward Wasiolek's *Tolstoy's Major Fiction*. There are a number of collections of essays on Tolstoy: *Critical Essays on Tolstoy* (Wasiolek), *New Essays on Tolstoy* (M. Jones), *In the Shade of the Giant: Essays on Tolstoy* (McLean), and *Cambridge Critical Companion to Tolstoy* (Orwin).

The periodical publication of the International Tolstoy Society, *Tolstoy*

Studies Journal, which has been appearing annually since 1988, is an invaluable
resource for bibliographies and surveys of ongoing research, and it represents
the best Tolstoy scholarship and criticism. Volume 8 (1995–96) is a special issue
on *Anna Karenina*.

There are two excellent omnibus collections of criticism: A. V. Knowles's
Tolstoy: The Critical Heritage includes a generous helping from the Russian
press, translated into English, as well as selections from the early critical response to Tolstoy in English; Gifford's *Leo Tolstoy: A Critical Anthology* is comprehensive through the 1960s and provides an array of responses to Tolstoy,
largely from well-known writers and literary critics. Harold Bloom's research
and study guide *Leo Tolstoy* in the series Bloom's Major Novelists includes excerpts from criticism about *Anna Karenina* (and *War and Peace*) as well as a
plot summary and a list of characters.

The story of Tolstoy's long life makes fascinating reading, and a number of biographies of Tolstoy are available in English. Short, generally favorable biographies were written early on by both Aylmer Maude and Edward Garnett. The
multivolume series by Boris Eikhenbaum, which includes *The Young Tolstoi,
Tolstoi in the Sixties, Tolstoi in the Seventies,* offers extensive information about
Tolstoy's creative and intellectual life. This series has been extremely influential
in Tolstoy studies. *Tolstoy in the Seventies* would be of most interest to the
teacher of *Anna Karenina*. There is a readable one-volume life and works study
by Viktor Shklovsky. The highly respected life and works by Ernest Simmons
has been followed by a number of popular biographies, the best of which is that
of A. N. Wilson.

Tolstoy's diaries and letters have been translated into English and compiled,
each into a two-volume set, with superb annotations, by Christian (Tolstoy,
Tolstoy's Diaries and *Tolstoy's Letters*). These are highly recommended reading
for those who want further insight into the life and mind of the creator of *Anna
Karenina*. Countess Sophia Tolstoy's diaries are available in the English translation by Cathy Porter (Tolstaia). For those interested in the countess's biography,
we recommend *Sonya: The Life of Countess Tolstoy* by Anne Edwards, as well
as Phyllis Rose's account of the Tolstoy's marriage in *Parallel Lives: Five Victorian Marriages*. Tolstoy's own semiautobiographical trilogy, *Childhood, Boyhood,* and *Youth*, as well as his *Confession,* can be useful in examining the life;
some teachers have used these works in classroom exercises exploring auto-
biography and the writing of fiction. Similarly, students often enjoy reading selections from Maxim Gorky's *Reminiscences of Leo Nikolaevich Tolstoy*.

Anna Karenina

C. J. G. Turner's *A Karenina Companion* is an invaluable guide to the novel,
covering the history of composition, the drafts, information about what Tolstoy
read from 1869 to 1877, a compendium of Tolstoy's statements on *Anna*

Karenina culled from his letters and diaries, notes on the new Russian and English editions, and extensive bibliographies.

Identifying monographs or collections specifically on *Anna Karenina*, many respondents referred to Amy Mandelker's *Framing* Anna Karenina: *Tolstoy, the Woman Question, and the Victorian Novel*. Also mentioned were Judith Armstrong's *Unsaid* Anna Karenina, Mary Evans's *Reflecting on* Anna Karenina, Sydney Schultze's *The Structure of* Anna Karenina, Elisabeth Stenbock-Fermor's *Architecture of* Anna Karenina, Anthony Thorlby's *Leo Tolstoy:* Anna Karenina, and Bloom's *Leo Tolstoy's* Anna Karenina. The treatment of *Anna Karenina* in Vladimir Nabokov's *Lectures on Russian Literature*, an edition of lecture notes from courses taught to American college students, is an excellent resource for teachers. Nabokov interprets the novel; offers discussion of its general features, such as timing and imagery; and makes detailed comments on cultural specifics in part 1.

Respondents to the survey identified several articles that have proved excellent starting points for launching classroom discussion: Kathryn Feuer's "Stiva"; Dragan Kujundžić's "Pardoning Woman"; Robert Louis Jackson's "Chance and Design in *Anna Karenina*" and "On the Ambivalent Beginning"; and Gary Saul Morson's "Prosaics in *Anna Karenina*," which initiated a series of provocative ideas that were developed further by Morson and Caryl Emerson in their *Mikhail Bakhtin: Creation of a Prosaics*. A debate of prosaics with reference to *Anna Karenina* was published in volume 8 (1995–96) of the *Tolstoy Studies Journal*. An excellent discussion of heroines' suicides in the nineteenth-century novel and *Anna Karenina* in particular is Margaret Higonnet's "Speaking Silences: Women's Suicides." The recent Anna Karenina *on Page and Screen*, edited by Helena Goscilo and Petre Petrov (2001), provides some perspectives on the novel that are applicable to the classroom.

Comparative Studies of Anna Karenina

Many of our survey respondents indicate that they teach *Anna Karenina* in courses that are either thematic or have a great-books focus, where recommendations of comparative studies of the novel would be welcome. Armstrong's *Novel of Adultery* places *Anna Karenina* in the context of other novels of adultery, as does Naomi Segal's *The Adulteress's Child: Authorship and Desire in the Nineteenth-Century Novel*. Although Tony Tanner's *Adultery in the Novel* does not focus on *Anna Karenina*, instructors have found its general discussion and commentary on other novels of adultery very helpful in teaching *Anna Karenina*. Elisabeth Bronfen's *Over Her Dead Body* offers a stimulating perspective on works of literature and art that culminate in the death of the heroine. French sources (Dumas fils, Hugo) for the themes and the poetics of *Anna Karenina* and its use of inner monologue are treated in Liza Knapp's "Tue-la! Tue-le!"

Many available studies compare *Anna Karenina* to Flaubert's *Madame Bovary* or Fontane's *Effi Briest:* Priscilla Meyer, J. P. M. Stern, Suzanne Osborne. *Anna Karenina* has been compared to English novels: Philip Rogers (*David Copperfield*), Rebecca Hogan (*Orley Farm*), Edwina Blumberg (*Middlemarch*), W. Gareth Jones (*Adam Bede*), George Zytaruk (*The Rainbow*). The essays by Blumberg, Jones, and Zytaruk have been collected in *Tolstoi and Britain*, edited by Jones, which also offers an extensive bibliography.

The Woman Question in Anna Karenina *and in Russia*

The classic feminist critique of *Anna Karenina* appears in Ruth Crego Benson's *Women in Tolstoy: The Ideal and the Erotic* (1973). Other sustained feminist readings of the novel are those by Armstrong, Evans, Barbara Heldt (her chapter "Tolstoy's Path to Feminism" in her *Terrible Perfection*), and Mandelker (*Framing*). For a more general book on the status of women in nineteenth-century Russia, we recommend Richard Stites, *The Women's Liberation Movement in Russia: Feminism, Nihilism, and Bolshevism*, and Barbara Engels, *Mothers and Daughters*. A more specialized history is available in N. N. Selivanova, *Russia's Women* (1923), and in Carolina de Maegd-Soëp's *The Emancipation of Women*. Also see Jane McDermid's "The Influence of Western Ideas on the Development of the Woman Question in Nineteenth-Century Russian Thought." For an analysis of the depiction of adulteresses in Russian literature, see Olga Matich's "Typology of Fallen Women" and the collection *A Plot of Her Own* edited by Sona Hoisington. Svetlana Grenier's *Representing the Marginal Woman* surveys the figure of the dependent single woman in Russian society and literature. John Stuart Mill's *The Subjection of Women*, which figured prominently in polemics about the woman question in the Russian press, may be used to inform class discussion of these issues. Mill's work comes up in the debate about the status of women at the Oblonskys' dinner party (pt. 4, ch. 12) as well as in the scene where Levin visits the Sviyazhskys (pt. 3, ch. 26). (For a discussion of Mill in Tolstoy, see Mandelker, *Framing* 21–25.)

Part Two

APPROACHES

Anna on the Installment Plan: Teaching *Anna Karenina* through the History of Its Serial Publication

William M. Todd III

The first aspect of *Anna Karenina* likely to strike contemporary teachers and students is its considerable length. Even by Victorian standards, it is a long novel, and dividing it into manageable reading assignments is the most practical of the many challenges it poses to a teacher. But as long as it is on paper—the first separate edition (1878) was a triple-decker (i.e., three volumes)—it extends no less impressively in the time it took to write and first be published. Modern teachers and students part company with Tolstoy's contemporaries in their encounter with the grand dimensions of *Anna Karenina*, as the novel's first readers experienced it over a lengthy two and a half years of serialization (Jan. 1875 to Apr. 1877 in the *Russian Herald*). By planning reading assignments to coincide with installment breaks, a teacher can help students share in the suspense and surprises the novel's first readers experienced and understand its hold over them despite the long process of serialization.

Anna Karenina may be taught (and therefore contextualized) in many kinds of courses: surveys of nineteenth-century Russian or European prose, thematic courses (e.g., on adultery in the novel), monograph courses on Tolstoy, seminars on theory of narrative, intellectual or cultural history courses, and courses devoted entirely to Tolstoy's novel, to name just a few possibilities. Each type of course offers a different scope for discussion of the novel's serialization. I suggest here several approaches and strategies that different courses might pursue. But no matter how limited the available class time or how broad or narrow the course's themes, attention to the novel's serialization offers a fascinating way for students and teachers to come to grips with the novel's creative history, its interaction with its reading public, and its engagement with the cultural controversies of its time. Not every course affords time to discuss these institutional and historical issues in detail, but it is a rare group of students who are not curious about them.

First, some general comments on the institutional issues. Serialization was the most common means of publishing novels in nineteenth-century Russia. With the exception of Nikolai Gogol's *Dead Souls* and Ivan Turgenev's *Fathers and Sons*, every novel that is likely to appear on a course syllabus met its first readers in irregularly spaced publication in parts (Alexander Pushkin's *Eugene Onegin*), irregular inclusion in a journal (Mikhail Lermontov's *A Hero of Our Time*, Mikhail Saltykov-Shchedrin's *The Golovlev Family*), or regular serialization (the major novels of Fyodor Dostoevsky, Turgenev, Ivan Goncharov). Gogol did not want to lessen the impact of his "epic poem" by allowing its readers to experience it over a long stretch of time; Turgenev's novel was short enough to fit into one issue of the *Russian Herald*. By the time Tolstoy began to write *Anna Karenina,* regular serialization dominated Russia's literary scene. A novelist would agree to provide a novel that would appear during the course of a subscription year; the journal would, in turn, advertise the novel to boost subscriptions. No novelist commanded the attention of Russia's small reading public more than Tolstoy, who could therefore demand the highest price of his time for his writing, 500 rubles a signature for the anticipated forty signatures of *Anna Karenina*, or 20,000 rubles in all. Students who follow the salary disputes of contemporary entertainers and professional athletes are usually intrigued to learn that Tolstoy's compensation was significantly higher than that of Turgenev (400 rubles per signature) and Dostoevsky (300 rubles). Lesser novelists and translators—"literary unskilled laborers," as one critic called them—might be lucky to receive 40 rubles a signature (Shashkov 33–35). This situation was less favorable for writers and publishers than was the novel trade in Victorian England, where a large readership and an extensive system of lending libraries provided economies of scale and relative stability. Yet in Russia publication in installments provided greater profit and commercial predictability than publishing novels separately.

In Russia the reading public for "high" literature, into which category such novels as Tolstoy's fell, was small. No proper surveys of literacy were conducted until 1897, but it is estimated that at most ten percent of the population of the Russian Empire was literate in the 1870s (Maguire, *Red Virgin Soil* 37; J. Brooks 3–34). Many of these Russians were not, however, literate enough to read imaginative literature or wealthy enough to afford books and journals, which were relatively expensive. Russian literature featured a mode of publication, "thick journals," which from the 1830s to the 1880s brought its small reading public together. These journals, of which the *Russian Herald* was one of the most long-lived (1856–1906), were not literary in a narrow sense but included a wealth of discourses—history; memoirs; fiction; literary criticism; analysis of foreign events; and material from the social, natural, and biological sciences. They attracted readers by promising a complete novel in the course of a subscription year, by featuring prominent critics with marked political tendencies, and by covering developments in so many fields of knowledge. The *Russian Herald* was remarkable for its outstanding fiction (by Tolstoy, Dostoevsky, and Turgenev, to name its stars) as well as for the conservative imperialist politics of its publisher, M. N. Katkov, an Anglophile whose journal also serialized translations of novels by eminent Victorian novelists.

Serialization in a thick journal often did not meet the goal of completion in a subscription year, but the progress of *Anna Karenina* was, even by this loose standard, slow and irregular.

Serial Publication of *Anna Karenina*

Installment	Month and Year	Parts, Chapters (in Modern Eds.)	Contents of Final Chapter in Each Installment
1	Jan. 1875	1. 1–23	Anna leaves the ball
2	Feb. 1875	1. 24–2:11	Consummation of Anna and Vronsky's affair
3	Mar. 1875	2. 12–29	Anna tells Karenin about her affair with Vronsky
4	Apr. 1875	2. 30–3.12	Levin sees Kitty in a carriage
5	Jan. 1876	3. 13–32	Levin thinks of death, goes abroad
6	Feb. 1876	4. 1–17	Vronsky visits Anna, who appears to be dying
7	Mar. 1876	4. 18–5.6	Kitty and Levin leave for the country
8	Apr. 1876	5. 7–20	Nikolai Levin dies; Kitty is pregnant
9	Dec. 1876	5. 21–33	Vronsky and Anna leave for the country after a scandalous scene in the theater
10	Jan. 1877	6. 1–15	Vasenka's expulsion from Pokrovskoe
11	Feb. 1877	6. 16–32	Anna and Vronsky leave for Moscow
12	Mar. 1877	7. 1–16	Birth of Levin and Kitty's son
13	Apr. 1877	7. 17–31	Anna's death

Katkov refused to publish the final part of the novel in the *Russian Herald*; it appeared as a separate brochure. See Evdokimova, this volume, for a discussion of the novel's ending.

This record of serialization can serve to initiate class discussion of Tolstoy's poetics and also of problems of authorial responsibility for the text. If this chart is distributed to the students (without the contents column if the teacher wishes their process of following the novel's events to approximate that of Tolstoy's first readers), they can immediately note two irregularities: the breaks during the summer and fall of 1875 and 1876 and the absence of part 8 from the journal. They will also note that the installment breaks coincide with the part divisions of the novel, as modern readers know it, only for installments 5, 9, 11, and 13. These irregularities afford the opportunity to explain to the class what Tolstoy called his "summer condition" (*letnee sostoianie* [*Polnoe sobranie* 20: 619]), namely, that during those months he oversaw and participated in the farming at his estate and pursued other activities he found pressing, including the education of the peasants. They also offer the class a chance to discuss *Anna Karenina* as a work in progress. While Tolstoy had drafted a considerable part of it before serialization commenced, he continued to revise the novel and add to it throughout the years it was being published. Part 8 includes passages on the unfolding war in the Balkans, which had not yet begun when the novel's installments began to appear. Tolstoy's negative treatment of the conflict, which Katkov and other contributors to the journal actively supported, led Katkov to refuse to publish the novel's conclusion and compelled Tolstoy to publish it as a separate brochure.

That the installment breaks do not coincide with the part divisions gives the class the opportunity to discuss Tolstoy's revisions of the novel for publication as a separate volume and the differences between the volume they are reading and the installments that readers encountered in the 1870s. The process challenges our modern sense of authorship, as at various times the *Russian Herald*, Tolstoy, and Tolstoy's friend Nikolai Strakhov made decisions concerning the shape and positioning of text. Judicious assignment of Tolstoy's letters to Katkov and Strakhov can show how Tolstoy's attitude toward serialization was at times highly artistic, at times unconcerned: he might insist that the journal retain his exact phrasing (e.g., when Katkov objected to the "graphic realism" of the scene following the consummation of Anna's affair with Vronsky [Tolstoy, *Polnoe sobranie* 62: 139]), or he might give Katkov carte blanche with the sequencing of chapters.[1] The preparation of the first separate edition shows a similar combination of insouciance and concern on Tolstoy's part. Strakhov sewed together the installments for Tolstoy, and the two of them by turns made corrections to the journal text. But Tolstoy relegated the checking of the final proofs to Strakhov, who missed many typographic errors. Modern editions, such as the Zhdanov and Zaidenshnur Academy of Sciences edition of 1970, have tried to separate out Strakhov's editing, uncovering as best they can the text that Tolstoy wrote and corrected.

Decisions regarding the text published in the *Russian Herald*, however, sometimes had to be made by its editors. Tolstoy was often late in returning corrections, forcing the editors to make decisions about sequencing and dividing into installments. Their decisions were not without consequence for their readers. The novel appeared only twice as a separate edition in Tolstoy's lifetime, both times in 1878. Readers who wished to read the revised version had to purchase it as part of Tolstoy's ten-volume collected works (eight editions, 1880–1910). Consequently, for many readers and critics the serialized version remained the familiar one.

Comparing the serialized version with the separate edition invites a class to appreciate the subtlety of Tolstoy's famous linkings, as he articulated them in the often cited letter to Strakhov (*Polnoe sobranie* 62: 268–69). Students will see that the final edition of the novel creates subtle comparisons between its two main plots (Anna's, Levin's) by juxtaposing long sections of each plot in each of the novel's eight parts. The individual installments that appeared in the *Russian Herald* rarely have the length to achieve this sort of linking, and its lack would have placed insurmountable cognitive obstacles before readers who wanted to read the novel as an integral work.

The novel's incarnation in the *Russian Herald*, instead, focuses on the sensational. Three installments, in particular, merit attention—2, 8, 12—because they end on events that strikingly violated nineteenth-century decorum: the consummation of Anna's affair, Nikolai Levin's death, and the birth of Levin and Kitty's son. The physical detail and emotional intensity with which they are presented would have made them arresting no matter where they were located, but in the separate edition they appear in the middle of parts, while the parts themselves tend to end on departures or moments of resolved tension. Ending the journal installments on such violent events made the serialized novel more sensational. It is hardly surprising, then, that these events drew criticism. The suspenseful or surprising endings also brought the novel into line with the serialization practice for novels by Wilkie Collins, Anthony Trollope, and Jules Verne, which appeared alongside *Anna Karenina* in the *Russian Herald*. They, too, were broken up at dramatic moments, a trick of the serial writer's trade that Tolstoy would have avoided if the serialization of the novel had coincided with his own division of it into parts.

Attention to serialization leads us from the poetics of the novel to pragmatics, the claims that *Anna Karenina* made on its readers. Reader-response theories—such as the one synthesized in Wolfgang Iser's *The Act of Reading* and practiced in his *The Implied Reader*—pay particular attention to gaps and shifts in narration, to "blanks," as Iser calls them (*Act* 182–203), moments in the experience of the text that call for particular cognitive effort on the reader's part because the flow of reading has been interrupted. Using some version of this approach, a class can follow its experience of the novel's themes, characters, and conflicts, correcting its initial understandings and anticipations with each new reading assignment.

A more historically oriented course can take a different approach to pragmatics, one that follows contemporary reactions to the novel as it was serialized and attempts to understand prevailing ethical and aesthetic values from them.

A thorough pursuit of this approach would require the resources of a research library and a class capable of reading Russian, but much can be done with existing scholarship and secondary sources to give students a sense of the contemporary expectations that *Anna Karenina* challenged. The most famous of these early critical reactions, Dostoevsky's, is readily available in the Northwestern UP edition of his *Writer's Diary* (February 1877 and July and August 1877). Its praise and critique of the novel give students a sense of the novel's ability to engage the incipient Russian public sphere. Other opinions may be found in A. V. Knowles's brief but useful survey of the first reviews ("Russian Views"). Books in Russian by E. G. Babaev and by V. Z. Gornaia present a more comprehensive account of contemporary reactions. Most of the responses that have survived belong to professional writers and critics, but one contemporary official, Prince V. M. Golitsyn, jotted down brief comments on eight of the thirteen journal installments in his diary, and they are available in English translation (Todd, "Reading"). These comments are invaluable not for their critical acumen but for the insights they offer into contemporary sensibility. Both Golitsyn and the professional readers were shocked by what he called the novel's "disgusting realism" (Todd, "Reading" 128). The critics, puzzled by the novel's intricate structure, tended to find the novel "formless" (Babaev 145–211). The more radical critics, politically speaking, noted the setting of the novel in high society and on country estates and found it a throwback to the drawing-room fiction of the early nineteenth century. Critics from the more moderate and conservative periodicals were no more respectful of the novel's art and its engagement with contemporary issues. And yet, as Strakhov noted in a letter to Tolstoy (7 May 1877), with each new installment of *Anna Karenina* the newspapers would "rush to inform the public as hastily and interpret as painstakingly as they would about a new battle or a new pronouncement by Bismarck" (Modzalevsky 116). The sensational nature of Tolstoy's installments and their sporadic appearance, however, clearly led both professional and amateur readers to link the novel to current events and situations and to ignore the linkings Tolstoy thought so crucial to an understanding of his novel.

Despite the critical charges that the novel was decidedly old-fashioned, such reactions suggest that it did serve to focus public discussion of pressing social, economic, political, and cultural issues. Here, too, a course that follows the serial publication can in several ways call students' attention to this critical function of Russian fiction in the 1870s. A more advanced course for students who read Russian can distribute the tables of contents for the issues of the *Russian Herald* in which installments of *Anna Karenina* appeared. In these issues they will find articles on topics discussed by the characters of the novel: education, spiritualism, hired labor, contemporary Russian and European politics, and the Russian Empire's treatment of the peoples it encompassed. They will find criticism of *Anna Karenina* by V. G. Avseenko and by Katkov as well as a novel by Avseenko, *The Milky Way*, which treats high society more respectfully than does *Anna Karenina*. If they examine the June 1877 issue, in which part 8 of

Tolstoy's novel was to have appeared, they will immediately see why Katkov found Tolstoy's treatment of the Balkan conflict so distressing. Fully three-quarters of the items in this issue addressed Russia's imperial ambitions and military activities.

Courses that do not have time for such a detailed examination of the medium in which *Anna Karenina* first appeared can nevertheless give students a sense of the novel's contemporary charge by assigning readings from readily available histories of Russia that give useful background information on topics that concern the characters of the novel and its readers.

In the century and a quarter following the serialization of *Anna Karenina*, the novel has become a canonical work, with all that this entails: assumptions of coherence, attempts at integral reading, respect for its art, rigorous interpretation and commentary, widespread familiarity. Numerous books and articles have sought—and found—the linkings that Tolstoy so enticingly and elliptically presented in his letter to Strakhov. At the same time much can be lost, especially a sense of the risks Tolstoy took in juxtaposing and intertwining two main plots, in challenging all social and cultural institutions, in developing characters who violate social norms, in voicing themes offensive to his publisher and readers. Attention to the novel as an unfolding event, as a serialized work, can help students appreciate Tolstoy's artistic daring and moral courage.

NOTE

[1]For a more complete discussion of sequence, division, and ideology, see Todd, "Responsibilities."

The Daily Miracle: Teaching the Ideas of *Anna Karenina*

Gary Saul Morson

Like the Russian public, American students tend to like literature with big ideas. But whereas the philosophical agendas of *Crime and Punishment* and *War and Peace* cannot be missed, *Anna Karenina* seems more a story of love and family, so common in the English novel. The trick in teaching this work, then, is to bring out the ideas that make sense of the whole and of so many passages that otherwise seem irrelevant.

Think of it this way: the entire Levin story concerns a man who seeks to answer large questions and who finds those questions so imperative that he contemplates suicide when the answers seem unavailable. He argues with his two intellectual brothers, debates social reform with Sviazhsky, and even discusses Plato with, of all people, Stiva. And perhaps strangest of all, we watch the progress of a book he is writing on reforming Russian agriculture. Now, Russian novels appear peculiar enough to Western readers for their long and explicit discussions of God, metaphysics, utopia, the nature of evil, the laws of history, and other such "accursed problems." But agriculture? Why devote so much space to such an obviously parochial and unpoetic topic? I think that the answer to this question can provide a window on one of the book's key themes: How can one make life better? Collectively, what is the best way to foster desirable social change, and individually, how can each of us become a better person? It would be hard to imagine a student not worried about one or both of these questions. In *Anna Karenina*, they turn out to be the same question, and Levin's book provides a key to both.

Like so many Russian landowners, Levin wants to modernize agriculture, on his own estate and in Russia at large. In so doing, he faces difficulties common to economic modernizers elsewhere and always; and one way to show the book's relevance is to point out that Levin's worries are still very much with us today, in Russia and in all modernizing countries. He tries, as do Sviazhsky, Vronsky, and so many others, to increase productivity and improve the welfare of the peasants by importing machinery, seeds, and methods that have worked so well in England, but he finds that "for some reason" (a favorite phrase of Tolstoy's) his efforts always fail. He later learns that all Sviazhsky's progressive reforms have actually reduced productivity. Why? To understand the answer is to grasp why most reforms fail and to realize what is most likely to succeed.

When Levin first returns to his estate after proposing to Kitty, "the bailiff came in and said that everything, thank God, was doing well; but informed him that the buckwheat in the new drying kiln had been a little scorched."[1] Levin, who has designed this kiln on scientific principles, knows that if the buckwheat was scorched, "it was only because precautions had not been taken for which he had hundreds of times given orders" (108; pt. 1, ch. 26). Also, his new English seed oats are ruined by "a touch of mildew" and his new hay-pitching machine breaks. And yet he knows that there is no question of conspiracy or sabotage on the part of the peasants, who like and want to please him (368; pt. 3, ch. 24). In much the same way, reformers of social institutions often find that the very measures they use to eliminate poverty either fail at great expense or actually increase poverty, and not because of deliberate subversion. Sviazhsky's explanation, which is characteristic of reformers, is that, if the reforms have failed, then they must be pursued even more rigorously and at greater expense until they succeed. Levin knows that such an approach is ridiculous, because it never allows the possibility that the reform itself may be misdirected and that, for all good intentions, it cannot succeed.

A key passage occurs when Levin is presenting some new ideas to the bailiff:

> The bailiff listened attentively, and obviously made an effort to approve of his employer's projects. But still he had that look Levin knew so well that always irritated him, a look of hopelessness and despondency. That look said: "That's all very well, but as God wills." Nothing mortified Levin so much as that tone. But it was the tone common to all the bailiffs he had ever had. They had all taken up that attitude toward his plans, and so now he was not angered by it but mortified, and felt all the more roused to struggle against this, as it seemed, elemental force continually ranged against him, for which he could find no other expression than "as God wills." (177–78; pt. 2, ch. 13)

The elemental force—or, as it is also called, the brutal force—is what reformers do not understand and what defeats their plans. Theorists usually imagine that behind the complexity of the world there are a few simple laws, as there are in planetary motion, and so they propose a few simple reforms. To them, because the world is fundamentally orderly, those who understand the laws behind it—that is, the theorist himself and his disciples—can remake it according to a plan. Since the seventeenth century, reformers or revolutionaries as diverse as John Locke and Jeremy Bentham, Karl Marx and Marquis de Condorcet have reasoned that way. Tolstoy, who at this time of his life could best be described as a radically nonconformist conservative, set himself against this whole approach to theory. To him, the world and the people in it are more complex than any theory and cannot be adequately comprehended by any set of abstractions; therefore, the world cannot be remade according to any blueprint or plan. It can be improved, but not that way.

What theorists fail to appreciate is the thoroughgoing contingency of the world. Contingency may be said to be Tolstoy's key idea, and when thinkers as diverse as the philosopher Ludwig Wittgenstein, the evolutionary biologist Stephen Jay Gould, the city planning critic Jane Jacobs, and the physicist Freeman Dyson take it seriously, they usually turn to Tolstoy, the concept's great exponent. Behind the disorderly phenomena of the world there is no set of a few simple laws; if one looks behind the diversity of things, one finds even more diverse things, and behind them still more. Complexity does not simplify, it ramifies.

In the social world, things never resolve into a simple pattern. Life is rather the accumulation of countless choices made with no larger purpose in mind, habits developed by local and accidental circumstances, and practices developed to meet particular needs and then applied to other needs. One adapts to the imperfect with the resources at hand; life is a matter not of optimal design but of tinkering. The force exerted by these multiple contingencies is not directed by anyone or to anything: it is elemental. In *War and Peace* Tolstoy argues that there can be no science of battle or any other social science analogous to a physical science; in *Anna Karenina*, he applies that lesson to everyday life.

The Roman emperor Caligula is supposed to have wished that Rome had a single head so he could cut it off with a single blow. So social reformers imagine that there is a single solution—apply English agricultural science, adopt socialism, whatever—to social problems. But if the reformers are at all open to feedback, they soon discover that almost every problem is really a hundred million problems. Despite the common rhetoric, there is usually no single root cause. Totalitarian regimes, when the reforms fail, apply greater and greater force, because they can only imagine treason or sabotage.

Why do English machines break in Russia? The answer pertains to Tolstoy's sense of psychology, which shapes the intensely realistic way he describes characters' thoughts and behavior in *Anna Karenina*. Like societies, people are accumulations of habits and practices. Attention is always a very limited resource, which is why we have habits. When you first learned to operate a car, you could not drive, talk, and listen to the radio at the same time, as an experienced driver can. The novice strains all attention to coordinate varied perceptions and actions that the expert does by habit, with attention left over. Acquiring such habits is part of what the famous mowing scene is all about (pt. 3, chs. 4–6). At first, Levin resembles a novice driver. Later, he can mow reasonably well by totally blanking his mind and letting what his body has learned take over, for in Tolstoy, not only minds but also muscles can learn, and the body has a mind of its own. But the experienced older peasant does not have to blank his mind. He can even stop and pick a mushroom for his wife without breaking stride.

All of us develop work habits to free our mental hands, so to speak. Now, we are creatures who live in a world of radical uncertainty, which is why our eyes and mind continually wander; it is almost impossible to focus one's attention on anything for very long without interruption. A machine will work if and only if what the worker does, when he is *not* paying attention, does not break the machine. Because Russian workers have different work habits from those of English workers, a machine that works well in one place will break in another. This is what Levin means when he disputes economic and agricultural theorists who treat laborers simply as providers of so many man-hours and what he means by saying that one has to take into account the particular culture of the laborer. Students in economics classes will recognize that the model Tolstoy criticizes has grown even stronger since he wrote. They may not be aware that, at the beginning of the twenty-first century, a trend of social thinkers has been insisting, Levin-like, that culture matters and that one model of development cannot simply be transferred wholesale from America to another country with a very different culture.

If one tries to make changes from the top down by applying a theory, the elemental force—the sum total of habits and practices that are life in all its messiness—will defeat one time and again. But that does not mean beneficial change is impossible. One can proceed from the bottom up. Levin learns to watch how the peasants actually work, to adapt machines and changes to their habits, and to choose the sort of new techniques that the peasants would have chosen had they known about them.

What is true of social change is also true of individual self-betterment. Kitty attempts to become a better person by imitating Mlle Varenka and Mme Stahl, that is, by borrowing a way of life wholesale. She even tries to walk like Varenka. She discovers that one can no more borrow or change a whole personality than one can borrow a foreign social model or change a whole society at a stroke. What Varenka does to help others actually causes harm when Kitty does it, as she is honest enough to see with the Petrovs. She recognizes, as she screams in a tantrum to Varenka, that what she did was all "fake" and concludes, a bit pettishly, that "I'll be bad, but anyway not a liar, a cheat" (269; pt. 2, ch. 35).

Just as it would be wrong for Levin to conclude from the failure of his changes that improvement is impossible, Kitty soon recognizes that she can make herself a better person in a different way. What one needs to do is proceed not from a model and imitate it—top-down thinking—but from an assessment of where one is and then, bit by bit, change bad habits and acquire good ones, a habit at a time. This is just what Kitty eventually does, and when we see her nursing Levin's dying brother, she has become very effective at helping another. She can even anticipate needs no one else can see and understand muttered words otherwise unintelligible, because she watches the small things— each small motion of the body—and so can guess what Nikolai wants. No theory of nursing would have helped as well.

Top-down versus bottom-up: the antithesis pervades the book and marks Tolstoy's belief that what we need is not what intellectuals usually offer—theories of society and ethics, whether Marxist or Hegelian or (in our day) Freudian or Foucauldian—but practical wisdom, which is acquired by learning to pay close attention to the small events and contingencies of the world before our eyes. Education may be described as learning better ways to pay attention so as to perceive more finely. Why is Mikhailov a fine painter and Vronsky a bad one? It is not because Mikhailov has "technique," as we are told (498): words like *technique, talent, genius* simply name something we do not grasp, as if mere naming were understanding. It is because he has learned to see.

When Vronsky and Anna go to Italy, they rent a palazzo, and Vronsky dons

Italian medieval dress, which Anna finds piquant. With nothing to do, Vronsky takes up painting:

> He had a ready appreciation of art, and for accurately and tastefully imitating it, and he supposed himself to have the real qualities essential for an artist, and after hesitating for some time about which style of painting to select—religious, historical, realistic, or genre painting—he began painting. He appreciated all kinds, and could have felt inspired by any of them; but he had no conception of the possibility of knowing nothing at all of any school of painting and of being inspired directly by what is within the soul, without caring whether what is painted will belong to any recognized school. Since he knew nothing of this, and drew his inspiration, not directly from life, but indirectly from life embodied in art, his inspiration came very quickly and easily, and as quickly and easily came his success in painting something very similar to the sort of painting he was trying to imitate.   (529–30; pt. 5, ch. 8)

Tolstoy was later to call such art by imitation "counterfeit art," which is to say, it is not really art at all (*What* 139). The same thing is true of thinking. Most people's ideas do not come from actually reflecting on their particular experiences but from learning a set of views held by people with whom they identify or wish to associate. Sviazhsky is just like that, which is why Levin cannot get through to him and why no counterevidence will ever matter. Or consider Stiva, who changes his views "only when the majority [his circle] changed them; or, more strictly speaking, they seemed to change of themselves within him" (9–10; pt. 1, ch. 3).

We all know counterfeit thinkers of this sort: having once identified themselves as liberal or conservative or radical, they will year after year reliably hold all those opinions that a liberal or conservative or radical is expected to hold. Such conformity cannot be the result of actual reflection on experience, because experience is too varied for one to reach predictable conclusions on all issues. This conformity is counterfeit thinking, as Vronsky's imitation is counterfeit art. By contrast, Tolstoy gives us Levin, who is always changing his mind, and the "reactionary landowner" with whom Levin does not agree but whom he tries to learn from and admires because

> the landowner unmistakably spoke his own individual thought—a thing that rarely happens—and a thought to which he had been brought not by a desire of finding some exercise for an idle brain, but a thought which had grown up out of the conditions of his life, which he had brooded over in the solitude of his village, and had considered in its every aspect.
> (379; pt. 3, ch. 27)

Real thinking grows out of the specific conditions of one's life, and since those conditions are different for each person, real thinking never fits a formula, much as Mikhailov's art fits into no school. Mikhailov is a fine painter because every prosaic minute of his life he is teaching himself to perceive—he remembers, for example, the chin of the shopkeeper who sold him cigars. When he contemplates a painting he has finished, "he had one conviction—that no one had ever painted a picture like it. He did not believe that his picture was better than all the pictures of Raphael, but he knew that what he had tried to convey in that picture no one had ever conveyed" (535; pt. 5, ch. 10). He can know this without having seen all the pictures ever painted because his art grows too specifically out of his experience, which he has taught himself to observe with a finely trained attention.

The landowner's ideas also grow specifically from his own particular experience. Levin knows that he can learn from them precisely for that reason. By attending to the landowner's ideas, Levin can grasp the circumstances that led to them and take those circumstances into account. In this way, Levin's own views become all the richer. Tolstoy is stressing the importance of not dismissing but seriously and empathetically attending to the opinions of those with whom we disagree. Sviazhsky, like most people, argues as if the point of exchanging ideas were to win a battle for one's own ideological camp, whereas Levin hopes to learn from his opponents and reach a more adequate position. For Tolstoy, a counterfeit thinker can be recognized at once by his failure even to imagine how an intelligent, honest, well-intentioned person might be on the other side of an issue. But those who are willing to seek out the thoughtful people on the other side, understand the experiences that have shaped their views, and modify their own views accordingly will arrive at solutions that are both more intelligent and less like those of other people.

When Levin at last finds faith, he does so not by finding a formula but by realizing that he has been asking questions the wrong way. Abstract questions like what is the meaning of life and death have no answer in that sense. But if one lives right, one senses the meaning. As Ludwig Wittgenstein, a devotee of Tolstoy, observed, "The solution of the problem of life is seen in the vanishing of the problem. (Is not this the reason why those who have found after a long period of doubt that the sense of life becomes clear to them have been unable to say what constituted that sense?)" (73).[2] Philosophical despair is a symptom, and the cure is to change one's daily life. Levin realizes that he has been living well even if he has been thinking badly; his despair has come from his belief that life must be justified by theory. He learns, in short, to apply the lessons of his book to his life and to place daily, prosaic existence first.

Levin can at last make both practical and ethical decisions well without applying any theory. Tolstoy describes Levin's ethical wisdom not by giving his principles but by enumerating examples: "To Piotr, who was paying a money-lender ten per cent a month, he must lend a sum of money to set him free. But he could not let off peasants who did not pay their rent" (894; pt. 8, ch. 10)— and so on, for a page. The point here is that there neither is nor could there be a theory of ethics. If there were, we could learn ethics by rote or program a computer to tell us what to do; but that is absurd. Goodness lies in a just appreciation of particular *cases*: Tolstoy is in the original sense of the word a casuist, thinking from the particular up. Indeed, one reason to read realist novels, and Tolstoy's above all, is that they give us extremely rich descriptions of specific cases.

Levin learns what the novel's real hero, Dolly, already knows: the importance of untheorized, prosaic daily life. Meaning is here, right in front of one's eyes, hidden in plain view: one must learn to see it. "And I watched for miracles, complained that I did not see a miracle that would convince me. And here is a miracle, the sole miracle possible, continually existing, surrounding me on all sides, and I never noticed it!" (899; pt. 8, ch. 12).

NOTES

[1]Page references in this article are to Tolstoy, *Anna Karenina* [Garnett].

[2]On Wittgenstein's debt to Tolstoy and to Levin's meditations, see Janik and Toulmin 161–66, 198–99, 204–05.

The Crisis in Tolstoy and in
Anna Karenina
Gary R. Jahn

"Without knowing what I am, and why I am here, it is impossible to live.
Yet I cannot know that, and therefore I can't live," [Levin] said to himself.
[. . . This thought] was the cruel mockery of some evil power [. . .]. It
was necessary to free oneself from that power. The means of escape were
in the hands of every man. An end had to be put to that dependence on
an evil power; and there was one means—death. [. . .] Levin was several
times so near to suicide that he hid a cord he had lest he should hang himself, and he feared to carry a gun lest he should shoot himself.

(714; pt. 8, ch. 9)

Few incidents in Tolstoy's life have attracted as much attention as his crisis and
subsequent conversion to a radicalized Christianity of his own devising. Although the origins of Tolstoy's crisis may be traced to the late 1860s or even earlier, its culmination in the mid-1870s is particularly relevant to *Anna Karenina*.
Compare the quotation from *Anna Karenina* given above to the following extract from Tolstoy's autobiographical narrative describing this crisis, *Confession*
(1879–82):

These moments of perplexity began to recur oftener and oftener, and always in the same form. They were always expressed by the questions:
What is [life] for? What does it lead to? [. . .] Try as I would, I could not
solve them. [. . .] My life came to a standstill, I could breathe, eat, drink,
and sleep, and I could not help doing these things; but there was no life,
for there were no wishes the fulfillment of which I could consider reasonable. [. . .] My mental condition presented itself to me in this way: my
life is a stupid and spiteful joke someone has played on me [. . .]. It had
come to this, that I, a healthy, fortunate man, felt I could no longer live:
some irresistible power impelled me to rid myself one way or other of life.
[. . .] And it was then that I, a man favored by fortune, hid a cord from
myself lest I should hang myself from the crosspiece of the partition in
my room where I undressed alone every evening, and I ceased to go out
shooting with a gun lest I should be tempted by so easy a way of ending
my life. ("Confession" 15–18)

When *Anna Karenina* is taught, attention to the connection between
Tolstoy's biographical crisis and his characters' fictional crises can lead to fruitful discussion—in particular, of the character of Levin. Talking about these con-

nections also offers an approach to one of the central problems of the structure of the novel as a whole, the relation between the stories of Levin and Anna.

Tolstoy's Crisis

The forces that drove Tolstoy to crisis and eventually to conversion were the fear of death and the inability to understand his life as possessing any meaning that would not be nullified by death. Judging by the pessimistic tone of his private papers of the mid-1870s, Tolstoy had begun to understand death as the only alternative, however undesirable, to the wholly unacceptable continuance of a life that seemed entirely circumscribed by the physical and completely devoid of higher significance. The only courageous course for a clear-thinking person seemed to be voluntary self-removal from life—suicide.

In *Confession* the power of death is represented as a stimulus that cannot be ignored and may be satisfied by only two responses: capitulation (i.e., suicide) or compromise. If we take Tolstoy's account of this crisis seriously, he was perilously close to capitulation, as the quotations given above suggest. In the end, however, he devised a defense against the power of death, based on his study of the Gospels. The new view of life and death, which he explained most completely in the lengthy treatise *On Life* (1886–87), recalls that view first presented through the character of Platon Karataev in *War and Peace* (in the late 1860s): death is a fiction, because true life is not bound in time and space. Tolstoy's concept of human life is decidedly dualistic. What Tolstoy called the "animal existence" of the body is contrasted to what he called the "true life" of the spirit. The former is transient and ultimately unimportant as compared to the latter, which cannot be endangered by any external force. Thus, in the logic of Tolstoy's reasonings, even the body's death is of no moment, since it affects only the animal existence.

Levin's Crisis and Tolstoy's

There are many similarities between the character of Levin and the person and experience of Tolstoy. To begin with, Levin's surname is made from the root of Tolstoy's personal name, *Lev* in Russian. Tolstoy also borrowed the general structure of Levin's life from his own: both author and character are orphans; both long for a family. After his marriage in 1862 to Sofia Andreevna Behrs, a woman half his age, just as Kitty is half Levin's, Tolstoy adopted the life of the active country squire, condemned the corruption and pointlessness of the urban life of the social elite, and proclaimed himself content to remain in a state of isolated rustication. He passed along all these characteristics to Levin. He also allowed Levin to share such of his own qualities as a predisposition toward radical (and unrealized) plans for a life of personal perfection, a conviction of his physical unattractiveness, and a fondness for gymnastic exercises with dumbbells.

Two of Levin's major scenes in the novel are closely connected to actual experiences of Tolstoy. The first is the celebrated scene of Levin's second proposal of marriage to Kitty (pt. 4, ch. 13). The young couple's astonishing and unlikely ability to understand rather complex sentences as revealed by no more than the initial letters of the words that comprise them is actually an idealized report of the manner in which Tolstoy and his future wife communicated to each other their mutual desire to become engaged. Also highly autobiographical is the scene in which Levin's brother, Nicholas, dies (pt. 5, ch. 20). This chapter, the only one in the novel to have its own title ("Death"), was inspired by Tolstoy's experience of the deaths of his brothers, Dmitry in 1856 and Nicholas in 1860 (for a detailed discussion, see McLean, "Truth.") The emotions and thoughts engendered by these deaths remained with Tolstoy in the mid-1870s and are clearly prototypes for the feelings of Levin in the novel. In a letter to his friend the poet A. A. Fet shortly after Nicholas's death, Tolstoy wrote, "It is true, as [Nicholas] said, that nothing is worse than death. But when one reflects well that that is the end of all, then there is nothing worse than life. Why strive or try, since nothing remains of what was Nikolai Nikolaevich Tolstoy? [. . .] And if he found nothing to cling to, what then will I find? Still less!" (qtd. in Simmons 207).

The connections between Levin and his creator are so numerous that Levin is often understood by students to be Tolstoy's spokesman in the novel. There is certainly some truth to this. But Levin does not take the final steps taken by Tolstoy in the resolution of his personal crisis. Tolstoy came to recognize a need for a complete break with his past and especially with the position in society that he occupied. Levin finds instead a balance point between the demands of social life (including the life of the family) and the intense inward desire for perfect and unfettered individuality. Tolstoy saw the center of the problem in the nullifying power of death; he sought a meaning for his life that would be able to withstand the challenge posed by the certainty of mortality. Levin, too, sees death as a barrier to meaningful life. Yet his overriding concern is not so much about his own death as about the metaphoric death represented by the intrusion of the social context in which he lives into his freedom to express himself as an individual. Levin brings the novel to an end not with his conversion to a radically revised understanding of life, a conversion that Tolstoy would eventually experience, but rather with his striking of a tentative and uneven truce between the competing forces of the pressures of his social context and his internal drive toward individuality.

As the novel ends, Levin reflects:

> This new feeling has not changed me, has not rendered me happy, nor suddenly illuminated me as I dreamt it would [. . .]. I shall still get angry with Ivan the coachman in the same way, shall dispute in the same way, shall inopportunely express my thoughts; there will still be a wall between my soul's holy of holies and other people; even my wife I shall still blame

for my own fears and shall repent of it. My reason will still not understand why I pray, but I shall still pray, and my life, my whole life, independently of anything that may happen to me, is every moment of it no longer meaningless as it was before, but has an unquestionable meaning of goodness with which I have the power to invest it.   (740; pt. 8, ch. 19)

Thus, while Tolstoy resolves the crisis radically, as a matter of the absolute integrity of the self, Levin finds a compromise in the search for an acceptable equipoise between the self as an individual, spiritual entity and the self as a social, physiological entity. His compromise may be understood as a stage on his creator's way to the final solution of his own crisis. The terms of Levin's solution, however, help us grapple with the most vexing artistic question raised by the novel—the nature of the relation between the stories of Levin and of Anna.

Levin's Crisis and Anna's

As early as 1878 Tolstoy was publicly reproached for "promising us one novel but giving us two" (A. Stankevich qtd. in Knowles, *Tolstoy* 294). S. A. Rachinskii expressed a similar concern in a letter to Tolstoy: "Two themes are developed side by side, and developed beautifully, but there is nothing holding them together" (Tolstoy, *Polnoe sobranie* 62: 378). Tolstoy dismissed these complaints, but readers have continued to perceive a radical division in the novel between the stories of its two protagonists. Edward Wasiolek wrote that "*Anna Karenina* is two novels: Anna's and Levin's" (*Major Fiction* 129).

Clearly, there should be some connection between these two characters. Approximately the same amount of space is accorded to each in the novel, and their appearing before the reader by turns is fundamental to the novel's organization. The scene in which Levin and Anna confront each other directly (pt. 7, ch. 10) provides a suitable, if perhaps tardy, basis for linking them together, but Tolstoy seems to have made little direct use of this opportunity. In teaching *Anna Karenina*, I have found that students experience the sense of disjunction between the stories of Anna and Levin very keenly. Their solution is very often the same as that adopted by the director of an early film version of the novel, starring Greta Garbo as Anna: Levin appears in the film for about thirty seconds and then vanishes forever.

The heart of the problem in teaching the novel is the perception that Anna's and Levin's situations are not morally comparable. The reader feels that Anna and Levin face such radically different circumstances that it is easy to contrast them to each other but difficult to see them as somehow involved in a shared dilemma. And yet there are visible signs of similarity between them—most strikingly, the moments of despair that each experiences.

Shortly before she kills herself, Anna thinks, " [. . .] I cannot imagine a situation in which life would not be a torment [. . .]. Yes, it troubles me very much, and reason was given us to enable us to escape; therefore I must escape! Why

not put out the candle, if there is nothing more to look at? If everything is repulsive to look at?" (693; pt. 7, ch. 31). This thought is highly reminiscent of
Levin's doubts about the value of life. Levin asks, "Without knowing what I am,
and why I am here, it is impossible to live. Yet I cannot know that, and therefore
I can't live [. . .]. In an infinity of time, matter, and space, a bubble organism
separates itself, maintains itself awhile, and then bursts, and that bubble is—I!"
This view represents life as "the cruel mockery of some evil power," and Levin
draws the same conclusion as Anna: "The means of escape were in the hands of
every man. An end had to be put to that dependence on an evil power; and
there was one means—death" (714; pt. 8, ch. 9).

Both protagonists are driven to despair; the question is, By what? I direct the
attention of my students to the precise terms of Levin's dilemma: How can one
maintain a tolerable individual presence in the world of social requirements in
which one must function? I then suggest that the character and experiences of
Anna can be regarded from this same point of view.

The class usually comes to see that it is Anna, rather than Levin, who is the
novel's clearest model of the human personality as a divided entity. Yearning for
the excitement and feeling of self-worth that come with the gratification of the
individual, she discovers that she cannot exist without the security and sense of
belonging that come with submission to the pressures of the social. Her highly
attractive naturalness and spontaneity, her "aliveness" (*ozhivlennost'*), the gen-
uineness of her passion, and her desire for freedom and dignity are all associated with her nature as an individual. In order to manifest these qualities in her
life she forsakes the restraint, suppression, and reasonableness that are required by the social dimension of the human personality and that are characteristic features of her initial portrait in the novel. The hypocrisy of perfunctory
concealment that enables those involved in illicit love affairs to maintain their
status as socially accepted persons is abhorrent and unacceptable to Anna. She
requires the full realization of herself as an individual and feels she can achieve
this only at the cost of divorcing herself from society. Unable to harmonize the
antagonistic components of her nature, she responds by choosing the individual
and rejecting the social. As she learns, however, it is one thing to reject the social and quite another to live without it.

At this point I try to redirect class discussion to Levin and how his life embodies the tension between the individual and the social, for the thorny problem of how his story connects to Anna's is the crux of any discussion of the
book's unity. At the beginning of the novel Levin is represented as someone at
odds with his society. His social clumsiness, the uncompromising strength of his
ideals as an individual, and his preference for the rural life all suggest as much.
Yet he never puts himself beyond the pale of society. Although isolated, his
country estate is nonetheless a social framework and one that is a genuine sub-
division of the society inhabited by the other leading characters. His desire to
marry and found a family begins as an attempt to realize himself fully as an individual (we need only recall that each of the Shcherbatsky sisters, in turn,

seems suitable to him in the role of helpmate and cofounder). He soon discovers, however, that marriage requires an increased acknowledgment of the social dimension of his being and entails an increased acceptance of external social pressures. Despite his disinclination, he endures the confessional, the marriage ceremony with its bustle and attention to fashion, and the obligatory calls that must be made following the honeymoon, to say nothing of the loss of the Levin way of putting up preserves in the onrushing tide of the Shcherbatsky influence (see 502–03; pt. 6, ch. 2). The narrator tells us that Levin is like a man who, having watched others skimming along the water in a boat, imagines that it is entirely pleasant, easy, and uncomplicated, only to discover on settling into the boat himself that it is an unremitting and arduous process to keep the boat moving along properly and that his hands and arms become extremely sore from rowing (436; pt. 5, ch. 14).

In short, just as Anna is beginning to discover the flaws of a decision to flee from society (her sojourn with Vronsky in Italy), Levin discovers the implications of his increased commitment to society. Both Anna and Levin pursue courses dictated by their desires as individuals and both learn as a result something more than they expected about the attendant social implications of their acts. Both become keenly aware of the dilemma that they face, and both are eventually driven to despair by their meditations on that dilemma. We must remember, however, that they view their mutual difficulty from contrasting points of view: Anna has turned her back on her social self in all respects but one (her relationship with Vronsky); Levin has ventured forth from relative isolation to a broader participation in the social context.

Students find enriching a discussion of the novel in this vein. It enables them to deal more effectively with the character of Levin, who without these connections seems either a supernumerary at best or the mouthpiece of the author's objectionable opinions at worst. Even more, it allows students access to a fuller and more nuanced approach to understanding the character of Anna. All too often they content themselves with the picture of her as the heroically suffering martyr to love, on the one hand, or as the bad woman who gets what she deserves, on the other. (I well remember one class discussion that contained the following interchange: Female student in a tone of outrage: "Anna gets just what she deserves; she's made her bed, and now she's got to lie in it!" Male student in a voice of anonymous, semisniggering aside: "And lie in it, and lie in it, and lie in it . . .")

Tolstoy's distress of the middle and late 1870s was a climactic point, a crisis, in a lifelong effort to grapple with the complex tension between his concept of himself as an independent individual and as a part of some larger all-embracing totality. Looking backward on his crisis, as he does in *Confession*, he seems most troubled by how the inevitability of death annihilates all hope of permanent significance or distinctive realization for himself as an individual. In *Anna Karenina* the fear of and despairing attraction to death is crucial to Anna, to Levin, and to the reader's understanding of those characters and of the unity of the novel. But in the novel Tolstoy goes beyond the specter of physical death and relates the despair of his main characters primarily to their unavailing attempts to realize themselves fully as individuals in the social and family context. Thus, the pressure of the social is itself a form of death.

In the decade following *Anna Karenina*, Tolstoy went on to find a new response to the death of the self: a radical reformulation of the meaning of life. But Anna, who capitulates, and Levin, who compromises, were forced to choose between the two responses that presented themselves to the author in the mid-1870s.

Law as Limit and the Limits of the Law in *Anna Karenina*

Harriet Murav

In teaching *Anna Karenina* in the North American university in the early twenty-first century, I find that it is likely that the students' experience of their own freedom and their belief in choice as a positive value will color their reception of the novel. Students want to know why Anna doesn't simply divorce Karenin, marry Vronsky, and get on with her life. The commonly held North American view that individuals define their happiness, under the protection of the law, which prevents one person's pursuit of happiness from interfering with another's, will be challenged by *Anna Karenina*. Tolstoy explicitly rejects a relativistic view of individually made happiness in the opening lines of the novel: "All happy families resemble one another, but each unhappy family is unhappy in its own way" (1; pt. 1, ch.1). This seemingly axiomatic statement implies that there is only one form of happiness: the family.[1] The abstract universal truth of the opening is realized in the concrete forms of the particular social world of late Imperial Russia. Tolstoy embeds in the fabric of the novel the sacramental meaning of marriage according to the Russian Orthodox Church and Russian imperial law. Brief excerpts from the Russian Orthodox marriage service, a concise summary of divorce law as enunciated by the "famous Petersburg lawyer" (332; pt. 4, ch. 5), and expositions of the law regarding the legal status of illegitimate children appear in the novel as part of the everyday world inhabited by its characters, who in their lives variously reflect on, struggle against, embody, and transform the significance of these laws and institutions. In the concrete social world of *Anna Karenina*, the differential weight of gender plays a central role in the forms of social agency and selfhood available to the characters.

The Problem of the Law

A brief overview of Russian imperial marriage and divorce law provides a framework for understanding its meanings in *Anna Karenina*. As William Wagner explains in *Marriage, Property, and Law in Late Imperial Russia*, the influence of the Russian Orthodox Church was felt in the ideology of marriage and family law and in concrete practice. Marriage was defined as the joining of two persons into one by God and the church. The civil code included a provision about a wife's "unlimited obedience" to her husband and her duty to "render him all pleasure and affection" (62).[2] This provision can be found in the text of *Anna Karenina* indirectly. At Kitty and Levin's wedding ceremony, we hear the deacon's admonition to the assembled guests: "Wives, obey your husbands" (415; pt. 5, ch. 6). The husband's obligations to his wife included the duty to "love his wife like his own body" and to "improve her faults" (Mikhailova 28).

The influence of the church could also be seen in divorce law. In part 4, chapter 5, Karenin acts on his threat that he will punish Anna for violating the rules of propriety by receiving Vronsky at home. He goes to a "famous Petersburg lawyer" for the purpose of obtaining a divorce. Imperial Russian law did not permit divorce on the grounds of the incompatibility of husband and wife or on the basis of mutual consent. The lawyer enumerates the permissible grounds for divorce in Russian law: "physical defect in husband or wife; five years' absence without news [. . .] and in cases of adultery" (335; pt. 4, ch. 5). Adultery (*preliubodeianie*) was defined as "an offense to the sanctity of marriage by the fact of a sexual relationship between one of the spouses and a third person" (Mikhailova 96). In order to be considered grounds for divorce, the adultery had to be intentional, conscious, deliberate, free, and not an attempt but a completed act. These same criteria were used to determine whether an individual could be held criminally responsible for any other transgression of the law. Indeed, a guilty party in a case of adultery could be subject to a criminal proceeding for "offending the honor of the sanctity of marriage," but then the victim lost all rights to use the spouse's acts as the grounds for divorce.

The famous Petersburg lawyer explains to Karenin that, in order to prove adultery, letters between the offending spouse and a lover are not sufficient. As Karenin learns, they may serve only as "partial confirmation, but direct evidence from witnesses must be produced" (336). According to the law, only the testimony of two or three eyewitnesses constituted sufficient proof that adultery had taken place. The deaf, the insane, "obvious adulterers," perjurers, relatives of the parties, and those receiving payment to provide testimony could not serve as witnesses (Mikhailova 101). To determine the veracity of the eyewitness testimony, a procedure known as *ochnaia stavka* (which can be translated roughly as "direct confrontation") was used in court. The witnesses were cross-examined at the same time before the allegedly guilty party to see if their answers matched the evidence they gave in pretrial proceedings. If the evidence of the witnesses matched the secondary evidence found in other supporting documents, such as letters, the judge had no choice but to consider the testimony "perfect proof" (Rozanov 1: 139). As critics of marriage and family law pointed out, the theory of proof behind this procedure was archaic and did not reflect changes initiated in other areas of the law in the reforms of 1864.

Divorce proceedings, including all the preliminary stages and the actual pleading, were controlled by and held in the offices of the diocesan authority. Again, to quote Karenin's lawyer, "cases of this kind, as you know, are decided by the Ecclesiastical Department, and the reverend Fathers in such cases are keenly interested in the minutest details" (336; pt. 4, ch. 5). Spouses were forbidden by law to live apart in the absence of divorce, and since husbands controlled the passports of their wives and children, without which the opportunities for travel, residency, and employment were extremely limited, separate residence did not provide a real alternative to divorce, except for the wealthy.

The law regarding children was similarly limiting. A woman living apart from her husband had no right to the custody of her legitimate children. If her husband granted her custody, she had no right to demand support for them. In the case of divorce, the children's presumed guardian was their legal, not their natural, father. Neither the biological father nor the biological mother of children born from an adulterous relationship had legal rights with regard to them (Wagner 72). Anna tells Dolly that the daughter she has with Vronsky is named "Karenin." Vronsky is far more emotional on this point. He hates the "falsehood" of his daughter's legal status as Karenin's child. He is particularly upset about the implications for his possible male heir. Vronsky, who flouts convention by pursuing a serious love affair with Anna, cannot imagine personal happiness outside the social and legal framework—"however happy we may be in our family life," says Vronsky, there will be "hardship and horror" in the absence of a legal bond between himself and his children (568; pt. 6, ch. 22). Vronsky's concern about his future possible son is abstract; Anna, by contrast, must live separated from the son she already has.

The Law in the Novel

At the time the novel was being written, new models of marriage were emerging. The model of companionate marriage, which emphasized the individual and relationships between individuals, challenged the sacramental model (Wagner 101–37). Tolstoy chose to conduct his inquiry on the meaning of sacramental marriage precisely at a time when it was under attack. The novel makes the controversies of its time explicit by staging debates between characters on such issues as the inequities of marital relations and the problematic absence of legal ties between parents and their illegitimate children. The dinner party given by Stiva Oblonsky in part 4 can provide a stimulus for classroom discussion about the problem of marriage in the novel as a whole.

The dinner-party conversation, as Karenin finds, does not help him solve his problem, because it does not take into account the complexity of his feelings. Tolstoy responds to the new models of marriage by dismissing their relevance to the problem he has created. He has his own way of attacking Russian divorce law. Karenin's visit to the lawyer, whom Tolstoy caricatures, is a case in point. The moth-catching lawyer tells Karenin that "[t]he most usual, simple, and reasonable way" of obtaining a divorce is "adultery by mutual consent"—a phrase that Tolstoy emphasizes by repetition (335). Since involuntary detection of adultery was highly unlikely, spouses resorted to agreements about who would play the role of the guilty party, hence adultery was "by mutual consent."

The novel's most profound exploration of marriage unfolds not at the level of society chatter and not in the lawyer's glib eloquence but in the interrelations between the Anna plot and the Levin plot. Anna and Levin inhabit the same social world. In the world represented by *Anna Karenina*, as in any other social world, law is a set of constraints, backed up by force, but at the same time it is a source of meaning (Cover). The law penetrates the characters' consciousness of themselves and their situation in the world. It functions both as a limit and as a language. This point is difficult to get across to American students, most of whom believe that their freedom has practically no limit. This belief can be expressed as follows: The law is outside me, saying no; it doesn't make me who I am. But making people who they are is just what the law does in *Anna Karenina*. The narrator and the characters engage with the discourse of the law; it enters their conversations and interior monologues and is subject to their shifting evaluations. Whether Anna and Levin have the same freedom to act in their shared social world and whether they are equally constrained by the law as a limit and have equal access to the law as a system of meaning must both be taken into account.

Law is both an external voice, like the one I described above, and an internal voice. Its significance changes. Students can be asked to trace the transformation from an external to an internal voice in Levin's engagement and marriage to Kitty, using language as a focus. When Levin attends church before his confession, the words of the service are nearly meaningless to him: "Lord have mercy upon us" sounds like "Lordvmercypons" (399; pt. 5, ch. 1). But later, during the marriage ceremony itself, the words acquire a reality that they previously lacked. Levin listens to the deacon's prayer that God send the new couple "help." He is struck by the correspondence between these words and his inner need—"Help is exactly what I need now!" He experiences a similar sense of inner congruence between his thoughts and the words of the church service when the deacon reads, "Eternal God who joinest them that were separate [. . .] and hast ordained for them an indissoluble union in love." Levin attaches great value to these words; he thinks, " 'Joined them that were separate'—what a depth of meaning is in those words, and how well they fit in with what I am feeling at this moment!" (411; pt. 5, ch. 4).

In everyday life, Levin finds, to his surprise, that the union of two persons into one does not grant him the happiness he expected. He and Kitty quarrel frequently. During one argument, "he first clearly understood what he did not realize when leading her out of church after the wedding: that she was not only very close to him but that he could not now tell where she ended and he began." Tolstoy uses several metaphors to describe the confusing sensations this realization provokes. Levin is compared to a man who receives a blow, but when he looks for his attacker, realizes he "accidentally knocked himself." He is also compared to a half-sleeping man who wants to tear off a part of his body that hurts but finds "on waking that the aching part was—himself" (438; pt. 5, ch. 25).

Just as Levin struggles to understand what marrying Kitty means, Karenin tries to decide what divorcing Anna means. The excerpts from the marriage ceremony inserted into the novel appear as a touchstone for both Levin and Karenin. Karenin can be all too readily dismissed as a mere creature of Petersburg officialdom. Encouraging a more sympathetic reading is important. By gaining a better understanding of Karenin's transformation—regardless of his subsequent reversal—students come closer to understanding the dilemma of divorce in *Anna Karenina*.

At first, the "religious meaning of marriage" is a pacifying abstraction for Karenin. It is one of the items he enumerates on his mental list: "First, the importance of public opinion and propriety; secondly, the religious meaning of marriage" (131; pt. 2, ch. 8). Later, in part 3, after Anna has told him about her relations with Vronsky, religion acquires slightly more meaning for him. As the novel unfolds, the meaning of religion acquires greater and greater internal significance for Karenin, culminating in his forgiveness of Anna as she lies dying of fever after childbirth. The law of forgiveness, which he previously regarded as impossible to fulfill with regard to Anna or to anyone else, becomes a reality in him: "He was not thinking that the law of Christ, which all his life he had wished to fulfil, told him to forgive and love his enemies, but a joyous feeling of forgiveness and love for his enemies filled his soul" (376; pt. 4, ch. 17).

Subsequently, in conversation with Oblonsky, Karenin reflects on the reasons against divorce. Religion and his religious obligation to his wife are uppermost in his mind. His "regard for religion" makes it impossible for him "to plead guilty to a fictitious act of adultery, and still less to allow the wife he had forgiven and whom he loved to be detected in the act and disgraced" (392; pt. 4, ch. 23). Again, the demands of divorce law at the time made it impossible for the guilty party to remarry. To free Anna even for a form of civil marriage not sanctioned by the church would require that Karenin pretend to be the adulterer. This is what the famous Petersburg lawyer meant by adultery by mutual consent. Furthermore, it seems to Karenin that divorcing Anna would harm her—she would be deprived "of the last support on the path of virtue." He remembers Dolly's words to him from their meeting in Moscow, at the dinner party during which Kitty and Levin became engaged. "What Dolly had said in Moscow, to the effect that in considering a divorce he was thinking of himself and not of Anna, who would then be irretrievably lost, had sunk into his heart." Dolly's words acquire the same emotional truth for Karenin that the text of the marriage ceremony acquires for Levin. However, in spite of these feelings, Karenin decides he must submit to "the coarse and mighty power which overruled his life" (392). He agrees to a divorce.

In an early draft of the novel, Tolstoy developed the plot differently. The Anna character obtains a divorce from the Karenin character, marries her lover, and has two children with him. The Karenin character visits his former wife and offers her religious advice:

> You are unhappy. Yes, more than ever. My dear, listen to me. Our union is unbroken. I understand that it is impossible. I am half, I am in torment, and now doubly so. I acted badly. I should have forgiven and driven [the Vronsky character] away, but not made a mockery of the sacrament, and we are all punished.   (*Polnoe sobranie* 20: 45–46)

The telegraphic quality of the draft adds to the pathos of the Karenin character. In the novel, Karenin usually speaks in full, complex sentences. Students can be asked to look for the parallel between his feeling about Anna and Levin's sense of connection to Kitty. After this exchange, the Anna character mocks her former husband, but he has touched a nerve. As in the final version, she commits suicide.

Adultery as Crime

Despite the narrow grounds for divorce and the other difficulties associated with it, divorce was nonetheless possible in the world represented by *Anna Karenina*. In the final version of the novel, Karenin knows of "very many" cases of divorce in the upper echelons of society (256; pt. 3, ch. 13). Varenka's guardian, Mme Stahl, for example, is divorced. As the draft plot shows, even divorce with remarriage does not solve Anna's problem. The possibility of divorce—and it was a very limited possibility—does not detract from the novel's fundamental principle that marriage is a sacrament. Marriage is not a privately agreed on arrangement, nor is it an absolute, imposed from without. Its meaning must be negotiated, felt, and lived. Levin's experience of his union with Kitty is too obscure to him to put into language. His marriage does not fulfill all his expectations, but he experiences, albeit painfully, its fulfillment. The text of the marriage ceremony becomes flesh in him.

Anna Karenina is a novel made of linkages, as Tolstoy famously wrote in a letter to N. N. Strakhov (750). The same source of meaning and value that enhances the marriage bond for Levin leads to the dissolution of the Karenin marriage. The happiness of one is the unhappiness of the other. The fulfillment of the sacrament and its breach are linked on the same plane of meaningfulness.

The violation of marriage by adultery is a crime, according to Russian imperial law, and adultery is represented as a crime in *Anna Karenina*. The narrator uses the metaphor of murder to describe Anna and Vronsky's first sexual encounter:

> She felt so guilty, so much to blame, that it only remained for her to humble herself and ask to be forgiven; but she had no one in the world now except him [. . .]. Looking at him, she felt her humiliation physically, and could say nothing more. He felt what a murderer must feel when looking at the body he has deprived of life. The body he had deprived of life was their love, the first period of their love. [. . .] But in spite of the murderer's horror of the body of his victim, that body must be cut in pieces and hidden away, and he must make use of what he has obtained by the murder.
>
> Then, as the murderer desperately throws himself on the body, as though with passion, and drags it and hacks it, so Vronsky covered her face and shoulders with kisses.

> She held his hand and did not move. [. . .] "Yes, and this hand, which
> will always be mine, is the hand of my accomplice." (135–36; pt. 2, ch. 11)

This is a difficult passage. Its complexities should be explored in detail. Part
of the problem is that Anna acts as both agent and victim of the crime. She and
Vronsky are "accomplices," yet her body is the metonym of their love and its
initial phase. Anna senses herself as a criminal at this moment because she has
violated the marriage bond with her husband. The line "She felt so guilty, so
much to blame" is more literally translated as "she felt so guilty, so criminal."
Her criminality, however, is uncertain, because her position swings back and
forth between accomplice and victim. The metonym of her body as the first period of love disrupts the stable categories by which the law defines an act.
Intentionality, deliberateness, and completeness are absent, because of the disjunction introduced among her body, her self, and her actions. She is not a
criminal in this narrow juridical sense.

The problem of Anna's criminality requires a reexamination of the function
of law in the novel. If the law is both a system of meaning and a force, the representation of Anna's experience suggests that the dual role of law as language
and limit splits along gender lines. Levin and Karenin encounter the law as language, but Anna encounters it as a force constraining who she is. The law defines her as a criminal. The first act of adultery takes away her voice: she fails to
put into words what she feels, and she never recovers the capacity. This depri-
vation is not Tolstoy's way of punishing her for her crime but a realistic depiction of the consequence of the destruction of her marriage. In late Imperial
Russia, marriage gave a woman a social self. Dolly's horror that Anna, divorced,
"will be nobody's wife" and therefore "ruined" is an apt description (359; pt. 4,
ch. 12). The loss of voice amounts to a loss of agency. Readers do not learn from
Anna in Anna's words why she does what she does. The lack of verbal self-
consciousness offers a striking contrast to Tolstoy's characterization of Karenin
and Levin.

In part 4, Anna refuses Karenin's offer of a divorce, even though he tells Stiva
that he is willing to give up their son. Anna goes to Europe with Vronsky, leaving Karenin behind in Saint Petersburg with Serezha. The reasons for her refusal are left unstated until she is in Italy. She reflects that since she did wrong,
she must suffer, both from the loss of her son and from her failure to obtain a
divorce (421; pt. 5, ch. 8). Anna's attempt even to suffer fails. She enjoys herself
in Italy. Suffering comes later. In refusing the divorce and failing to pursue
what is in her own best interest, she does not act as students might expect.
Anna Karenina requires a critical reappraisal of the so-called liberal self, the
model on which law in American society is based.[3]

There are other reasons for Anna's refusal. To agree to Karenin's offer of a divorce is to put herself utterly in debt to him. The marriage bond, severed by divorce, would be replaced by another form of obligation, no less real for its lack

of outward ceremony. This is not the freedom Anna seeks. Furthermore, accepting Karenin's act of goodness would be a way of condemning herself and of confirming her sense of herself as a criminal.[4] If she were to agree to a divorce, Karenin would have to assume the role of adulterer, with all the consequences. Anna is still a moral being, with scruples and a sense of justice. She may not want Karenin to have to endure the scandal. The moral self with a sense of justice that she still possesses, and to which Karenin appeals, cannot take concrete form in the social world Anna inhabits.

After Anna and Vronsky return to Russia, she worries that Vronsky is losing interest in her and agrees to marry him. In part 7, she writes Karenin to ask for a divorce, without success. Apart from the letter, she is powerless to negotiate for herself. Her dependence on Karenin has not decreased since her separation from him. Her actions and the particular nature of Russian divorce law, parodically rendered as "adultery through mutual consent," place her outside the law, depriving her of her status. She cannot speak, and she cannot act. The same law that expels her gives other people acting in private the power to assume an enhanced role, not only as active agents but as de facto legal officials, who inflict on her the force of law. Stiva, attempting to negotiate for Anna, tells Karenin "it's like keeping a man condemned to death with the halter round his neck for months, promising him either death or a reprieve!" (655; pt. 7, ch. 18). Stiva uses the comparison to describe the agony of the wait, but it has broader implications.

By the end of the novel, Tolstoy subjects his axiom to a series of questions. Levin, married and the father of a son, "hid a cord he had lest he should hang himself, and he feared to carry a gun lest he should shoot himself" (714; pt. 8, ch. 10). Both Levin and Anna live in fear of the halter around their necks. Levin finds a way to extricate himself, at least temporarily, but Anna does not. The problem is not her passion, sinfulness, or even the backwardness of the divorce law, which exacerbates but is not the whole of the difficulty, as C. J. G. Turner ("Divorce") points out. The problem stems from the intertwined religious, social, and legal meanings of marriage and from the differential constitution of the female and male social self in the world of *Anna Karenina*. If marriage is the joining of two persons into one, then the loss of the marriage is a loss of the self that was joined to the other spouse. The Karenin character in the draft says pathetically, "I am half." But he can still act and move about in society, and his power over Anna, is, if anything, increased. Anna's act of adultery is a harm inflicted not only on Karenin and not only on that part of herself joined to him but also on the social, active, vocal self that marriage afforded women in late Imperial Russia. The conjoined functions of law as force and law as system of meaning break apart in her case. For Anna, by the end of the novel, law is only force, an inert weight that kills her.

NOTES

[1]Tolstoy helped his sister try to obtain a divorce in 1864, before the writing of *Anna Karenina*. He wrote to his sister's husband to negotiate the specific terms between the estranged spouses, including a proviso that the children remain with their mother and be supported by their father. See Turner, "Divorce" 99–100.

[2]For a discussion in English of Russian family law, see Wagner; Stites 181–82; for discussion in Russian, see Mikhailova; and Brun's entry under "razvod" (divorce) in the Brokgauz-Efron encyclopedia. Rozanov's study is fascinating although idiosyncratic. For a specific discussion of *Anna Karenina* and Russian divorce law, see Turner, *Karenina Companion*.

[3]This model of the liberal self has been challenged by feminist critics, for example, West (179–249).

[4]Dostoevsky explores a similar problem in the relationship between Prince Myshkin and Nastasya Filippovna in *The Idiot*.

Motif-Mesh as Matrix: Body, Sexuality, Adultery, and the Woman Question

Helena Goscilo

The Bird's Claw

In comparison with the spacious universe of sunlit plenitude inscribed in *War and Peace*, *Anna Karenina*'s world seems ominously shadowed and corseted, primarily because Tolstoy casts a conceptual net over the novel that binds images and motifs so tightly as to court psychological and stylistic claustrophobia. Whether readers view the novel as rigorously constructed or ruthlessly constricted hinges on their aesthetic assumptions. Few phenomena in the text exist as merely part of the world's furniture. Even an ostensibly minor hunting episode, where Laska's reluctance to disobey her canine instincts ("if I go forward, I shall not know what I am doing [. . .]. [I]f he wishes it, I will, but I can no longer answer for anything" [539; pt. 6, ch. 12]) echoes the terms of Anna's flight to Saint Petersburg ("doubts kept occurring in her mind as to whether the train was moving forwards or backwards, or standing still [. . .]. Something seemed to draw her to [these delirious thoughts], but she had the power to give way to them or to resist" [92–93; pt. 1, ch. 29]), neatly fits into Tolstoy's larger concern with disorienting temptation, moral responsibility, and the spatialized Voltairean wisdom of cultivating limits: the garden of one's immediate, familiar, or familial realm. Since virtually all aspects of the novel are functional, subsumed by presiding ideas larded with strictural values, *Anna Karenina* stylistically anticipates what serves as the monitory epigraph of Tolstoy's signally titled play, *The Power of Darkness* (1886): "When just one claw is caught / The whole bird is doomed." In the novel, that synecdochic principle likewise governs morality, and obtains a fortiori when the bird is female and her claw inexperienced. Yet the preponderance of dense motif-meshes facilitates analysis of *Anna Karenina*, for tracing connections not only pleasures the hermeneut seeking structural unity but also leads to a confrontation with the novel's major concepts. Indeed, the inextricability of the two vouchsafes the inner continuity on which Tolstoy prided himself. Among these meshes, the most revelatory, arguably, is that of body-appetite-sex-marriage-adultery–the woman question.

Tolstoy's Anatomical Anathemas: The Appetite-Driven Body

The novel begins and ends with plump bodies and consciousness. The opening establishes the body as an indicator of appetite (culinary and concupiscent) the moment Stepan Oblonsky's ample, pampered, self-indulgent, adulterous flesh awakens to cognizance of its pleasure in itself and the consequences of its heedless chase after gratification (1–9; pt. 1, ch. 1–4). By contrastive analogy, the conclusion dramatizes Mitya Levin's access to awareness (he recognizes "his own people" [737; pt. 8, ch. 18]) as his mother bathes his equally plump but innocent baby body (see Kovarsky, this volume). Others attend to the immediate well-being of these two plump but differently signifying bodies: whereas the first scene registers inwardly projected consciousness in circumstances that threaten the future of family life, the second marks the birth of an outwardly projected consciousness in circumstances promising family continuity. In between, Tolstoy pointedly indexes characters' morality through legible bodily signs, pitting against bodily excess a spiritually affirmative lack of flesh or seeming independence of it: the faded-flower Varenka's attenuated thinness (196; pt. 2, ch. 30), Lvov's refined visage, Karenin's boniness, Dolly's emaciated fingers and thinning hair, Serpukhovskoy's "delicacy and nobility" of face (281; pt. 3, ch. 21), and Kitty's "clear, truthful" eyes and diminutive proportions ("girlish," "childlike," "slim," "little feet" [26; pt. 1, ch. 9] and "little head" [70; pt. 1, ch. 22]). Examples of excess include Sappho Stolz's "shapely, well-developed and much-exposed bust" (272; pt. 3, ch. 18); Anna's full figure, suppressed energy, and unruly black curls, which exteriorize her finally unleashed, unappeasable sexuality ("If I could be anything but his mistress, passionately loving nothing but his caresses—but I cannot and do not want to be anything else" [690; pt. 7, ch. 30]); and the fat-calved virility of the novel's improvident sybarites: the chest-expanding Oblonsky; the red-necked, strong-toothed Vronsky; and the voracious, parasitical Veslovsky—all appetite-driven carnivores associated with special foods or edacity (Oblonsky's gourmandizing, Vronsky's beefsteak, Veslovsky's gluttony—"he flourished on underdone beef, truffles, and Burgundy" [272; pt. 3, ch. 18]).

Bodies speak in the novel, usually before their owners do (Veslovsky's hefty thighs always precede him), conveying copious and sometimes superfluous—hence emphatic—information. Levin's frequently noted strong muscles confirm his moral, as well as physical, fitness, both forms of health achieved through exercise and meaningful labor: weight lifting, gymnastics, skating, mowing. By contrast, Yashvin, "a man [. . .] with bad principles," displays and senselessly dissipates his extraordinary physical strength chiefly in his card playing and "his ability to drink like a fish" (161; pt. 2, ch. 19). Levin possesses moralized muscles; Yashvin is the hulk-hedonist. Varenka's indifference to self-adornment, her plainness, her constant physical exertions in the service of others, as well as her asexual fadedness signal a strenuous self-denial on all fronts (as with Sonia in *War and Peace*). Grinevich's and Veslovsky's long fingernails (16; pt. 1, ch. 5; 523; pt. 6, ch. 8), Lisa Merkalova's languid body, and Sappho Stolz's grotesquely reconfigured body all indicate their remoteness from useful physical effort ("here people purposely let their nails grow [. . .] to make it quite impossible for them to use their hands!" [33; pt. 1, ch. 10]). For Betsy Tverskaya, corporeal endowments exist solely to be paraded in public, a credo that requires her to be "befittingly nude on returning [. . .] into the glare of gas-light and the gaze of all eyes" (119; pt. 2, ch. 5). Tellingly, the novel's ideal couple, the peasant Parmenovs, incarnate pure energy in self-oblivious, body-intensive labor à deux, their rare harmony stemming, Tolstoy implies, from their continence: "All the first year [of marriage] he didn't understand anything"(250; pt. 3 , ch. 11), whereas for Levin and Kitty "the honeymoon—the first month of their marriage [. . .] remained in both their recollections as the most oppressive and humiliating time of their lives. They both tried in later life to efface from their memories all the ugly shameful circumstances of this unhealthy time" (439; pt. 5, ch. 14). Physical vitality channeled into productive toil systematically contrasts with energy expended on exhibitionism or random sensual gratification, and occupies a higher rung in Tolstoy's ironclad moral hierarchy.

Adulterated and Adulterous Sexuality

Body language enables us to deduce characters' morality above all in questions of sex—Tolstoy's bête noire and the hub of the novel—bracketed with the themes of marriage, adultery, the family, and the woman question. Sex in some form, personally or intellectually, preoccupies the majority of characters. For Tolstoy as lascivious puritan, only reproduction justifies sexual intercourse, hence the disputable family status of such childless couples as the Sviazhskys, Baroness Shilton and spouse, and other representatives of Saint Petersburg's haut monde, antipodes to the Shcherbatskys and the supremely familial, self-abnegating Lvovs (616–18; pt. 7, ch. 4). Failure to procreate implies a betrayal of the sole possible dispensation for the grossness of coupling. By the time of *The Kreutzer Sonata* (1890), of course, not even procreation will legitimate the sexual activity Tolstoy so enjoyed and abhorred.

In a society founded on family structures, sex inescapably entails the problem of violated marriage vows. While Anna's adultery and others' reactions to it compose the novel's polemical centerpiece, marital infidelity reticulates throughout with obsessive regularity, interconnecting diverse individuals analogized primarily or exclusively through moral turpitude: Stiva Oblonsky, the perennial philanderer; Vronsky's debauched mother and profligate older brother; the dissolute Baroness Shilton; Lisa Merkalova; Sappho Stolz; and unnamed or hearsay characters whose conduct Anna refuses to condemn ("No, I am not going to throw the first stone" [72; pt. 1, ch. 22]). Over such characters spouses either fight duels to protect their putative honor (Vasya Prachnikov, who reportedly kills Kvitsky [356–57; pt. 4, ch. 12]; Daryalov, who appears in Karenin's reflections on an entire catalog of husbands cuckolded by "modern wives" [255; pt. 3, ch. 13]) or lodge official complaints (the incident of Titular Councillor Wenden and his young wife, involving Petritsky, with Vronsky in the unlikely guise of propitiator [119–20; pt. 2, ch. 5]).

Regardless of the mental acrobatics performed by critics intent on allying Tolstoy with feminism, in sexual matters, as elsewhere, he advocates a double standard: premarital male sexual experience springs from biological necessity (even Levin succumbs to it, presumably for reasons of health—to emerge unscathed) and therefore may be extenuated (Kitty's "Yes, I have forgiven you" [372; pt. 4, ch. 16]), whereas sexual desire in women is unnatural and degrading. Anna's beauty coarsens under its corruptive impact: "Both morally and physically she had changed for the worse" (326; pt. 4, ch. 3). This essentialist gendered binarism explains why Levin's "tainted past" does not prevent his union with Kitty and her "dovelike purity" (372; pt. 4, ch. 16), though a role reversal would be unimaginable. Few novels betray such a visceral fear and disgust of female sexuality as *Anna Karenina*, where, in addition to traditional thermal metaphors for passion, Tolstoy resorts to the derogatory fin de siècle metaphor of the "fallen" woman as spider (38; pt. 1, ch. 11) and to the reductive, demeaning symbol of the little red bag for Anna's awakened carnal desire (91; pt. 1, ch. 29; 691; pt. 7, ch. 30; 695; pt. 7, ch. 31). As the plastic constellation of bodies immediately following the physical consummation of Anna and Vronsky's love illustrates, women who surrender to passion replicate the original sin of the lapsarian myth (135; pt. 2, ch. 11). The men enabling their irreversible fall, however, merely compete in a socially sanctioned chase that never dooms *them*, though it destroys their partners in crime (the inequity symbolized with crude prophetic explicitness by Frou-Frou's death in the overly allegorized horse race). Tolstoy's revulsion against women's libidinal urges compels him to sexualize Anna posthumously in a disturbing final image, mediated through Vronsky's pained recollections, of her sinful, lifeless body "stretched out shamelessly [sic] before the eyes of strangers" (707; pt. 8, ch. 5). It is impossible to conceive of an adulterous male body being subjected to such textual representation, which carries the weight of a moral autopsy.

Marriage, like sex, is fundamental to the novel's themes, and the sheer number of pages devoted to the Orthodox ceremony that eternally conjoins Kitty and Levin (as well as the decelerated, particularized description of elaborate preparations for it) conveys the primacy of this sacramental union. Aptly, it deprives Levin of all appetite and elevates him to the transcendent: he cannot sleep; eats nothing; contemplates church domes, crosses, stars, and doves, "sure that he could fly upwards" (365–67; pt. 4, ch. 14–15). Marriage is Levin's subjective utopia, which the novel, despite itself, endorses. Summatively analyzed as a parental dilemma in the context of Kitty's marital prospects, matrimony serves as the subject of frivolous conversation among the glitterati congregated around Betsy Tverskaya ("I know of happy marriages, but only such as are founded on reason" [125; pt. 2, ch. 7]); prompts extended ruminations on the part of Karenin, Levin, Koznyshev, Dolly, and even Stiva; and receives passing but weighty commentary from such characters as Serpukhovskoy: "But I am married, and believe me, that 'knowing only your wife, whom you love'—as somebody once said—'you can understand all women better than if you knew thousands' " (284; pt. 3, ch. 22). That *profession de foi* directly challenges the numerically oriented Don Juanism favored by Stiva, Betsy, Lisa Merkalova, and Vronsky's set (104; pt. 1, ch. 34).

For Tolstoy, marriage is a prelude to family, the optimal unit for human existence and social organization, faute de mieux, inasmuch as the single state eventually conduces to desiccation (Varenka, Koznyshev), childlessness results in the stasis of frivolity, with nugatory enjoyment as the overriding criterion for actions (the Sviazhskys), while full-time engagement in sociopolitical and religious causes leads to patina and falsity (Mme Stahl, Lydia Ivanovna) or withdrawal from living life into abstraction (Karenin, Koznyshev). Koznyshev, tellingly, "was intelligent, well-educated, healthy and active, but did not know how to employ his energy," hence his "superfluous leisure and mental energy" (697; pt. 8, ch. 1). Whereas Levin thrives in his own fields and woods, Koznyshev futilely seeks satisfaction in common ideas and words—an ontological category that, in the value system underpinning *Anna Karenina*, lies outside one's garden and cannot substitute for genuine (i.e., family) happiness. Such happiness resides beyond language, for *Anna Karenina* belongs to that huge repository of verbal texts that, paradoxically, articulate a profound skepticism of words. What finally matters is deeds, which is why Levin, who acts right but thinks wrong ("he had lived well, but thought badly" [721; pt. 8, ch. 12]), attains the only possible Tolstoyan version of truth and fulfillment: felt and enacted insight.

In *Anna Karenina*, as in *Family Happiness*, the Tolstoyan woman ultimately realizes her true self through maternity and family life, composed of breast-feeding and raising children, sorting linens, making jam, nursing the sick, listening to her husband's doubts and diatribes, coping with his jealousies or infidelities, supervising meals and accommodation for guests—all those duties that the Shcherbatsky sisters fulfill, with their husbands' help (Nataly and Kitty) or without (Dolly, for whose children Levin becomes a surrogate father-educator). Tolstoy freights breast-feeding, which he adamantly urged on his own ailing, constantly pregnant wife, with mystical significance, for, according to Levin's epiphany, "spiritual truths [. . . are] imbibed with [. . .] mother's milk" (722; pt. 8, ch. 12), a discovery that Kitty experiences personally when her lactating breasts bind her morally to her milk-hungry baby son: "she knew surely by the flow of milk within herself that he was wanting food." "[F]or his mother he had already long been a moral being, with whom she had already had a long series of spiritual relations" (708, 709; pt. 8, ch. 7). In accordance with the novel's device of simultaneously moralized and biologized juxtapositions, Anna's refusal to bear more children and failure to breast-feed her daughter, Annie, are concrete evidence of her rejection of maternal obligations—an inevitable consequence, Tolstoy would have us believe, of her arachnoid fall.

Although *Anna Karenina* acknowledges sexual energy as a requisite (if pernicious) life force, it nonetheless insists that men and women sublimate or harness it, respectively, to productive and reproductive labor. Consequently, female pursuit of interests or employment outside the home constitutes delusion (Anna's involvement with the construction on Vronsky's estate) or compensation (Varenka's caretaking). Critics applauding Tolstoy's so-called feminist inclinations (Heldt; Mandelker, *Framing*) ignore the discrepancy between the gendered spheres legislated in the novel: the circumscribed domain of the household for women and the incomparably broader arena of estate management for men (service in the government and army receives short shrift, as corrupt and corrupting, severed from life's pulse). As the conclusion of *Anna Karenina* attests, successful nonpeasant marriage necessitates the coexistence of separate, but adjoining, gendered domains. According to Serpukhovskoy, to acquire a certain independence "and to love in comfort and unhampered, the only way is to marry! [. . . W]hen I married [. . .] I suddenly had my hands free" (284; pt. 3, ch. 22). Marriage liberates man from a depleting focus on the object of his love but redeems woman from "the humiliation of being an old maid" (361; pt. 4, ch. 13) while imposing on her an endless series of household duties and, if Dolly's case is representative, successive pregnancies. Tolstoy deems anything outside married maternity synonymous with compromise or failure in a woman's life. Though the novel occasionally verges on recognizing that social prejudice decisively shapes such coercive gender paradigms, it ultimately retreats to the conventional position of naturalizing gender disposition on biological grounds.

The Woman Question, according to Man

At the memorable Oblonsky dinner that decides Kitty and Levin's conjugal fate, women's estate is the chief topic of heated debate, raised by Pestsov as spokesman for equal rights: "We must not forget that the subjection of women is so widespread and so old that we often refuse to recognize the abyss that separates them from us. [. . .] Duties are connected with rights, power, money, honours: that is what women are seeking'" (353–54; pt. 4, ch. 10). Here Pestsov, sounding suspiciously like John Stuart Mill, recasts notions implied, provisionally formulated, or polemicized in the 1830s society tales of Elena Gan, Vladimir Odoevsky, Evdokiia Rostopchina, Vladimir Sollogub, and countless others—and in Karolina Pavlova's *A Double Life* (1848); Alexander Herzen's *Who Is to Blame?* (1848); Aleksandr Druzhinin's *Polinka Saks* (1847); Evgeniia Tur's *The Niece* (1851); and, most forcefully and programmatically, in Nikolai Chernyshevsky's *What Is to Be Done?* (1863). Tolstoy's fictional treatment of women's emancipation recalls Fyodor Dostoevsky's dismissive satire in *The Possessed*, which likewise diminishes the issue's profound and far-reaching complexities through trivialization and arbitrary hyperbole. Pestsov's sound argument—that women's exclusion from education deprives them of fundamental rights and vice versa—elicits Prince Shcherbatsky's startlingly tasteless quotation of the old proverb "Women's hair is long, but their wits short," followed by his illogical (Tolstoyan!) confusion of civil rights with biological capabilities: "It is just as if I were to strive for the right of being a wet nurse, and were offended because they pay women for it and won't pay me" (354; pt. 4, ch. 10). Pestsov's subsequent contention that gender inequality, far from being "in the very nature of things," as Karenin claims, in fact derives from "the infidelity of a wife and that of a husband [being] unequally punished both by law and by public opinion" (356; pt. 4, ch. 12) muddles cause and symptom but gets to the heart of the novel's matter (and merely states what the cases of Stiva and Anna concretize).

Education in the world of *Anna Karenina* belongs to men, for even intelligent women cannot be entrusted with something as rudimentary as children's home lessons: Karenin, not Anna, supplements Serezha's tutorials with his own assignments and tests; Levin shoulders that duty with Dolly's children; Arseney Lvov alone supervises his sons' learning (616–17; pt. 7, ch. 4). All women in the novel except Anna remain happily impervious to any and all intellectual pursuits, and Tolstoy frames her efforts to understand, share, and contribute to Vronsky's estate management in an unambiguously negative light. To what extent the mandate that women be virginal and ignorant, with no access to education, excludes them from exchanges about politics, social conditions, and virtually any serious problem emerges grotesquely at the Oblonsky dinner party, when discussion of women's rights grinds to a halt because of "some questions not freely to be discussed in the presence of ladies concerning the inequalities of marriage relations" (356)—precisely those relations that Tolstoy touts as intrinsic to women's self-realization!

If the irony of this passage encourages the conclusion that Tolstoy champions enlightened reform for women's emancipation, the remainder of the novel effectively demolishes that surmise. Theodor Fontane, whose *Effi Briest* (1895) parallels the approximate trajectory of Gustave Flaubert's *Madame Bovary* (1857) and *Anna Karenina*, envisioned multiple scenarios for extramarital passions: his earlier *L'Adultera* (1882) ends not with the heroine's inevitable death but with a fulfillment of human aspirations through an illicit liaison. The problem with *Anna Karenina* is not the wayward heroine's doom but the novel's inflexible closedness from the very outset to alternative plot developments and resolutions. In questions of gender, *Anna Karenina* combines structural rigor with conceptual rigor mortis.

Agrarian Issues in Tolstoy's *Anna Karenina* as a "Mirror of the Russian Revolution"

Mary Helen Kashuba and Manucher Dareshuri

In a course entitled Conflict and Peacemaking, we approach the French, Russian, and Iranian Revolutions by reading literary, political, and economic thinkers whose ideas reflect the unrest of the times, foreshadow the upheaval to come, or propose a brighter future. This interdisciplinary, undergraduate seminar is based on discussion and led by two professors, one from literature and one from economics. In studying the French Revolution, we discuss such works as Molière's *Le bourgeois gentilhomme*, Voltaire's *Candide*, Jean-Jacques Rousseau's *Discourse on Inequality* and *The Social Contract*, and articles in the *Encyclopédie* (Diderot et al.). For the Russian Revolution we read, among other works, Nikolai Gogol's "Overcoat" and *Inspector General*, Ivan Turgenev's *Fathers and Sons*, Leo Tolstoy's *Anna Karenina*, Boris Pasternak's *Doctor Zhivago*, as well as selections from Karl Marx, Friedrich Engels, and Vladimir Ilich Lenin. The course ends with a study of the Iranian Revolution, through the short stories of Samad Behrangi and Jalal Al-eh Ahmad, the poetry of Foruq Forrokhzad, and classic and contemporary films. Students are thus invited to discover the inner workings of each country, to analyze the events leading to each revolution, and to see its consequences.

Agrarian issues are an important economic factor in all three prerevolutionary societies. We use *Anna Karenina* for its depiction of these issues in the Russian context. Students are already familiar with Rousseau's idealization of rural life; thus they can be directed to compare and contrast his ideas with those of Tolstoy's Levin. In their readings of Lenin's essay, which is provocatively titled "Tolstoy as the Mirror of the Russian Revolution," students discover Tolstoy as "the spokesman for those ideas and feelings which took shape in millions of Russian peasants" (Lenin qtd. in Knowles, *Tolstoy* 432). As Lenin noted the contradictory elements in Tolstoy's thought, so students need not be surprised to see incomplete theories but brilliant insights throughout the novel, half of which is devoted to the story of Constantine Levin, who—as Gary Jahn points out in this volume—reflects Tolstoy's own struggles and discoveries during the 1860s and 1870s. Such critics as Boris Eikhenbaum (*Tolstoi in the Sixties*) and Ernest Simmons reinforce the autobiographical elements in the novel.

Students begin by exploring two distinctive characteristics of Levin: his inclination to country life and his preoccupation with agrarian issues. Early in the novel, he dines with his future brother-in-law, Stiva Oblonsky, and reacts negatively to city life (30–39; pt. 1, chs. 10–11). The inane conversation of the salons, the lavish dinners, the expensive wardrobes contradict the values that he seeks. Like Rousseau, Levin prefers the country, for he sees the city as a place of contamination. Yet he neither abhors pleasure nor regrets the aristocratic lineage "to which I too belong, and to which, in spite of the merging of the classes, I am very glad to belong. [. . . T]o spend like a nobleman is their business—only the *noblesse* know how to do it" (155; pt. 2, ch. 17). However, he seeks his personal fulfillment only in the harmony of work and land, and eventually in marriage, where the fertility manifested in the birth of children mirrors the fruitfulness of the earth.

Through the eyes of Levin, Tolstoy shows the Russian agrarian system in a state of crisis. Students easily discover some of its problems in parts 2 and 3. When Levin returns home to his estate, he speaks with his steward about the condition of the farm. As in most farms, mismanagement reigns. The machinery is in disrepair, the fields have not been plowed properly, only one-third of them have been sown (140–43; pt. 2, ch. 13). If things were bad under serfdom, they are not any better now. The peasants have an instinctive distrust of their masters; they want to work the least amount of time for the most pay; they are a drunken and aimless lot (301; pt. 3, ch. 27). Give them a new machine, and they immediately break it, or they ignore it and do their work the way it has been done for generations (292–93; pt. 3, ch. 24).

One of these problems, namely, the destruction of machines, finds echoes in *The Communist Manifesto*, which students have already read and analyzed and can easily apply here. According to Marx and Engels, at the initial stages of capitalist development, "workers direct their attacks [. . .] against the instruments of production themselves; they destroy imported wares that compete with their labor; they smash machinery to pieces." Marx and Engels see this as an attempt by labor, which is alienated from its *product,* "to restore by force the vanished status of the workman of the Middle Ages" (17).

Students see the difference between Levin's solution and that of Marx and Engels by studying chapter 25 of the first part of *Anna Karenina* (80–83). Levin and his brother Nicholas both believe that "our workmen and peasants bear the whole burden of labor" and "all this surplus value is taken away by the capitalists" (80). Levin also agrees with Nicholas that there is no sense in social institutions. Like Nicholas, he wants to see a change in this system, but not an association, "in which all the products and profits and, above all, the instruments of production will be common property" (81). Even on his deathbed, Nicholas returns to his communist gospel (319–20; pt. 3, ch. 32). The novel's only communist is portrayed as a sick, ineffectual man whose ideas are an impractical vanishing dream and whose death is the death of the utopian socialist ideal. Students compare Nicholas's ideas with Engels's in *Socialism: Utopian and Scientific.*

Having identified some problems in the agrarian system, students then begin to speculate on the solutions proposed by Tolstoy for the renewal of agriculture in Russia. The following three ideas emerge as central: (1) Human activity is motivated by self-interest. (2) Labor is an essential element in agricultural production and must operate in a system that gives the worker the opportunity to participate in planning and producing through some form of private ownership.

(3) Technology must be compatible with the sociocultural background of the country. Students do not necessarily arrive at these points by themselves but will express them in some form as the teachers lead them through the steps that follow.

Levin states, "I think that no activity can endure if it is not based on personal interest" (224; pt. 3, ch. 3). Students list numerous examples of the self-fulfillment and pleasure that he derives from his farm. He enjoys mowing with the peasants (pt. 3, chs. 4–6). Earlier, on a beautiful spring day, he returns to his farm after Kitty has rejected him. He thinks of "all sorts of plans for the estate"; he dreams of cultivating his farm with "not a single desyatina exhausted" (142, 143; pt. 2, ch. 13). It is not just the physical exertion that brings pleasure but also the planning and managing of one's own work motivated by self-interest, a point also noted by Denis Diderot ("Luxury"), with which students are familiar.

Levin is also inspired by the self-interest shown by other farmers, notably when he stops at the home of a well-to-do peasant on his way to see Sviyazhsky in the Surovsky district (295; pt 3, ch. 25). The house is clean, the yard tidy, the women ruddy and happy, and the farm prosperous. Despite problems with hired laborers, common to most farms of the day, the peasant has found a way to cope. "We look after everything ourselves. If a laborer is no good, let him go! We can manage for ourselves" (297). Levin thus begins to understand the necessity for collaboration between landowners and workers.

The visit to the peasant's house forms another building block in Levin's plan to improve agriculture. Levin sees that private ownership can become an important factor in motivating the farmers. Under the existing system, the farmers work only for their wages, which are the same regardless of how much they produce. The result in Tolstoy's time was often laziness, drunkenness, and cheating. Later in the course students read Anatoly Genatulin's "Rough Weather," a modern short story which shows that the same conditions prevailed in the Soviet system and produced similar results. If farmers were given the opportunity to plan and manage their work, they would have more confidence in its productivity. Students also draw parallels and contrasts with peasants in the works of Gogol and Turgenev.

Levin considers labor an important factor in the economic growth of Russia. He does not favor class antagonism in the Marxist sense. By contrasting him with his brothers, students observe that he does not see the peasants collectively as a class, as does Nicholas, who views them as a homogeneous association of people antagonistic to the association of property owners who exploit them. Nor does Levin share the opinion of his half brother, Koznyshev, who boasts that he knows and likes the peasants. Levin "regard[s] the peasants as the chief partners in a common undertaking" (216; pt. 3, ch. 1). To him they are human beings, with their strength, meekness, and fairness as well as their carelessness, untidiness, and drunkenness. Like all people, they have their good and bad points, and he treats each one as an individual. He condemns industrialists, who "get their money in ways that earn contempt," and believes that "every acquisition out of proportion to the toil contributed is dishonorable" (532; pt. 6, ch. 11). The third element of Levin's plan is compatibility between technology and socioeconomic background. Part of the success that Levin observes at the well-to-do peasant's farm is due to the peasant's use of modern machinery. On Levin's estate, however, machinery does not bring success (pt. 3, ch. 24). Give the workers a new machine, and they break it, because they want to rest and not be obliged to think. They ruin everything you put into their hands, because they hate whatever they are not used to (303; pt. 3, ch. 27). Machines stand idle while farm laborers continue the time-consuming, unprofitable, traditional methods.

At this point students are invited to speculate on the reasons why the farmers dislike the machines. Is it rebellion, as Marx noted, or is there another reason? The class generally concludes that if the workers see the advantage of using the new machines, they are willing to try them, as in the well-to-do peasant's farm, or even in Vronsky's experiment with a model farm (583; pt. 6, ch. 25). Contrasts with Rousseau as well as with Marx bring out Tolstoy's position. Students observe that Tolstoy was not against material progress, as was Rousseau, who idealized an earlier, perhaps unreal, period in human development in his *Discourse on the Origin of Inequality*, which they have studied. Teachers can add that he was far from Rousseau's idyllic, static vision of country life as expressed in *La nouvelle Héloïse*, a work most students have not read. Students note that Tolstoy did not favor the revolt of the proletariat in revolutionary Marxist ideology, with which he was no doubt familiar through Petersburg journals; his travels abroad; and his knowledge of revolutionary thinkers, such as Nikolai Chernyshevsky and Aleksandr Herzen. Herzen was the first to publish Mikhail Bakunin's translation of *The Communist Manifesto* into Russian around 1869 (Eaton 108). Students then conclude that Tolstoy was essentially an evolutionary thinker who favored the gradual improvement of the peasant's life.

For technology to flourish, both technical knowledge and human cooperation and readiness are necessary. Technological progress assumes both improvements in technique and the advancement of the organizational structure embracing it. Students are asked to study carefully part 5, chapter 15, where Levin reflects on these issues. He feels that an agricultural policy, successful in the West, has been falsely imposed on Russia. Industry, railways, credit facilities preceded rather than followed a secure agricultural system, as they did in the West.

Although the mechanical aspects of modern European agricultural techniques were introduced into Russia, no attempt was made to reform the organization of production, distribution, and consumption of agricultural products. Thus, laborers were not ready for the new technology. New machines only complicated their work; they were a burden, not a relief. Peasants, seeing no economic justification for the new technology, either ignored or intentionally destroyed it.

There are many similarities between the current issues involved in the transfer of technology to underdeveloped countries and the ones in rural Russia as described by Tolstoy. When students later study the Iranian Revolution, they are asked to compare the situation described in *Anna Karenina* with what happened when modern equipment was sent by the United States to Iran. Technologies developed in industrialized nations can operate efficiently only in an industrial environment. Lack of cultural preparedness, skilled labor, adequate markets, and compatible infrastructure hinders the use of these techniques in an underdeveloped country, whether it is nineteenth-century Russia or twentieth-century Iran.

Reading *Anna Karenina*, students also see that Levin's struggle to find the best way of managing his farm is part of the spiritual quest for meaning that consumes him, most poignantly at the end of the novel. Levin finds that his plans to reform his estate and perhaps all of Russian agriculture need to be grounded in spiritual and ethical values. Although he has determined that self-interest is important to economic ventures, he will not let self-interest become selfishness. We use this feature of Tolstoy's novel to engage the students in discussion of how economic and political programs interact with belief systems.

By focusing on the agrarian issues of this great novel, students can see the problems of Russian rural life in the nineteenth century as it faced growing industrialization. Tolstoy's vision of a new life—of self-satisfying activity for all who engage in it; of collaboration between laborer and landowner in work that profits both; of private ownership; of a prudent use of technology in an appropriate setting; and, most important, of labor that includes spiritual and ethical values—can be seen as an ideal not only for Russia but for any society in the process of transformation.

Tolstoy's Antiphilosophical Philosophy in *Anna Karenina*

Donna Orwin

When I discuss the role of philosophy in *Anna Karenina* with students, I first must deal with an obstacle that its author has set in my way. Here, as elsewhere, Tolstoy foregrounds his disagreements with philosophy. The novel contains lampoons of professional philosophers, and in part 8 Levin states explicitly that philosophy, even as practiced by such nonmaterialists as Schopenhauer and Plato, cannot explain life (713; ch. 9). In fact, Tolstoy's attitude toward philosophy is more complex than he would have us believe. True, philosophy for him was legitimate only when it served practical, moral goals. At the same time, he took thought very seriously, and his opposition to philosophizing in the novel was itself part of a principled philosophical position. As is typical of Tolstoy, moreover, his attack on false philosophy (*filosofstvovanie*) is accompanied by a vigorous if muted defense of what he regards as the real thing. In what follows, I explain the contradiction between his private and public stance toward philosophy and then reconstruct parts of the philosophical scaffolding that he used to build *Anna Karenina*. I trace the origins of his antiphilosophical philosophy to two thinkers whom he read carefully—Jean-Jacques Rousseau and Plato—and discuss them in some detail.

Tolstoy's antiphilosophical stance, partly rhetorical and partly serious, goes back to his immersion, in his student days, in the writings of Rousseau. In his *Confessions*, Rousseau explains how he educated himself by reading all the modern philosophers, Locke, Descartes, Leibnitz, "and others" (246). In the *First Discourse*, he criticizes these same philosophers as "extravagances of the human mind" and "aberrations of human reason" (*Discourse on the Sciences* 20). Rousseau's reasons for this attack are in part rhetorical and have to do with the status of reason in the human soul. According to Karl Barth, Rousseau brought the Enlightenment to a close and inaugurated the "age of Goethe" by his focus on the individual self (Melzer 38). Tolstoy, Rousseau's faithful student in this regard, writes confessional literature himself and appeals to each of us as a particular individual. He engages us by starting with the ultimate source of our particularity, our bodies, and the senses that are our first access to the external world. Through the vicarious experiences that we have from literature that applies this strategy, the feelings of the writer, so Tolstoy hoped, would reverberate in the soul of each reader. As for thoughts, Tolstoy believed that if we as readers did not think that they originated with him, we would not believe them. If we did not ourselves feel their truth as a result of our own experience, we would never truly accept them. While writing *Anna Karenina*, he praised his friend Nikolai Strakhov's article on Darwin and predicted at the same time that it would have little impact on the general public (*Polnoe sobranie* 62: 67; 13

Feb. 1874). The implication is that only art will convince people of the truth of Strakhov's argument. Not logic but feelings communicated through art move readers. In his fiction, Tolstoy wants us to believe that his ideas are not derived from books of philosophy; he wants them to be inscribed in our souls, as they are in his.

Students are enthralled with *Anna Karenina,* just as we teachers were when we first read it. To help them think about how Tolstoy enchants them, I step back from the song to the Pied Piper. His public stance notwithstanding, Tolstoy read philosophy throughout his long life. As a thinker, he was a product of the nineteenth-century philosophical movement that Maurice Mandelbaum has called metaphysical idealism. Metaphysical idealists believed that "within natural human experience one can find the clue to an understanding of the ultimate nature of reality, and this clue is revealed in those traits which distinguish man as a spiritual being" (6). According to Tolstoy's brand of metaphysical idealism, poets, who seek out and represent natural human experience as fully as possible, are the ones who have access, albeit partial, to ultimate truths. Metaphysical idealism called for a unique relation of the particular to the general, in which generalizations might extract certain truths from particular details, but the details represent reality more completely than can any rational generalization about them.

Returning from author to text, I show the students how Tolstoy's art operates from the bottom up, from details to generalizations rather than the other way around. This method initially strikes them as paradoxical, especially as regards *Anna Karenina,* which seems much more tightly structured than *War and Peace. Anna Karenina* commences with a kind of overture in which the basic elements of the structure are laid out and their relations established. (See Holland, this volume, for a discussion of the novel's opening.) But in the opening the shifts from one level of generalization to another do not flow smoothly. On the greatest level of generalization there is the epigraph itself—"Vengeance is mine; I will repay"—the relation of which to the text is as enigmatic as that of God to the world created and ruled by him. Then, as Robert Jackson has pointed out, the emphasis in the first paragraph on happy families and togetherness gives way immediately in the second paragraph to unhappy families and the isolation of individuals in them ("Ambivalent Beginning" 345–53). None of the different structural elements of the novel introduced at its beginning coexist harmoniously with one another, and therefore they raise more questions than they answer. All the levels of discourse are true in some way, but it is not always easy to explain exactly how and why they fit together. But the poet need not explain. God, standing outside life and inexplicable to the human mind, will take care of final judgments and appropriate sentences.

After I have taken my students through the complexities (and perplexities) of narrative levels in the beginning of *Anna Karenina*, I tell them that this formal element of the novel reflects Tolstoy's philosophical beliefs. Specifically, it presents reality from the point of view of metaphysical idealism. Tolstoy drank deeply at the sources of this school, in his reading of Rousseau starting in the 1840s and also in his discovery, in the early 1850s, of Plato, whom he first read in the translation of Victor Cousin.[1] Less obvious than the many thematic connections to Plato in Tolstoy's oeuvre is the debt that Tolstoy owes to the genre of the Platonic dialogue (see Evdokimova, this volume). The beginnings of this influence can be detected in his early stories, especially "The Raid," but *Anna Karenina* actually contains an embedded narrative that is both a tribute to Plato and also an explanation of his "Tolstoyan" significance.

The relevant Platonic dialogue in *Anna Karenina* is one of Tolstoy's favorites, the *Symposium* (see Plato, *Lysis*). In it, Pausanias's definition of the two kinds of love, a low one associated with the body and sex and a high one associated with virtue and the soul, is tested in the other speeches and also by the dramatic situation. Pausanias wants to convince the handsome young Agathon, with whom he is in love, that his love is the higher kind. Disguising his snickers as hiccups, Aristophanes laughs at Pausanias's self-serving high-mindedness and deflates it later with a myth about love as longing for the half of our bodies lost when the gods split us in two as punishment for our hubris. Socrates counters this comic view of love as entirely self-absorbed with an explanation (attributed to the wise Diotima) of love as longing for the beautiful. Just as Aristophanes is about to defend his speech, the drunken Alcibiades bursts into the gathering and tells stories about Socrates that partly support and partly contradict the earlier speeches, including even the one by Socrates. We are left with the impression that there are two kinds of love but that it is difficult to define what the higher one is or even to distinguish it completely from the lower one.

As always when I teach about the relation between philosophy and literature, I stay as close as possible to the writer's interpretation of the philosopher, no matter how eccentric or partial that may seem. My abbreviated summary of the *Symposium* is intended only to demonstrate that it is what we would call a philosophical drama, not a tract. It is the mixture of Socratic dialectic and poetic exposition in the Platonic dialogue as a genre that appealed to Tolstoy, and in tribute to this form he created just such a philosophical drama in *Anna Karenina*.

In the novel Plato is invoked on three different occasions, which together constitute a philosophical subplot about Levin's search for the proper relation of the details of his life to its fundamental organizing moral principles. Plato first comes up in part 1, during a restaurant dinner (chs. 9–11) that is itself an allusion to the *Symposium*. Like the participants in Plato's banquet, Stiva and Levin discuss love, and Levin provides a definition of it drawn from the *Symposium*. Later, during his spiritual crisis, which climaxes in part 8, he consults philosophical texts in a futile effort to find a justification for living. The houses of cards constructed from artificial chains of thought by various nonmaterialist philosophers, including Plato, all collapse because they do not directly engage life, which is anterior to reason and not the same as it (713; pt. 8, ch. 9). When Levin does recover his belief in the possibility of a moral life a few pages later, however, it is because he hears of a virtuous peasant named Platon,[2] who "lives for his soul and remembers God" (719; pt. 8, ch. 11).

Coming at the beginning and end of the novel, functioning as they do respectively as opening, crisis, and denouement, the three Platonic moments bind the novel together on the level of thought. In this subplot, the name of Plato is implicated in both the problem and its solution. At the restaurant, Levin makes two related but different claims about Plato. In the first place, he says that, according to Plato in the *Symposium*, there are two kinds of love. This statement is shown to be true and thus, as Irina Gutkin has claimed, is one key to understanding the organization of the novel. The relation between this philosophical statement about love and its dramatic exposition is that of a maxim to its illustrations. The two kinds of love are physical and spiritual, corresponding to Tolstoy's dualism, which Tolstoy believed Plato shared with him. Plato's definition as Levin first states it does not, however, rank the two loves morally; Levin immediately does this by designating the higher, spiritual love platonic and the lower, bodily one, not platonic. In a slight but significant shift, he now associates Plato with a love of virtue and wholeness, the relation of which to reality is unclear. He admits also that his own past behavior does not harmonize with his preference for platonic love. This inconsistency creates a drama that would not exist if ideals and reality simply coincided, as Levin is temperamentally inclined to assume they do. Once he remembers his own misdemeanors, he twice says that he doesn't know what to think (36, 39; pt. 1, ch. 11). Moral generalizations in which he wholeheartedly believes do not organize the details of his life.

So the knot is tied in this episode, and the philosophical subplot is launched. It consists of a search for what, if anything, might make the life of an individual meaningful, that is, capable of the higher, disinterested love of others called agape. Even Gutkin has to conclude, however, that if these categories, which she calls fleshly and spiritual, organize and explain the content of the novel, they do so only to a certain extent. The love of Kitty and Levin is "more Platonic"; that of Vronsky and Anna "explicitly erotic" (90). In the poetic narrative, not a single important character fits exclusively into Levin's category of high or low, platonic or unplatonic, lover. The novel contains a veritable catalog of mixes of the two, and there is no sense that this catalog is exhaustive. Anna expresses the truth about the mixed character of reality when she says, "I think . . . if it is true that there are as many minds as there are heads, then there are as many kinds of love as there are hearts" (125; pt. 2, ch. 7).

Plato as he is invoked by Levin in the restaurant supplies definitions of what love is and what it ought to be. What he does not explain is love in its particular manifestations. The philosophical search for meaning resumes in part 8, with Levin's crisis. The platonic wholeness or purity for which he longs and with which he identifies in his original discussion with Stiva is unattainable: therefore no philosophical tract, not even a nonmaterialist one, can bridge the gap between general ideals and reality. Levin escapes his suicidal despair only when he realizes that what he seeks is inaccessible to his intellect but visible in a life well led. And whereas Plato is mentioned among those philosophers who fail Levin, another Plato, a Russian peasant bearing this name, comes to his rescue. The peasant appears not as a thinker, who as such must labor in the limitations of the inherent laws governing the intellect and therefore knows that he knows nothing about ultimate truths, but as a character whose actions bear witness to the capabilities of the human personality.

The second Plato, that peasant Platon who appears as a character in the novel, represents the positive side of Plato the philosopher as Tolstoy understood him, namely, his knowledge and love of the good, and it is Platon who is platonic in the moral sense in which Levin uses the term in the conversation with Stiva in part 1. Plato as Tolstoy understood him was able, like Levin, to know the good and act on it, because Plato could rely on a moral instinct. In a revealing letter to Strakhov contemporary with the writing of *Anna Karenina*, Tolstoy placed Plato among the true philosophers, because he "does not correct the original and simplest concepts of [his] listeners, but seek[s] out the meaning of life without breaking down into constituent parts those essences of which life is composed for every person" (*Polnoe sobranie* 62: 222). Along with selfishness, goodness, or "life for the soul" such as Platon lives, is one of the "essences" of human life from which true philosophy, instead of deconstructing life, should "seek out the meaning of life," as Levin does.

Platon proves the existence of platonic love by demonstrating its effect on his actions. When Tolstoy says that Plato practices true philosophy, he means that Plato starts philosophizing from the ground up. Rather than apply abstract categories to explain behavior, the true philosopher arrives at them through the analysis of experience and constantly returns to that experience to check the truth of his conclusions against it. In *Anna Karenina* Tolstoy follows a similar path, moving from description to analysis of phenomena and revisiting the same phenomenon obsessively until he has supplied a comprehensive account of it. Comprehensiveness is more important to him than interpretation. That life comes before thought is reflected by the relation between the dramatic context that adequately captures life as it is and explanations of life supplied by characters or even an omniscient narrator. Not bound to the principles of reason, broader and deeper than a rationalizing philosophy because less abstract, the novel imitates before it analyzes life, which therefore is never completely explained by analysis.

So we are back at Tolstoy's antiphilosophical philosophy in *Anna Karenina*. When I teach the novel, however, I find that I cannot stop here, because Tolstoy himself does not. On the one hand, he rejects any systematizing philosophy; on the other, he does generalize and even appeals to what he regards as true philosophy, which, I repeat, is always in the service of morality. His technique is to make the reader aware of clashes of interests among characters, moral contradictions that call out for solutions.

The first, jolting example of such a clash is at the beginning of the novel, when the narrative switches abruptly from Stiva's to Dolly's point of view. Another occurs in part 6, between Levin and his guest Vasenka Veslovsky. Veslovsky appears with Stiva and functions as his simplified and completely comic double. Even more than Stiva, Veslovsky, whose very name in Russian connotes merriment, lives at the level of the raw emotional content that makes up existence, and he declines to think about life. Watching Veslovsky with the pregnant Kitty, Levin feels jealous pangs. Then on the hunt (521–41; chs. 8–13), he unreservedly admires Veslovsky for his charm and his zest for life, and it is important for us to understand the conditions of this admiration. The hunt is a natural activity that takes place outside the conditions of civilized life. The hunters jostle good-naturedly to outdo one another at sport, and Levin does not take much offense when Veslovsky and Stiva between them—Veslovsky taking the lion's share, so says Stiva—devour all the food Kitty has prepared. When Stiva and Veslovsky go off to dally with peasant girls, Levin does not reproach them. Their dalliance works to his advantage the next morning, when they sleep in and he has a successful hunt without them; after it he enjoys Oblonsky's envy at his catch. In his later philosophical tract On Life (1887), Tolstoy acknowledges that the self-centered view of life taken by a Stiva, a Veslovsky, or Levin on the hunt is natural. (Laska, Levin's dog and his partner in the hunt, similarly has no moral qualms as she stalks birds, whom she mentally designates as others, them.) The problem for human society is that the natural inclination for each individual to be self-centered leads to conflict. So, when the hunters return home and Veslovsky flirts again with Kitty, Levin's mood turns ugly (541–48; ch. 14). Levin may laugh indulgently at Veslovsky's conduct with other women, but he does not laugh when, as he sees it, that conduct compromises his own wife. In chapter 15, while consulting Dolly about Veslovsky's behavior, Levin pleads with her to forgive little Masha for some childish sexual experimentation carried on in the bushes (i.e., in nature). Dolly tells Masha she may go, but the child, feeling guilty, lingers, catches her mother's eye, and bursts out crying. Dolly caresses her, and Levin leaves, thinking, "What is there in common between us and him [Veslovsky]?" (546). He has witnessed a moment of moral education, in which a child learns from a beloved teacher that she must not do certain things even though her desire to do them is natural. Such restraint does not exist for Veslovsky, but it is necessary if human society is to cohere.

The outcome of the subplot of Dolly and Masha is satisfying both because Dolly does the right, moral thing and because this right thing is tailored so specifically to the circumstances that require it. Before Levin comes into the room, Dolly is a prisoner of her anger at Masha's transgression, which must remind her of Stiva's philandering. She softens and forgives Masha as part of the process of assessing Levin's problem. Masha, standing in the corner, notices her mother's "scarcely perceptible smile" at the stock comic situation of the jealous older husband (545). Masha turns around, and Dolly orders her back, but the little criminal has truly gauged the sea change in her mother's mood and soon rides to safety on the wave of Dolly's horror that Levin may overreact, breach social decorum, and throw Veslovsky off his estate. Masha is saved by coincidence, of course, but Dolly forgives her daughter in obedience to the laws of noncontradiction. Responding to an unexpected turn of events, comparing the two scenarios fortuitously entwined, she realizes that she cannot in good conscience go on blaming Masha even as she excuses Veslovsky.

The little drama between Masha and Dolly illustrates how moral decision making takes place in the chaos of ongoing life. On the hunt, Stiva and Levin have a conversation, echoing their earlier one at the restaurant, about the possibility of morality. Once again Levin is forced by his worldly interlocutor to acknowledge an inconsistency between his moral beliefs and his life: he knows that his relations with his peasant workers are unfair, but his obligations to his family make it impossible for him to change them. But whereas this troubles Levin (although he can put the question aside during the hunt), for Stiva it is enough to admit his injustice in order to be able to go on committing it. Like Levin, the reader recognizes and forgives Stiva's inability to choose the good of others over his own. As each of us knows from experience, in individual consciousness the rules of noncontradiction do not yet apply: what we want takes precedence over what makes sense. Tolstoy hopes to wean us eventually from the bedrock of irrational consciousness. His text is built on individual instances of it, however, and only a willingness to submit to a dialectic based on the laws of reason will lead readers finally to the level of generalization necessary for moral rectitude. At any point, readers (like some of Tolstoy's characters) can refuse to go along, and many have refused. The amazing verisimilitude of Tolstoy's fiction depends at every level on its rootedness in the realities of individual consciousness.

Stiva and Veslovsky are amiable hedonists. The opening sally in the novel is especially daring, because Tolstoy maneuvers readers into identifying with Stiva when this character is behaving unfairly. Everyone likes Veslovsky; even Levin feels sorry as he expels him. In the utmost self-absorption, characters may also behave admirably, as Dolly does in the example just discussed. In fact, every moment of moral significance in the novel, for good or for evil, occurs at that same level of irrational consciousness to which we are introduced through Stiva. The standards, or ideals, inhere in the very raw material of the soul that they shape morally. To behave badly, even Stiva, so in tune with everything, has occasionally to ignore the voice of conscience, and he is shown ignoring it in certain key episodes in the novel. (One of these is when he tries to convince Karenin to grant Anna a divorce.)

Tolstoy's belief in inherent moral standards is evident already in his 1847 reading of Rousseau's *First Discourse*. According to Rousseau there, God has placed the thoughts necessary for our happiness and virtue within us, in the form of conscience:

> O virtue! Sublime science of simple souls, are so many difficulties and preparations needed to know you? Are not your principles engraved in all hearts, and is it not enough to learn your laws to return into oneself and listen to the voice of one's conscience in the silence of the passions? That is true Philosophy, let us know how to be satisfied with it.
>
> (*Discourse* 22)

In 1847 Tolstoy began a commentary, both defiant and reverential, on the first and second discourses of Rousseau. The nineteen-year-old Russian student asserts his independence from his French master by taking issue with parts of the *First Discourse*, but one major strand of the argument, about the status of "true Philosophy," he swallows whole. The commentary sounds the first notes of the notorious Tolstoyan assault on books: "[. . .] all philosophical questions for the resolution of which so many have labored and so many [useless] books have been written, all these questions, I say, can be reduced to simple beginnings. [. . .] The leaves of the tree please us more than the roots" (*Polnoe sobranie* 1: 222).

Thirty years later, in *Anna Karenina*, we find Levin following the Rousseauesque path to "simple beginnings" first suggested in these words. Inspired by the peasant Platon, Levin finds in his own heart the "true Philosophy" that has eluded him in books. Although he is looking for "something more important in life than reason" (713; pt. 8, ch. 9), his renewed confirmation of life comes from thoughts that are innate: "At the peasant's words about [Platon] living for the soul, rightly, in a godly way, dim but important thoughts crowded into his mind, as if breaking loose from some place where they had been locked up, and all rushing toward one goal, whirled in his head, dazzling him with their light" (719; ch. 11).

Despite his belief in the incomprehensibility of life, as a thinker Tolstoy was not simply an irrationalist. He was a kind of transcendentalist—in V. V. Zenkovsky's apt conception, a mystic of the mind (29)—and both his reading of Rousseau and Plato and his own artistic practice reflect this. He believed that the fundamental precepts of ethics, or practical reason as he understood it, were available to people not from the intellect but, as he would put it, from the heart. Rather than ascend to truth through dialectic, people descend to truth by listening to voices that well up in their soul. These voices compete with others in the soul. Therefore moral truths, as Tolstoy understood them, do not so much shape reality as add a dimension to it that allows human beings to behave morally while remaining free not to do so. We know that such voices exist, because we hear them speaking in us and, just as important, see their effects in our actions and those of others.

In *Anna Karenina* as elsewhere in his writings, Tolstoy rejects Enlightenment thought but still privileges reason and hence the practice of philosophy.
The contemporary philosophy that he condemns as merely logical, systematizing, and abstract does not account for the facts of life. Real philosophy, as
Tolstoy understands it, has limited, ethical goals. Because human beings are
sentient, not rational creatures, they accept direction from poetry, which ad-
dresses feelings, rather than from philosophy, which speaks to reason. Ultimately, however, Tolstoy equated moral truth and reason. Like Rousseau in that
seminal passage from the *First Discourse* quoted above, Tolstoy both deni-
grated philosophizing and equated "true Philosophy" with the conscience,
which for him represented the voice of transcendental reason. In the case of
Levin, the mind searches for its moral compass, without which a thinking person cannot live, and discovers it both in the individual soul and manifest in the
deeds of good people.

NOTES

Part of this essay appeared in Russian: "Zhanr Platonovykh dialogov i tvorchestvo
Tolstogo," *Russkaya literatura* 44.1 (2002): 38–45.

[1]Tolstoy did not actually read the most important influence on metaphysical idealism,
Immanuel Kant, until 1887. On Kant's debt to Rousseau and Tolstoy's own discovery of
Kant, see Orwin, *Tolstoy's Art* 192–95. Tolstoy read both Rousseau and Kant through the
prism of German idealist thought as it was taught in Russia in the 1840s, and his ties to
German idealism were strengthened in the 1850s through his friendship with such men
as V. P. Botkin (51–81).

[2]Platon is a common peasant name that is the Russian version of Plato. The Maude-
Gibian translation of the name is "Plato."

ANNA KARENINA IN THE LITERARY TRADITIONS OF RUSSIA AND THE WEST

Tolstoy versus Dostoevsky and Bakhtin's Ethics of the Classroom

Caryl Emerson

In classrooms the world over, it has long been the practice to distill the age of the great Russian novel into Dostoevsky versus Tolstoy. We say "versus," because very early on, while Tolstoy was still alive, critics saw these two titanic contemporaries—who never met but whose work was often serialized in the same journals—as creators of profoundly incompatible worlds. Dostoevsky was a "seer of the spirit," Tolstoy a "seer of the flesh."[1] Dostoevsky resolved his great novels with religious revelations, both tragic and triumphant. Tolstoy, wherever possible, resolved his with physical reproduction. As writers, both are massive, philosophical, deeply serious (prompting Vladimir Nabokov's cover term for the two of them, "Tolstoevsky"), but by and large, readers prefer one over the other. One world seems more real.

When this difference is taught in anglophone cultures, Dostoevsky's mystical, theosophical spirit is often aligned with such writers as Herman Melville and Edgar Allan Poe. Like them, Dostoevsky was deeply influenced by European Romanticism and cast his writings in the fantastic, ecstatic intonation common to Gothic literature. (He retained this habit even after he had enriched his plots with the metaphysics and ethical philosophy that were to make him Russia's greatest novelist of ideas.) Dostoevsky's most memorable heroes are drawn from the urban underclass or the eccentric rural gentry and depicted in an unstable, liminal phase of their lives. The brief slice that we see is already under great pressure; it is being tested at an extreme threshold moment. This pressure can erupt into tragedy or comedy—for Dostoevsky is a great comic writer—but importantly, it erupts rather than leaks out or fuels its human carriers at a steady pace. One of Dostoevsky's favorite words is *vdrug* ("suddenly"). In such an environment, natural and biological cycles are muted. In the course of a narrative, families tend to break down. Although focal events in a Dostoevskian novel are relatively few (one big murder, scandalous marriage, or disputed inheritance), what does occur, or is rumored to have occurred, becomes the focus for an extraordinary amount of talk: provocative; freestanding as philosophy (consider "The Grand Inquisitor" chapter from *The Brothers Karamazov*); and, more often than not, inconclusive. Dostoevsky's characters are rarely shown going to work, raising children, eating or sleeping at regular times, living by a schedule. Their energy is spent elsewhere. To teach Dostoevsky, most would agree, is to teach the life of the spirit, its struggle with eternal moral questions under conditions of crisis ethics, and not to teach the routine maintenance required by the life of the body.

By contrast, Tolstoy sees and registers the needs—often overwhelming—of mortal and enfleshed beings. Since these needs arise out of our most basic anxieties and hungers, he treats them as panhuman. Aspects of Tolstoy recall John Steinbeck, Ernest Hemingway, Doris Lessing. Although the texture of his novels is neither placid nor complacent and personal crises can be terrible in their local force, Tolstoy places high value on the reflexes, rituals, and habits developed in the course of everyday life. Thus a Tolstoyan novel usually feels more filled in than a Dostoevskian one and tends to proceed at a more measured, epic pace. Convictions, like families, coalesce gradually, on the basis of repeated contact and experience. Nature and natural processes of maturation play a prominent role; the novels spread out in a biologically rooted way. (If Dostoevsky's favorite word is "suddenly," then Tolstoy's is *vsegda* ["always"]). Humor can be exuberant in Tolstoy, but in him there is nowhere near the range of the comic that we find in Dostoevsky. And while tragedies certainly occur—consider Anna Karenina's awful end—and can even be sudden, they are (except on the battlefield) never really a surprise. Since an individual's fate is the result of tiny daily decisions, all lovingly documented by the novelist, miracles can neither ruin us nor save us. Thus what appear to be irreversible threshold moments in Tolstoy are often tucked into the middle of the novel and end up changing very little in the lives of the heroes, who revert to their routines once the crisis has passed (consider Anna's birth-and-deathbed epiphany and the reconciliation of husband and lover, so dramatic and so temporary). What is more, Tolstoy does not tolerate a lot of abstract philosophy from his characters. For all his reputation as a preacher, it is difficult to extract coherent philosophical arguments from his fictions and anthologize them on their own. Quite the contrary: centrally important events, such as Kitty and Levin's engagement around a chalkboard, seem to transcend the need for talk and even to make explanations and ideas superfluous. In part for this reason, a Tolstoyan narrative (and Tolstoy labored mightily to bring this illusion about) feels universal and accessible. Although precisely placed in Russian space and time, it can be grasped without extensive glosses on Russian politics, social history, European philosophy. To teach Tolstoy is to teach long-term survival strategies that work wherever we are. No matter how distant the Karenins' Saint Petersburg or the Oblonskys' Moscow might become to future generations, Tolstoy designs his characters to lead lives that we sense (rightly or wrongly) we ourselves could live.

In 1959 the critic George Steiner, building on the work of Georg Lukács, canonized the difference between these two great novelists for the Western world in his best-selling study *Tolstoy or Dostoevsky*. With its acute observations and robust binary contrasts, it has long served teachers as a useful handbook. Dostoevsky, Steiner argues, is a tragic dramatist, Tolstoy an epic poet in the Homeric style. Dostoevsky builds scenes that culminate in crowded scandals and dramatically focused acts, after which the major protagonists explain themselves out loud and at length (a theater-friendly trait); Tolstoy constructs intricate multiple plots over a wide terrain that require, for their proper telling, many years' duration and austere authorial distancing. To be sure, there are problems with Steiner's thesis. What are we to do, for example, with the fact that actual dramatizations of Dostoevsky's novels (not only the numerous popular films but also serious attempts by thoughtful philosophers, such as Albert Camus's stage adaptation of *Devils*) are almost always miserable failures? Scenes and events might be preserved in the play text, but what matters most has disappeared. And Tolstoy, for all his epic love of sensuous objects and his unsentimental, authoritative narration, treats personality in a very different way from the ancients. Nor, of course, does he share their honor code on heroic slaughter and military glory. But most important, when these two Russian novelists are explicated through Steiner's dichotomy—that is, when they are retrofitted to the two genres most central to a classical poetics: epic and tragedy—we and our students are invariably distracted from the fact that Dostoevsky and Tolstoy were writing novels. In the shadow of those classical prototypes, the specifically *novel* aspect of their craft is overlooked. Overlook that, and once again the classroom is back to discussing "real life," existential philosophy, ethics, anything but art. Such slippage out of art and into the reader's real life has long been both the drawing card and the curse of realism. Acts of identification must happen, for they are at the beating heart of the genre, but they must be supplemented and disciplined. The modern critic who has probably done the most to provide that discipline, to equip us with aesthetic tools that can help us teach the form—not just the feel—of novels, is the Russian philosopher Mikhail Bakhtin.

Bakhtin wrote provocative books on Dostoevsky (*Problems of Dostoevsky's Poetics* [1929, rev. ed. 1963]) and François Rabelais (*Rabelais and His World* [1965]), as well as a lengthy draft of a study of Goethe and the bildungsroman. He did not devote a book-length study to Tolstoy, nor does that writer's genius appear to have fired his imagination. But Tolstoy is a steady minor presence in Bakhtin's work. As part of an informal Home Course on Russian Literature (enrollment: three) in Vitebsk, Belorussia, in the spring of 1924, Bakhtin delivered four lectures on Tolstoy, remarkable for their insight and evenhandedness. After his linguistic turn in 1929, however, and the discovery of polyphony and dialogism in Dostoevsky, Bakhtin began to employ Tolstoy largely as a negative example—the losing side, as it were, of a literary quarrel. Like Steiner, Bakhtin juxtaposes the two great Russian novelists in a binary, schematic way. Since these distinctions work as well for the translations as for the original Russian texts, they can help teachers grasp and transmit that most elusive quality of the novelist's art, the formal aspect of genre.

Before we consider Bakhtin's specific contributions to teaching Tolstoy, however, a word is in order on Bakhtin as pedagogue. He was a legendary lecturer and deeply beloved teacher throughout his life, from the Home Course he conducted in the Russian provinces and Leningrad in the 1920s to the lectures in world literature delivered to large classes at Mordovia State Teachers' College in Saransk (later upgraded to a major provincial university). By all accounts, Bakhtin's classroom manner—with three students or three hundred—was utterly magisterial. According to one memoir from the post–World War II period, he would hobble into the auditorium, greet the class, invariably ask the same question ("Where did we stop with you last time?") and, on receiving the answer, would nod ("Yes, yes . . .") and then suddenly change his tone and stance from the everyday, dialogic present tense of classrooms to an inspired, distanced voice that saw and heard only the world he was transmitting, not the world he was addressing.[2] The students were thrilled by these epic presentations. Bakhtin never used notes. He was proud of his photographic memory, which worked equally for prose (in several languages) and poetry; he could recite verse in Russian, German, and French for hours and could remember pages of Rabelais verbatim after a single reading. The eventual erosion of this ability was deeply embarrassing to the septuagenarian Bakhtin, his only recorded instance of personal vanity.

Bakhtin's competence in this performative realm—his ability to assimilate without effort the authoritative texts of others and to recite them flawlessly, with passionate conviction—is intensely revealing. In cultures such as our North American own, with its post-Dewey reflexes and open-classroom aspirations, memorization in the schools is often equated with sterile rote learning and reckoned a disservice to the emerging personality. Dialogism and a nurturing of the student's own word has been enthusiastically embraced by the progressive wing of English composition studies over the past two decades, in part because it is so thoroughly in keeping with traditional American pedagogical doctrine. Bakhtin's method for teaching adults was quite different. He was more old-fashioned, more rooted in continental European habits, academic in the tradition of the nineteenth-century German professoriat. (A helpful analogy here is the famously self-enclosed lecture style of the Russian émigré aristocrat Nabokov at Cornell.) Bakhtin's unapologetic recitation method, which set off to such stunning advantage the richness of the worlds he carried around intact in his head, might encourage us to reconsider the famous dichotomy in the essay "Discourse in the Novel" between "authoritative" and "internally persuasive" words (*Dialogic Imagination* 342–48). Bakhtin, it appears, took for granted that any personality genuinely serious about realizing its potential would be eager to absorb verbatim the authoritative words of its culture's great classic texts. When building up one's own verbal self, how could one hope to improve on the diction and style of the acknowledged masters? What is more, the fictive worlds contained in these masterworks deserved to be experienced in their full integrity, without any premature admixture of one's own, more confused word. As department chair at Mordovia State, Bakhtin frequently complained about overly lax standards for students and their inadequate immersion in art. In his view, we are obliged to master not only speech acts as genres of expression (relatively easy to do, because they are selfish and in the present tense), but also listening acts as genres of concentrated attention, which means attuning ourselves to the intonationally distinct worlds created by the great writers of the past. A serious student must live there in that world for substantial amounts of time. Rights to dialogue are acquired only later, after our vocabulary and genres of response have grown disciplined, flexible, complex—that is, after we have liberated ourselves from the arbitrary constraints and urges of our immediate environment with the help of the glorious repertory internalized from art.

Such reflections on Bakhtin's ethics of the classroom set us up for the vexed issue of Tolstoy's authoritative word. Theoretically, Bakhtin resists it. Authoritarian narrators, in his view, crimp the freedom of fictional characters to grow and restrict the free response of readers. But in practice, as a pedagogue, he greatly admired this style of thought. He found the faithful reproduction of ingested texts both easy and pleasant, recommended this mode of literary education to others, and was himself revered for practicing it. Since the dialogue he really valued was already locked inside the literary text, the primary task of students was to appreciate that dialogue, not dilute it with interventions of their own. Whole worlds came out of Bakhtin's mouth, worlds it would take even the best class some time to assimilate. The audience risked losing a great deal if it sought too quickly to remove the footlights.

This much said, let us return to Bakhtin on Dostoevsky versus Tolstoy. In Bakhtin's hands, as in Steiner's three decades later, the juxtaposition produces some splendid initial insights of a binary nature: dialogism versus monologism, double-voiced versus single-voiced, internally persuasive versus authoritative, the eternal life of the word versus the mandated death of the body. But these initial binaries soon reveal internal paradoxes—and contradictions—even more compelling. After considering these paradoxes (of which Bakhtin's personal monologic style, mounted on behalf of dialogic forms, is exemplary), we try them out on a scene from *Anna Karenina*. The easy dichotomies corrode. And Bakhtin becomes more provocative as an aid to teaching than might be suggested by the multiple clichés now associated with his name and method.

Bakhtin's "Tolstoy or Dostoevsky" differs from Steiner's in several ways. First and most obviously, Bakhtin would not endorse the retrofitting of any nineteenth-century novel into the poetics of a much earlier time—and especially not into a classical or neoclassic poetics of epics and tragedies, from which, in his view, novels of all sorts are pointedly excluded. As a genre, the novel always stands in the now and is oriented toward the immediate future. One of Bakhtin's best-known essays, "Epic and Novel" (1940–41), draws categorical distinctions between these two forms of literature (and philosophies of life): novels are multilanguaged, structured to feel like the present, and take place in a zone of maximal contact with their readers; epics are national-unitary in scope, structured to feel like an absolute past, and separated from their audience by "absolute epic distance" (*Dialogic Imagination* 13). Epics look backward for justification and welcome authoritative perspectives; novels look forward, tend to outgrow every authority represented in them, and undermine pretensions to single-voicedness. Bakhtin is equally unsympathetic to the other half of Steiner's dichotomy: a dramatic prototype for novels. In his view, works for the stage (including classical tragedy) know only "dramatic dialogue" (*Problems* 17)—which, by uttering words out loud in alternating lines, flattens their potential dialogism and diminishes the degree and variety of multivoicedness that resonates in a given utterance. The glory of the novel (not lost on a citizen of Stalinist Russia) is its almost subversive privateness, its muteness, its illicit creation, as one critic has put it, of "subjects without obligation to enunciate" (see Lock, esp. 85). Bakhtin would understand absolutely why stage plays carved out of Dostoevsky's polyphonic novels are miserable failures. Dialogism is not about surface levels of talk. It is about our silent competence, as readers, to discern the multiple personalities packed into a communication and our ability to place our own intonational quotation marks around patches of novelistic text. Bakhtin believes in the hard work of the author-narrator who structures a world, and he believes as well in the work of the reader who personalizes that world through acts of reading. He would not want authorial presence shorn off, peeled away, or replaced by the more consumer-friendly, passively assimilable images of screen or stage.

Let us now narrow the focus. Bakhtin opens his magisterial study of Dostoevsky's poetics with the observation that readers of Dostoevsky tend to polemicize directly with the characters (Raskolnikov, Ivan Karamazov, the Grand Inquisitor), not with their author. This unmediated quality of the novels testifies to their polyphonic construction. As a literary device, Bakhtin intimates, polyphony is the most subtle, selfless authorial position a novelist can adopt. In committing to it, Dostoevsky resolved to reduce to a minimum his own authorial surplus of vision and consequently his control over ultimate meaning (*Problems* 73). Having constructed his great fictional personalities around specific ideas in dialogue (what Bakhtin calls "voice-ideas" or "persons born of an idea" [85–91]), he then turns over to them the knowledge about themselves that—for him as author and perhaps for the anguished characters as well—would have been easier, and far less painful, to retain for himself. Thus his fictional works resemble a highly democratic, still unfinalized universe, in which consciousness is forever being individualized, disunified, and concretized in discrete personalities. Its truths are multiple. For proper access to them, dialogism is indispensable.

The opposite sort of universe Bakhtin associates with Tolstoy. It is permeated with a unified, "monologically naive point of view" that produces generalized, centralized, impersonal truth (56). It is authoritative, presided over by the voice of a person in control of contexts and ultimate values, who speaks not from a delimited perspective (where genuine surprises and mistakes can always occur) but from outside and beyond. From the much admired first sentence of *Anna Karenina* onward, we are not invited to doubt the author's grip on facts or his absolute access to the reality of his characters' minds. Genuine conflict and paradox are certainly present in Tolstoy and described with intricate care, but what the characters conclude about these situations is not allowed to rest solely with them. Their authority is insufficient. In Bakhtin's version of this point, what most characterizes Tolstoyan narrative is the absence in it of any autonomous, equally weighted voice that might compete with the author's.

Bakhtin has in mind more than merely the author's pressure in shaping dialogues and ethical outcomes, something felt in all well-crafted realist prose. He refers to the specifically Tolstoyan didactic repetitiveness that can so undermine the autonomy of the characters' utterances that willy-nilly, even if narrator and character are in agreement over the wisdom of a scene, readers are deflected from the fictional world and turn (in irritation or in awe) toward its author. Consider Vronsky's surprise visit to Anna on the day of the steeplechase. While waiting on the verandah for her son, Serezha, to return from his walk, Anna informs Vronsky of her pregnancy. Tolstoy tells us that the presence of Serezha is an embarrassment to the two lovers, evoking in both of them the feeling that a sailor might have after glancing at his compass and confirming that indeed he has strayed from the proper course—but the sailor cannot stop, because to stop would mean to acknowledge that he is lost (169–70; pt. 2, ch. 22). This observation is then immediately repeated, not as a feeling experienced by the characters but as a truth in its own right: "This child with his naïve outlook on life was the compass which showed them their degree of divergence from what they knew, but would not recognize, as the right course" (170).

The texture of Tolstoyan narrative is saturated with such redundancies and confirmations from above. Those who prefer Dostoevsky's more puzzling epiphanies usually consider this moral lecturing inappropriate for a realist novel and condescending to the reader. They would argue, in the spirit of the European Romanticism so precious to Dostoevsky, that every individual life has its own compass. But Tolstoy was the first major Russian writer not to pass through the Romantic school. His business was with Truth. And the truth of art, he came to believe, lay not in art's ability to multiply the number of fictions, positions, and voices in the universe (this was Dostoevsky's passion) but rather in its efficiency at eliminating those multiple fictions. Diverse experiences could be shown to reveal eternal truths. If for Dostoevsky art should posit a hero striving toward some personal vision, so complex that certain angles of it might be hidden even from the author, then for Tolstoy art is authentic when it infects its audience with the same emotion that seized the artist-author. The very purpose of art, in Tolstoy's mature view, is to unite artist-author, narrator, performer, and spectator-reader in a single emotional experience. If no such flush of oneness comes about, either the artwork is counterfeit or else we can be shown to be not in our right mind—drugged; drunk; corrupted by upper-class life; stupefied or over-stimulated by cigars, caffeine, lust. Tolstoy's later anarchic tracts against church and state and his polemical treatises against the consumption of alcohol, tobacco, and meat (prefigured in Levin's distrust of politics and in his devotion to clean country living in *Anna Karenina*) all have this moral subtext: the proper path is clear. Each of us carries the same compass, which is conscience. We can pollute ourselves and thus blur our vision, we can turn away from the compass or even deny its existence, but such actions on our part affect neither the truth of the compass nor the orienting poles of the objective world. Tolstoy speaks through, and for, everyone. As Bakhtin put it in a preface commissioned in 1929 for a new edition of Tolstoy's late novel *Resurrection*, such a monologic approach can only result in a tendentious "socioideological" novel—not, to be sure, unimportant as a model for the new Soviet literature but clearly not what novels are best designed to do ("Preface" 257).

In the early 1960s, while revising his Dostoevsky book (*Problems*), Bakhtin returned to this issue of dialogic Dostoevsky versus monologic Tolstoy. Here his focus is on death—and, he intimates, Tolstoy is obsessed with it. Whereas Dostoevsky depicts dying matter-of-factly, from the outside looking in (i.e., from the perspective of those who will remember the life and words of the departed), Tolstoy manages to be on both sides of the boundary, morbidly tracking the dying consciousness from within. As it moves toward its own light, this consciousness needs other people less and less. (Think of Andrei Bolkonsky's slow decline and withdrawal after the Battle of Borodino; of Ivan Ilyich's final torments, salvational to him in proportion to his disgust or indifference to those around him; and of Anna Karenina's internal monologue, vortexing bitterly toward an isolated suicide. Then compare those scenes with Stavrogin, watched constantly up to and after he is found hanging in a garret, or with the Elder Zosima, whose luminous departure is silent but whose bodily decay creates a scandal for the survivors.) Tolstoy might be a seer of the flesh, but, more important for Bakhtin, he is a singer of death. So potent for Tolstoy are the experiences of the mortal body that death, when it comes, utterly blacks out a character's significance—unless, of course, the transcendent author steps in and keeps it alive.

It is Bakhtin's thesis that this Tolstoyan way of dying was deeply alien to Dostoevsky. Since in Dostoevsky's world nothing substantial can be accomplished by a single isolated consciousness, dying people cannot complete themselves from within. Others will do that for them, afterward; others, and not the depersonalized voice of the author, will love them and keep them alive. Thus for Dostoevsky, our need of the other is absolute. For Tolstoy, despite all his Herculean strivings and preachings on behalf of love, the primary aim is to generate a loving attitude within the self toward the outside world. Whether that world needs this love, understands it, responds to it, is helped by it or made better by it turns out to be secondary. That world could even be a rock or a sunset; strictly speaking, people are not necessary to it. What matters to Tolstoy is the orientation of the singular, autonomous, striving self. The contours of Bakhtin's larger critique now become clear. It surpasses mere irritation at bossy narrators or a preachy style. If every other were to attend, as its sole order of business, to its own self-absorbed moral center and if those selves were presumed to be morally identical, dialogue would be painless—and superfluous.

The immense difference between these two positions, intimated by Bakhtin and expanded on here, offers a paradigm as fertile as Steiner's two-pronged tragedy versus epic. But is it correct? Bakhtin's binary opposition has come under much suspicious scrutiny. Can it really be said that Dostoevsky's characters (or, for that matter, his cosmos) are saved by dialogue alone? Doesn't Bakhtin undervalue the desperation, hallucination, brain fever, and private underground hell of these heroes and heroines, with their disjointed states of mind from which no double-voicedness or communality will rescue them? Conversely, can it be said that the great Dostoevskian heroes (Raskolnikov, Ivan Karamazov, even the kindly Elder Zosima) really listen to others, or need to listen? These personalities, caught in the spiritual grip of their own idea, are remarkably free of outside influences; others cannot do things to them. Dostoevskian heroes grab at labels and internalize them according to their own idea. Does Raskolnikov really learn from others' words? Or the ecstatic Dmitry Karamazov? In certain ways Dostoevskian characters come to themselves through self-absorbed monologue far more profoundly than Tolstoyan ones do. At the tenderest moments in the lives of Tolstoy's most beloved creations (Natasha Rostova, Princess Marya Bolkonskaya, Constantine Levin), it is the love streaming from *their* eyes, not the author's, that accomplishes a transfiguration in the other. Or put another way: Tolstoy might tell you what he thinks (about this he is never shy), but does that really control what we think or what his characters—having come to vibrant life in the presence of their cocharacters—are experiencing?

Try an experiment. Ask your students what Raskolnikov stands for, and they will be able to say. Ask them what Levin or Anna Karenina stands for, and they will draw a blank. Tolstoyan characters are too much like us. They are trying to get through the day. Their environment grinds them down, they are constantly disillusioned and reillusioned, and they embarrass themselves too often in public to want to talk about what they live by. In discussing *Anna* in his *Tolstoy or Dostoevsky*, Steiner remarks, "The most stringent test of the aliveness of an imagined character [. . .] is whether or not it can grow with time and preserve its coherent individuality in an altered setting" (qtd. in Tolstoy, *Anna Karenina* 812). Tolstoy's creations do persevere and grow in that way, adjusting to alterations in their daily settings so gradual and formless that no philosophy can emerge from it. It could be argued that the unrelieved life-confusion of your typical Tolstoyan hero or heroine is more genuinely open, vulnerable, and in process than is the more articulate idea-confusion of any voice-idea in Dostoevsky.

Tolstoy commented in print only cautiously on his great contemporary, but (of course) he was a strong critic. In a late essay entitled "Why Do People Stupefy Themselves," he remarked that Raskolnikov did not kill the old pawnbroker with an ax on the day of the murder; he had been killing her for months, lying feverishly on his couch in his garret, making the possibility of that murder a habit of mind. After Dostoevsky's death, Tolstoy conceded that Dostoevsky's novels contain powerful spiritual messages (indeed, the last piece of fiction Tolstoy experienced was most likely Zosima's meditations from *The Brothers Karamazov*, a novel that lay open on his bedside table in October 1910, when he fled Yasnaya Polyana). But late in life Tolstoy professed surprise at Dostoevsky's "careless," often "monotonous" narrative style.[3] The charge seems odd, given the brilliant argument and manifest excitement of those crisis-strewn Dostoevskian lives. An answer might lie in the fact that for Tolstoy, crisis and hysteria are rather monotonous, homogenizing behavioral states. During them, people sound and act alike—regardless of what has triggered their distress. Since what shape our personality and create genuine heterogeneity are stable forms of living, interacting, and talking, mere ideas (and even more so, ideas in extremis) cannot differentiate us in vital ways. As we follow Anna or Kitty chapter by chapter, each new experience brings in its wake a revised idea—and the more painful the experience, the more defensive will be the idea that shields it from inner and outer scrutiny. For, Tolstoy insists, we are not run by the overt objective philosophies we devise for ourselves. We are run by our subjective needs, and an idea can always be recruited to cover for them. How often in Tolstoy we witness one of his favorite characters attending not to the content of an idea but to its effect on its carrier. For example, when at the beginning of *Anna Karenina* Levin walks in on his half brother's discussions with a professor of philosophy, we are supposed to see interlocutors driven by logic alone as slightly ridiculous (21–23; pt. 1, ch. 7); as he does with Natasha at the opera in *War and Peace* (bk. 8, ch. 9), Tolstoy turns off the sound. Why such hostility to rhetoric? Tolstoy, whose aesthetic sense was so excruciating that he broke down and wept during performances of music, distrusted as well the beautiful sound of a flow of ideas. He would warn us against the mesmerizing, tyrannical effect of such abstract intellectual flow on human behavior. And he suspected, perhaps unfairly, that the most passionate and intimate relationship experienced by a Dostoevskian hero was with an idea, not with another human being.

It is thus an exquisite classroom paradox that Tolstoy probably would not have wished his novels to be taught at all. Teaching entails the reduction of a complex narrative texture to its key ideas, patterns, philosophies of life. In that manageable form we can bring our students in. In his famous letter of April 1876 (qtd. in Anna Karenina 750), Tolstoy resolutely asserts that the "idea" of *Anna Karenina* is unextractable; to express it, he would have to "write the same novel all over again." Only the tiny linkages matter, and "this linking is based not on an idea, but on something else." Very possibly, he would have considered the ideal teacher of his novels to be Bakhtin, one of his least sympathetic readers. For Bakhtin must have known his Tolstoy essentially by heart (as he knew every prose text on his syllabus); he would comment, yes, but he would also recite him page after page, all linkages intact, to a silent and awestruck auditorium.

In closing, let us take one famous scene in *Anna Karenina* from the perspective of both writers: Dostoevsky who read it, Tolstoy who wrote it. In his *Writer's Diary* for February and then for July-August 1877, Dostoevsky published a two-part review of *Anna Karenina*.[4] In it he expressed some irritation at that "stallion in uniform" Vronsky and the "Epicurean egotist" Stiva Oblonsky (2: 870, 872); he found the inner life of these pampered aristocrats rather tedious. But he confirmed that in its treatment of sin and guilt, the novel was an event of all-European importance. In his judgment the most profound scene in the novel is the spiritual reconciliation of Vronsky and Karenin, humiliated lover and deceived but resurrected husband, at Anna's bedside, after the birth of her daughter and on the brink of her anticipated death (372–96; pt. 4, chs. 17–23). These scenes in Tolstoy have everything that Steiner and Bakhtin encourage us to look for in Dostoevsky's art: high drama, a compressed threshold moment, a crisis during which people change abruptly and reveal their truer, more potent selves. Unforeseen options open up at the breaking point of very great pain. Dostoevsky believed that the sinner's path, or progress, could not be softened or abbreviated. Only the full experience of transgression could provide all the knowledge and strength of will necessary to abhor the transgression. It made complete sense to him that Anna, having sinned, now craves Karenin ("That other is not I" [375]); Karenin, in turn, is seized by Christian ecstasy and forgives his erring wife unconditionally.

Tolstoy was surely gratified by this warmly appreciative review. Nevertheless he must have debated Dostoevsky's reading, because this childbirth-deathbed crisis scene does not end anything in the novel, nor does it stand timeless and alone. Since crises in Tolstoy's world are deformations, not formations, we should attend to the cooling periphery of a trauma, not to its hottest point. What is more, Tolstoy would argue that there is no need to experience a sin fully in order to despise it. Quite the contrary: experience, once indulged, can create habitual appetites that then dull the ability of the spiritual self to discipline the body's animal sides, which is a task that requires our constant vigilance. Within several pages, the epiphany has passed. Anna's survival seems likely; old habits of mind and body reassert themselves. Vronsky must now live with the memory of his "shame-suffused face" (378). Karenin is again shut out. Indeed, this crisis succeeds only in making an illicit routine, once resumed, all the more necessary, passionate, real. And what are we to make of the fact that Tolstoy came to write the aftermath of this scene by a method Bakhtin would have reserved solely for his polyphonist of choice, Dostoevsky? A cornerstone of Bakhtin's judgment against the monologic Tolstoy is that his characters are mere funnels through which the author speaks. But according to Tolstoy's own testimony, this segment of the novel was prompted wholly by the heroes' inner life, whose obedient transcriber he considered himself to be. As he writes in his letter of April 1876, "completely unexpectedly for me, but quite certainly, Vronsky started to shoot himself." It was "organically necessary" (qtd. in Anna Karenina 750).

At base, then, Tolstoy and Dostoevsky have profoundly different views about organic necessity. One writer might be of the flesh and the other of the spirit, one might be more epic and the other more dramatic, one tends toward monologue and the other toward dialogue, but these rubrics do not exhaust the meaning of any one scene. Underlying those binary distinctions is a more basic debate over what endures in a real or fictional world and how much freedom we have to define it. "Where am I? What am I doing? Why?" Anna asks at her final moment of consciousness, before the candle "lit up for her all that before had been dark" (695; pt. 7, ch. 31). Tragic Dostoevskian characters are allowed to live by their philosophical wisdoms and visions; Tolstoyan characters, more rooted in their body's needs and more suspicious of words, are permitted to glimpse this wisdom only as life is being left behind.

NOTES

[1]The terms belong to the Russian critic and Symbolist poet Dmitry Merezhkovsky, whose massive study *L. Tolstoi i Dostoevskii* was published in 1902–03. In the preface to the third part of that work, he argues that the Holy Spirit and the Holy Flesh are equally precious to the church—and thus Dostoevsky and Tolstoy are both Christian writers (1: 193–203). For a survey of the evolution of Merezhkovsky's extremely hostile, then curious, then finally grudgingly appreciative attitude toward Tolstoy from 1896 to 1919, see Rosenthal.

[2]I draw here on one representative source, Viktoria A. Mirskaia, whose lecture notes and reminiscences of Bakhtin as a teacher of ancient and medieval literature are published in Bakhtin, *Lektsii*.

[3]The reminiscence is from the diary of V. F. Lazurskii (entry for 10 July 1884; qtd. in Remizov 86).

[4]Dostoevsky's subtitles in this entry are fascinating. In the first part, they are: "One of Today's Most Important Questions," "The Issue of the Day," "Dissociation Again: Part 8 of *Anna Karenina*," "Confessions of a Slavophile," "*Anna Karenina* as a Fact of Special Importance," "A Landowner Who Gets Faith in God from a Peasant." The second part, targeting Tolstoy's position on the Serbian War that Dostoevsky chauvinistically sup-

ported, contains these subtitles: "The Irritability of Vanity," "Tout ce qui n'est pas expressement permis est défendu," "On the Uneducated and Illiterate Russian People's Unerring Knowledge of the Real Essence of the Eastern Question," "Levin's Agitation: A Question: Does Distance Have an Influence on Love for Humanity? Can One Agree with the Opinion of One Turkish Prisoner on the Humaneness of Some of Our Ladies? So What, Then, Are Our Teachers Teaching Us?"

Anna Karenina and the Novel of Adultery

Judith Armstrong

The very existence of *Anna Karenina*, a novel of adultery, should come as a huge surprise to anyone at all familiar with the Russian literary tradition. Its status as a world classic obscures its essential atypicality in its own country.

To grasp an anomaly unfamiliar to many established readers, students require some explanation of where the novel lies in relation to two basic issues—literary genre and national cultural identity. Both are essential and connected, and I address them first. I then propose a lateral interpretation of Anna that has, in my experience, proved provocative to students: it rejects her conventional position as heroine-culprit-victim of the classical novel of adultery and poses her as the true and only hero of Tolstoy's great work.

In regard to the issues of genre and cultural identity, I assume that students have some understanding of the history and development of the European novel, as covered in generalist courses. The task of the *Anna* teacher is to slot into this overview the development of the genre in Russia and to consider the course of the subgenre, the novel of adultery.

When the novel form arrived in Russia in the last quarter of the eighteenth century, it implanted itself there in defiance of both the nation's isolation from the West and the strict censorship exercised by church and state. Historically, the Russian novel that rapidly grew up was formally dependent on western European tales of romance, which crossed the national borders via Poland. These tales of romance held far greater appeal than the didactic reading matter available to Russia's aristocracy (the only members of the population, apart from the clergy, who were literate). The tales caused a momentous change in public sensibilities, but the resulting body of indigenous literature did not become a carbon copy of the European model. Throughout the nineteenth century the Russian novel flourished along its own magnificent lines, but the subgenre with which we are concerned, the novel of adultery, was unable to put down many roots in the black earth of Mother Russia. *Anna Karenina* was virtually the only one of its kind.

For students to understand why this should be so, they must know a little about the development of *Anna*'s European antecedents, while the teacher must point out that in nineteenth-century Russia issues of genre and cultural identity were inextricably mixed.

The historical timescale with which we are concerned ranges from the eleventh to the nineteenth century; the geographic span ranges from Languedoc in the south of France to much of western and, later, eastern Europe. Of course, the existence of passionate extramarital love is so old as to be undatable, but the concept, as distinct from the emotion or the activity, was linked to the eleventh-century rise of the phenomenon called courtly love. This extraordinarily intense cult of romantic passion has never been fully explained, but it seems to have been in large part a by-product of the Crusades, when landless knights, restless squires, and young pages were left at home in French castles and manors with a small number of elegant ladies awaiting the return of their husbands from the Holy Lands. Many of these younger men transferred their vassalic devotion to the lady of the castle, expressing their adulation in romantic love lyrics learned from the troubadours, those originally Provençal minstrel-poets whose sole theme was perpetually unsatisfied love. This adoration was an outpouring of a romantic love that occurred by definition outside marriage. Those caught in its toils deliberately cultivated an unfulfillable passion, languishing after desire for its own sake.

The church fought to defend itself against this subversion of Christian marriage by outlawing the troubadours, while society used a different strategy of containment. The age-old invention of myths had long provided a method of dealing with supernatural powers and natural forces that could not be completely understood by the human mind. Since time immemorial, stories had been created that familiarized society with potentially threatening phenomena and to some extent defused the uneasiness they engendered. The origin of fire, for example, was "explained" by the myth of Prometheus. Similarly, a much later myth was invented to contain the destructive effects of courtly love. Its most recognized form was the story of Tristan and Isolde: two lovers, fatally smitten by mutual passion and adulterous love, seek each other out to lie together, yet always separate their two bodies with a sword. Their love of passion for its own sake, forever unconsummated and forever prolonged, impels them to find ways of obstructing the normal course of love, marriage, and procreation. When no further earthly means are available, the lovers choose death—the ultimate obstacle to the fulfillment of love. Therefore, as well as dealing with passion, the myth also romanticizes, enacts, and palliates the seductive linkage between passion and death.

In their different ways, church and society did their best to ensure that the dangerous, life-opposing values of courtly love were suppressed; but the myth only went underground, out of sight for about seven hundred years. In the nineteenth century it reappeared in the newly popular novel, with the figure of the adulteress now incarnating the overt, social threat to regular marriage. A less obvious aspect of her dangerous charm was the invitation she continued to extend to passion and death. In France, the well-established novel of adultery dealt with matters that were of national interest because of the predominance in that country of the arranged marriage, in which property settlements superseded natural feelings. Under these circumstances, the existence of love outside marriage was an accepted norm, so long as the mistress remained powerless. If it looked as though she might upset the property settlement, she had to be eliminated. Novels in which the adulterous woman was punished or destroyed (e.g., Flaubert's *Madame Bovary*, 1856–57) became a staple of a west European body of literature differentiated by national characteristics.

In Russia, the cultural context was different. Marriages were normally arranged by matchmakers but assumed to engender marital fidelity. The chronicles and the oral tradition, both of which were rich and strong, focused almost exclusively on the warlike deeds of national heroes, who at the conclusion of their exploits returned home to faithful wives. The few early Russian chronicles that deal with domestic arrangements are typified by the tale of Peter and Fevronia, in which the couple are buried separately but keep turning up in the same grave. The Russian mentality, unlike that of western Europe, was largely innocent of romantic love.

When Western literature infiltrated the country, it was obliged to conform to local norms. Although the amorous intrigue became a stock-in-trade of the burgeoning indigenous tale, it usually represented a lighthearted premarital play culminating in legal marriage and wedded fidelity. The couple were never to part, or to stray. Thus Tatyana, the heroine of Alexander Pushkin's *Eugene Onegin* (1823–30), remains faithful to her lawful but unloved husband despite bitter temptation. Although she becomes a literary template, she does not in fact depart from the model of the faithful wife of the chronicles. The novels that followed *Onegin* had just as little truck with adulterous behavior. The European theme of passionate, self-obstructing love held little interest for the Russians.

In this context, the question "Why, and how, *Anna Karenina?*" begs to be asked. The answer is to be found partly in an understanding of the foreign influences working on mid-nineteenth-century Russian society and partly in the conscious views and subconscious fears of *Anna*'s author.

As Western social ideas continued to penetrate the Russian mind through fictional tales, the traditional arranged marriage began to be called into question. The issue grew more urgent as the novels of George Sand, in which the arranged marriage always creates unhappiness, became increasingly available in Russia. Both sides of the debate were aired, but without resolution. We see that Tatyana's mother was happily married off, but not so Tatyana. Other characters in *Eugene Onegin* are said to marry honorably, for love, and certainly Pushkin himself did, though with a tragic outcome. The breakdown of Lavretsky's marriage in Ivan Turgenev's *A Nest of the Gentry* is ascribed to its being a love match; the breakdown of the hero's marriage in Alexei Pisemsky's *In the Whirlpool* is ascribed to its not being a love match. The increasing difficulty of choosing between the arranged marriage and the love marriage is vented in *Anna Karenina* by Princess Shcherbatskaya, who accepts that the Russian habit of using matchmakers is out of fashion but cannot decide whether to select suitable husbands for her daughters in the French fashion or leave them the freedom of choice customary in England.

Tolstoy, anxiously aware that the whole pattern of how marriages were made and maintained was under challenge, felt impelled to write a novel on a subject virtually untouched by Russian literature hitherto. The connection he made in his own mind between the sexual emancipation of women, à la Sand, and the degeneration of family life caused him intense personal anguish, but in the novel he veils his subjective position under apparently objective moral and social judgments. He shows that Anna and Vronsky were both morally disadvantaged by being brought up without good family structures; when Anna comes to marry, the stuffy, incompatible Karenin is selected by her pragmatic aunt for reasons of social suitability and financial security.

Vronsky ironically remarks elsewhere, "How often the happiness of marriages founded on reason crumbles to dust because the very passion that was disregarded makes itself felt later" (125; pt. 2, ch. 7). His statement should not confuse the reader: it is not an argument for passion but rather an expression of Tolstoy's belief that marriage—the rock on which the family is built, the cornerstone of the social fabric—should be based on something more spiritual than reason or pragmatism. In which case, "disregarded" passion will have no occasion to raise its ugly head. Extramarital love, whether genuine or passing, must provide no solution at either the social or the personal level. Tolstoy underlines his point by pouring contempt on Vronsky's professed moral code, by which only ridiculous fuddy-duddies believe in marriage while the bold pursue every passion. Vronsky's intrusion into Anna's legal union with Karenin is depicted as heinous, even though Tolstoy has clearly shown the poverty of the marriage. At her first sexual encounter with Vronsky, Anna experiences not ecstasy but degradation; Vronsky feels like a murderer. Anna begins to make such a huge investment in their love that it outweighs every good, including life itself. Tolstoy does not spare Anna a single one of the escalated emotions that adultery brings in its wake. Lust, possessiveness, insecurity, anger, and despair follow one another in needless but compelling succession.

In subjecting Anna to this fate, Tolstoy appears simply to follow the scenario established in western European novels of adultery. However, I believe that his judgment of her originated in his intensely conflicted subconscious, where another motivation, secret and unacknowledged, underlay his stalking of the adulteress. Family structures were for Tolstoy not merely a social glue but also a means of containing the horror of rampant sexuality that obsessed him, less out of concern for society than because of his own sexual urges, which he strove to repudiate.

Evidence for this assertion can be found in the ambivalence toward women that characterizes Tolstoy's diaries, letters, and other fictional works. He idealized his mother, who died when he was only two years old, enshrining her as the epitome of feminine purity; the evidence shows that thereafter no living woman could equal the image he retained in his mind, while almost any woman could arouse his lust. In his early life he was compulsively attracted to the kind of woman who was the opposite of pure—serf girls, prostitutes—and the hold such women exerted over him appalled him. He diarized promises to abjure their company, but every time he broke his vow and immediately loathed himself. The temptation represented by impure women was inextricable from the horror evoked by his uncontrollable sexuality, by his regular falls from his ideal of purity.

As an adult, Tolstoy desperately wanted to believe that marriage would cure the lust he expended on low-class women, but it did not. He was as demanding of his wife, Sonya, as of any prostitute—and despised himself commensurately afterward. The last few of his thirteen children were fathered as he publicly preached the virtue of abstinence. Uncontrollable sexual dependence on his wife provoked feelings of personal humiliation and resentment not only toward her but also toward any woman in life or literature who might represent temptation. When he went to the local railroad station to view the body of Anna Pirogova, the mistress of a neighbor who had cast herself under a train because she had been thrown over for a governess, he saw, besides a pitifully mangled corpse, the inevitable consequence of illicit and intemperate sexual passion.

Students might object that if Tolstoy had wanted simply to show that such a love was out of place in Russian society, Anna's ostracization and unhappiness would have been enough to make the point. But the author of *Anna Karenina* was determined to do more than that: his heroine must administer to herself the punishment that he felt *he* deserved. In killing her, he was attempting to kill his own sexuality. Other characters before and after Anna reveal some projection of the loathing in him generated by sexual lust, but in earlier works such as *Family Happiness* and *War and Peace* he was able to channel the unsuitable infatuations of his heroines into acceptable outcomes; in the later "Kreutzer Sonata," suspicion of an adulterous affair results in murder.

Tolstoy also had to show how good women can avoid the primrose path trodden by Anna. Kitty, the virgin bride, must almost immediately become the young mother, her sexuality sublimated by motherhood, her personal life subsumed in love for her child(ren), as is her sister Dolly's. When Anna, in contrast, discards the roles of wife and mother, she loses her only possible source of salvation. Tolstoy viciously strips her of the moral props of domesticity and motherhood he hands out so peremptorily to Dolly and Kitty. This is why Vronsky is allowed to run the household; why Anna's love for Serezha, the child of her purer past, trickles away; why for Annie, the child of her adultery, Anna never develops any enduring maternal feelings.

Students might further object that if Tolstoy's aim was to show the danger posed by passionate women, he would have done better to create a less sympathetic heroine. There is indeed evidence in the early drafts of the novel that Tolstoy started out to make Anna unattractive, vulgar, and crudely voluptuous; but as he worked on successive versions of his sexually explicit character, he constantly rewrote her, each time making her more beautiful in every way, and ended up with a woman so enchanting, she tempted him beyond his powers of resistance. Falling passionately in love with his creation, he was unable to eliminate from her character or her story a sexuality that he was bound to abhor even while prey to it. Anna thus came to represent an appetite that he could at least kill in her and with her, even if he could not root it out of himself. In throwing his heroine under a train, he was willing the redemption of his own life.

Paradoxically, Anna does save him, or at least she saves the writer. The magnificence of the artist triumphs over the anxieties of the moralist and didact—a feat that Anna helps achieve by refusing to play the victim role assigned to her by Tolstoy. Anna outwits her creator and becomes one of the greatest literary characters of all time, precisely because she is not a mere heroine in Levin's story, as is Kitty, but the hero of her own novel. As such she is hugely privileged by the text she inhabits.

The twentieth-century theorist Iurii Lotman explains how Russian medieval texts depicted the world as a static space over which a small number of characters could travel, crossing frontiers and doing deeds. These active, mobile, dynamic beings were the essentially male heroes of the texts. The space they traveled was static, and the immobile characters who inhabited it were static: fixed, female characters construed as mere elements of plot-space through which the heroes moved and acted. These distinctions continued into nineteenth-century fiction, although the field was now semantic rather than geographic. Anna, a transgressor, crosses social, marital, and moral boundaries; through this deliberate mobility she becomes an active principle, a woman who wills her own destiny. The process begins as soon as she acts in defiance of the normal kinship customs by which a woman is given in marriage; allotted to Karenin, she nevertheless desires and chooses Vronsky. When she becomes his partner, no institution such as marriage or family guarantees her that position, only she herself. It is true that her mobility is frustrated by the social norms she challenges and that, branded as an outcast, she is forced to wander around the plot-space until the social barriers become the final frontier of death itself. But, once again, it is she who chooses to cross that frontier.

Kitty and Dolly, in contrast, are the classical objects of male desire and choice, the princesses whose hands are won, the socialized good wives and mothers constructed by a patriarchal society. They rear children, let out dresses, and make jam; they are true heroines. But Anna, at Vronsky's estate, shows an informed knowledge of architecture, farm machinery, and the depth to which foundations should be poured. She has developed a male intellect. Tolstoy even allows her the supremely male activity that he himself excelled at: Anna starts writing a book (for children)—but only after she has imposed her own pattern on her life story.

In part 1, when Anna is still a mere reader (in the train), she expressly longs to act as freely as the heroine of the book she is reading (see Sloane, this volume). The book is specified as an English novel—England being the country, in Princess Shcherbatskaya's eyes, where girls are excessively free and even choose their own husbands. During the course of Tolstoy's novel, Anna's insistence on acting for herself is a kind of Anglicization. To make sure the point is not missed, the little English girl she takes into her house is called Hannah; Hannah replaces Annushka, the unsuccessful native-born guardian of Anna's red handbag, the red bag of passion. (The dearth of Christian names in the novel—two Alexeys and four variations on Anna—says more about projected aspects of a single personality than about an authorial lack of imagination.)

Unaware that he was dealing with a hero rather than a mere heroine, did Tolstoy perceive that he had as little control over his heroine as Annushka does over her mistress? Although his alter ego, Levin, dominates the majority of chapters in the novel, is it not Anna who claims the title role? She not only outshines the other women, she eclipses every male too, rising above the flawed, would-be heroes Karenin and Vronsky, because she is more vivid, more vital, more passionate than any of them. Only she is worth being struck down. Even the passive voice is inappropriate: Tolstoy sees to it that Anna is destroyed, but she kills herself; she is actor, not object.

Anna has therefore mobility, desire, intellect, imperiousness, creativity, Englishness, animation, passion, and the title role. She is even successful in killing herself (both Levin and Vronsky bungle their attempts at suicide). She is the true hero of the novel, in Lotman's sense of the word *hero*.

Anna Karenina is always high on the list when critics or readers are asked to nominate the best novel they have ever read, and so we are all used to its special position in purely literary terms. But students might be introduced to further reasons why the novel should be seen as unique in the context of traditional Russian literature, for in the novel Anna singly defeats both her author and the conventions of the western European novel of adultery.

Anna Reading and
Women Reading in Russian Literature

David A. Sloane

In the 1930s, long before reader-response criticism became popular, Louise Rosenblatt urged her literature students at City College of New York to trust their reactions and be creative readers. This essay is intended as a companion to her work (see her *Literature as Exploration*) for teachers doing an undergraduate survey of Russian literature or the European novel.

Anna Karenina, perhaps more conspicuously than any other work Tolstoy wrote, problematizes the act of reading. Whereas *War and Peace* appears to spell out truth in lengthy digressions, *Anna Karenina* from the outset presents us with short ambiguous pronouncements—whether in the epigraph or in the novel's opening sentence—that occupy an uncertain relation to the rest of the text. The novel immediately challenges the reader to fill in spaces left open by the author and thus involves us in the task of co-creation. The novel's meaning, to a large extent, is what we ourselves put into it.

Many of us find unforgettable the scene where Anna reads an English novel on the train (91–93; pt. 1, ch. 29). (For another analysis of this scene, see Jackson, this volume). It is one of many moments in the novel when a character interprets a text, a piece of music, or a painting on the basis of personal experience and makes self-revealing inferences. Gina Kovarsky points out that such interpretive activities are analogous to the way characters continually read one another in the novel, attempting to discern the inner world of an other through their own selective lens (67–68). Such efforts succeed to the degree that readers (and people in everyday life) allow themselves to be infected with the feelings of others. But they also carry a portion of the viewer's own experience and, therefore, must always be unique.

As Tolstoy expects us to be, Anna is an empathic, creative reader. Many things in her experience color the way she responds to the text before her. After her brief but passionate flirtation with Vronsky, she is rushing home to a joyless but secure marriage. For eight years she has been a faithful wife, and now she tries to forget the events of the previous evening and reimmerse herself in the stable routines of her daily life with Karenin. At home she would read English novels to relax, finding Victorian mores soothing, and here she chooses to do the same. Contrary to expectation, however, the reading disturbs her:

> [A]t last Anna began to read and follow what she read. [. . .] Anna read and understood, but it was unpleasant to read, that is to say, to follow the reflection of other people's lives. She was too eager to live herself. When she read how the heroine of the novel nursed a sick man, she wanted to move about the sick-room with noiseless footsteps; when she read of a member of Parliament making a speech, she wished to make that speech;

when she read how Lady Mary rode to hounds, teased the bride, and as-
tonished everybody by her boldness—she wanted to do it herself. But
there was nothing to be done, so she forced herself to read, while her little hand toyed with the smooth paper-knife.   (91–92)

What happens to Anna is familiar to anyone who appreciates fiction. We
imagine ourselves into the work by empathizing with characters and sharing
their experience. Going one step further, we may close the book and project
these roles onto our own lives, fancying ourselves for a moment as Robinson
Crusoe surveying the island or Jane Eyre waiting for Rochester. And all this is
perfectly normal. Yet as Tolstoy's novel unfolds, Anna makes the second illusion
into an elaborate conceit that ultimately engulfs all she thinks and feels. She
chooses to follow an overpowering imperative, coming from deep inside her, to
aestheticize life, to make her life into an artistic creation. More than any other
major character in the novel, Anna is by nature an artist, and she feels eternally
deprived of the opportunity to fulfill this latent gift. Were she a writer, she
might infuse a novel with her experience; were she a painter, she might identify
with people in her paintings, as Mikhaylov does. But her calling is to be a poet
of life—like a magician, she restores tranquillity to the Oblonsky family, she enters the salons of Saint Petersburg like a diva, and she knows how to charm the
unwitting Levin with her voice. Anna walks through life with an air of theatri-
cality, mesmerizing everyone in her presence and subjugating all to the unstud-
ied poetry of her performance. This explains why "the key word in *Anna
Karenina* is *drama*" (Orwin, *Tolstoy's Art* 171), and why Anna, unlike Emma
Bovary, flaunts rather than conceals her adultery.

Anna's flair for spectacle, held in check throughout her life, is now set loose
by her reading. In her mind she begins to formulate a new, creative relation to
life, freely based on various artistic models. Her actions will not conform rigidly
to the plot of an English novel; indeed, her subsequent behavior in many respects subverts the conventions of that genre (Mandelker, *Framing* 59–63).
Nor does she simply act out a generic tragedy, although the tragic model ultimately predominates (Sloane 14–16; Morson, *Narrative* 71–77). Anna transforms her essential mode of being in the world from one of reading to one of
authoring, from passivity to action, from the principle "We are what we read" to
the maxim "We are what we do." And at each point she makes choices, shaping
her fate in much the same way an author or artist works on recalcitrant material, welcoming the agency of fortuitous insight.

Anna's way of reading has many literary precedents. If, as I believe, comparison of like things always brings out the unique features of each, it is useful as a
teaching strategy to target such points of convergence for detailed analysis.
Especially rich for such an exercise is *Madame Bovary* (1857), which Tolstoy
knew well (Meyer 243–47). Worth examining in particular are those chapters
where Gustave Flaubert's heroine mines her reading for fantasies about life

(pt. 1, ch. 9; pt. 2, chs. 9 and 15). But there are also Russian texts, available in translation, which serve the same function and can be included in a typical survey course on Russian literature. Alexander Pushkin's *Eugene Onegin* is an excellent choice, because Tolstoy clearly had its heroine in mind when writing *Anna Karenina* (Sloane 11–12), hence students might contemplate, as with Flaubert's novel, the nature of Tolstoy's response to Pushkin's novel in verse.

As we first encounter Tatyana, she is a dreamer and a loner. She prefers sitting by the window reading novels to playing and chatting with her friends, and in this solitary activity she enters a vast world of imagination, embellishing it with the richness of her own feeling: "She came to like the novels early on; / For her they took the place of everything; / She fell in love with fabrications / Of Richardson's imagination, of Rousseau's pen" (ch. 2, st. 29). Like Anna, she places herself inside the experience of her favorite characters:

> Imagining herself the heroine
> Of her beloved authors,
> Clarissa, Julia, Delphine,
> Tatyana wanders through the quiet wood,
> Alone with her dangerous book.
> In it she seeks and finds
> Her secret passions, her dreams,
> The fruits of feeling's abundance.
> She sighs and makes her own
> An other's joy, an other's pain,
> And whispers in delirium
> A letter to her hero [. . .].   (ch. 3, st. 10)

Like Anna, Tatyana projects her fantasy onto life, making Onegin (whom she does not know at all) into a Grandison or Lovelace, that is, a Prince Charming or a villain—these the only stereotypes she knows from her reading.

Tatyana too, like Anna, harbors within herself a stifled poetic gift. On occasion she is ready to compose verse, and Pushkin describes these moments as he describes his own lyric inspiration elsewhere (e.g., "The Poet"):

> Love's agony drives Tanya on,
> She walks into the garden grieving,
> And suddenly her vacant eyes point down.
> She halts forgetting how to step.
> Her breast is heaving, her cheeks
> With fire tingle,
> And breathing ceases on her lips.
> Her ears are filled with sound, her eyes are flashing [. . .].
>   (ch. 3, st. 16)

Cognizant of the fact that writing poetry (in her time) was reserved for men, Tatyana redirects her lyric impulse into a socially acceptable genre—she writes Onegin a love letter in "prose" (ch. 3, st. 26). That she initiates the courtship at all is a brazen violation of marital etiquette. By scribing the initials of her beloved on the window glass, she reasserts her determination to make choices that social custom denies her:

> Tatyana stood before the window,
> Exhaling vapor on the icy glass.
> Engrossed in thought
> Her charming finger scribed
> The sacred monogram EO
> Upon the foggy pane.   (ch. 3, st. 37)

Tatyana's reading has been a stimulus to action and authorship, and in this respect her behavior prefigures Anna reading, imagining, and wishing to author the drama of her own life. On the train, Anna first picks up her penknife to use for reading ("Anna [. . .] took a paper-knife and an English novel from her handbag" [91]), but moments later she is drawing it across the window in self-reflective anticipation of ecstatic transport ("She passed her paper-knife over the window-pane, then pressed its cold smooth surface against her cheek [. . .] with unreasoning joy" [92]). Moving the knife across the glass symbolizes her desire to move beyond the confines of her former life, represented by the window. In this rebellious gesture she resembles Pushkin's Tatyana seeking release from society's prescribed roles.

As each novel unfolds, however, the rebellious, self-affirming, and creative impulses in Tatyana and Anna chart very different trajectories. Tatyana tames her unrealizable desires and reconciles them with reality. A turning point for her is the visit she pays to Onegin's library (ch. 7), where she sees the relics of a reader's misguided hubris. She discerns the absurdity of a Romantic's mimicry of art. Onegin, she realizes, is a "parody" of literary prototypes (st. 24), and she chooses not to follow his poor example. Instead, she marries a man she does not love and accedes to society's expectations of her. Privately, she still nurtures her romantic dreams, but she does not expect to reify them. In her Petersburg salon (ch. 8), surrounded by Russia's intellectual elite, she has discovered her own art form, that is, as William Todd writes, "the highest form of creativity open to a women at this time," which gives her the opportunity "to unite, if not 'magic sounds' [. . .] then thoughts and feelings and good conversation" (*Fiction* 129). Hers is a realistic, healthy accommodation to life. Anna, by contrast, who spent her youth forcing obstreperous passions into a square container, now experiences an untimely adolescence and lets passions reign uncontrollably over every aspect of her life. Her sole meridian is her aesthetic vision, and it is this Baedeker that she chooses religiously to follow. That she is on a collision course with reality makes no difference to her, because the idea of authoring a life is more important to her than life itself. For Anna suicide is, paradoxically, a life-affirming gesture, because it gives expression to the creative impulse that has become the source of her spiritual freedom.

Tatyana and Anna represent two paradigms of intelligent women reading in a repressive society. Tatyana's way is benign compromise, Anna's is pathological extremism. These two ways were the norm in literary portrayals of Russian women for the better part of the nineteenth century. To be sure, reading was not important for all female heroines (Tatyana's sister Olga, for instance, does not care about reading at all), but the genuinely inspired readers tend to follow one of these two paths, neither of which is a truly happy alternative.

For comparison, I would suggest a few other works in Russian literature that are easily accessible. The orphaned heroine of Ivan Turgenev's story "Asya" (1858), for instance, having grown up without role models, tries to acquire so-cially acceptable womanly behavior by mimicking female characters in the books she reads. As childish as her efforts are, she appears destined for a healthy accommodation with life at the end, when she recites Tatyana's farewell to Onegin and proclaims, "I would like to be Tatyana" (my trans.). Masha, the nar-rator of Tolstoy's short novel *Family Happiness* (1858), also reads literature as life's script (*Great Short Works* 67–69). She resembles Emma Bovary more than any other character Tolstoy created, and she very nearly ruins her life in the same way Emma does. *Family Happiness* would read almost like an es-quisse for *Anna Karenina*, were it not for the fact that Masha's way at the end is essentially Tatyana's.

The tragic, nonadaptive path Anna represents can be found in two Gothic tales by Turgenev, "A Quiet Spot" (1854) and "Faust" (1856), about women who are poisoned by their reading and ultimately commit suicide. A more interesting jux-taposition would be Anna Karenina and Nastasya Filippovna from Fyodor Dostoevsky's *The Idiot* (1868). Although Dostoevsky does not tell us much about Nastasya's reading, we learn from her sketchy biography (pt. 1, ch. 4) that she was educated in the manner of Russian noblewomen, had an experienced Swiss gov-erness, and had access at home to a library suitable for young girls. At the very end of the novel (pt. 4, ch. 11), we learn an intriguing bit of information when Prince Myshkin visits Nastasya's quarters at the rooming house in Saint Petersburg: "[H]e noticed an open library book on the little table, the French novel *Madame Bovary*, bent the corner of the opened page, and [. . .] ignoring objections that it was a li-brary book, slipped it into his pocket" (637). A fascinating topic for discussion or a short paper is lurking here: What page in Flaubert's novel was Nastasya reading just before her suicide? A more formidable topic (for a longer paper) would be a psychological comparison of Anna, Nastasya, and Emma.

A world that offered intelligent, creative young women two paths—fulfill-ment through marriage on the one hand, spiritual isolation on the other—is not one that could satisfy educated women in the changing economic, social, and political climate of the mid–nineteenth century. In Russia, the turning point was 1855, the year of Nicholas I's death, which ushered in an era of liberalization and emancipation. New career possibilities opened up to women (secular teacher, writer, editor, cashier, notary, salesperson). Marital customs, conventions of courtship, educational opportunities, property law, serfdom—a vast number of social institutions were held up to critical scrutiny and debated more or less openly for the first time. These changes (and even more so the whole atmosphere of the time) had a profound influence on women's choice of reading and the role models they sought in books.

Judging from the Russian novels that appeared on the cusp of this new era (many of which, unfortunately, remain untranslated), young women had lost interest in sentimental novels and romantic plots. Goethe, Pushkin, Heinrich Heine, Walter Scott, Ann Radcliffe, and George Sand had become passé. By contrast, the English Victorian novel—which readers associated with practical, mercantile, industrialized life; social progress; and women's emancipation—became the rage. In the fifties, sixties, and seventies, Russian translations of George Eliot, William Thackeray, and Anthony Trollope were appearing in journal installments almost simultaneously with the English originals. (We cannot be certain, therefore, whether Anna reads her English novel in Russian, English, or French.) Aside from novels, women took to reading history, philosophy, and political theory. There is also a tendency for the heroines of the new Russian novels to despair that there is nothing available to read that truly relates to their current interests and ambitions.

An amusing passage in Nikolai Chernyshevsky's *What Is to Be Done?* (1863) shows how women's reading habits had changed. The heroine of the novel, a budding socialist named Vera Pavlovna, has taken to reading books on political philosophy. Her mother, finding them around the house and suspecting they contain something seditious or immoral, asks a hapless family friend to translate the foreign titles. To her surprise they pass muster:

> Mikhail Ivanych [a middle-aged man] was paying a call on Marya Aleksevna [Vera's mother]. Marya Aleksevna picked up some of these books and brought them in to show him.
>
> "Have a look, Mikhail Ivanych. I've almost figured out the title of this French book all by myself: Drawing Room, that must mean it's a manual on social etiquette . . ."
>
> "No, Marya Aleksevna, it's not Drawing Room, it's Destinée, that means destiny." [The book is *Destinée sociale* by the French socialist Considérant.]
>
> "What kind of destiny? Is that the title of a novel, a fortune-telling guide, or a book on dream interpretation?"
>
> "Well, [. . .] let's have a look. [. . .] Most of it deals with series, Marya Aleksevna. It's a scholarly book."

"Series? That's good—that means how to conduct monetary transactions."

"Yes, that's what it's all about, Marya Aleksevna."

"Well, and what about the German book?"

Mikhail Ivanych read the title slowly: "On Religion, by Ludwig, that is, by Louis XIV, Marya Aleksevna. It's a book by Louis XIV. He was king of France . . ." [The book is *The Essence of Religion* by Ludwig Feuerbach.]

"That's good . . . I know that Dmitry Sergevich [Vera Pavlovna's tutor] is a respectable young man . . ."   (112; slightly modified)

Many young heroines of this new era, like Vera Pavlovna, read books that help them participate in the construction of a new social and economic order. Others give up reading entirely because they find nothing in fiction but idle dreams. For whatever reason, female heroines seek to enter society as makers and achievers. Reading is no longer an escape of either the benign or the pathological kind. It has become, rather, a preparation for life, a tool to understand life. Or it has become irrelevant to life. Either way, the heroines of this era choose to subordinate reading to doing, as for instance Vera Pavlovna or Elena Stakhova in Turgenev's *On the Eve* (1860).

Anna Karenina does not fit easily into these new categories, because she is not socially responsible. What she does have in common with this new generation of women readers is her dissatisfaction with escapism. She wishes to be active, to write something on the text of life. There are suggestions of other, more satisfactory ways for her to do this: she starts writing a book for children, talks about starting a school and doing "useful work" (pt. 7, ch. 9)—activities that are entirely possible for women in Russia of the 1870s. But these inclinations come to naught. What is it about Anna that makes it so hard for her to find a happy and productive niche in life? To some extent, the answer to this question can be found by examining how she reads.

One can gain insight into other characters in much the same way. It would be fruitful, for example, to ask undergraduates to write a brief reaction paper (preferably ungraded) about the reading habits of Oblonsky (5–6; pt. 1, ch. 3), Levin (87; pt. 1, ch. 37), Karenin (102; pt. 1, ch. 33; 129–31; pt. 2, ch. 7), or Vronsky (159–60; pt. 2, ch. 19). What these characters read and how they read show us a great deal about who they are. Teaching students to focus on such small portions of text and draw larger insights out of them is one of the most important things we do in our profession. It lets them see that in great works tiny windows open on to vistas of great depth.

Reading Anna:
Opera, Tragedy, Melodrama, Farce

Julie A. Buckler

When I teach *Anna Karenina*, I use an approach that counters the persistent view of Tolstoy's fiction as perfectly transparent realism. As Henry James famously wrote, "Tolstoy is a reflector as vast as a natural lake; a monster harnessed to his great subject—all human life!" (qtd. in Knowles, *Tolstoy* 433). Matthew Arnold similarly declared that "we are not to take *Anna Karénine* as a work of art; we are to take it as a piece of life" (qtd. in Knowles, *Tolstoy* 353). Accordingly, students tend to resist reading Anna Karenina herself as a literary or artistic construct rather than as a real person who comes to life in the novel's pages. Without denying students the pleasures of character and plot, I contend that Tolstoy's realism points to the ways in which art structures life.

In *Anna Karenina*, Tolstoy explores the relation between theatrical genre and social convention. More precisely, his novel represents the social world of nineteenth-century Imperial Russia in terms of theatrical forms derived from the neoclassical system of genres: opera, tragedy, melodrama, and farce. Opera and tragedy, which the novel links with its heroine, represent the upper ranges of the available generic spectrum. But the novel also makes abundant references to less elevated theatrical genres that simultaneously shape the stories of the literary protagonists. All these theatrical genres were familiar to readers of Tolstoy's time. Most important, the characters themselves in Tolstoy's novel use these diverse theatrical categories to interpret their experiences and structure their behavior. A multiplicity of generic paradigms contributes to the extreme mysteriousness of Anna, who—as is often noted—has hardly any biography and remarkably few memories of her girlhood. As close readings of selected passages and extratextual references can show, she is a cipher who lends herself at different moments to the surrounding contexts of multiple dramatic modes.

Opera

Although Tolstoy held opera responsible for Natasha Rostova's near ruin in *War and Peace* and condemned opera in his treatise "What Is Art?," he never denied the power of this definitively public art form to influence human response to seemingly stock situations. Students can be led through close readings of the two famous opera-house scenes in *Anna Karenina* (pt. 2, chs. 4–8; pt. 5, chs. 32–33) to see how he establishes this generic space for Anna (Buckler, ch. 6). During the first opera-house scene, Vronsky and Princess Betsy discuss Vronsky's prospects with Anna. During the second opera-house scene, Anna rebelliously attends the theater and becomes the focus of social disapprobation, eclipsing the soprano's performance. In fact, the reader's very first glimpse of Anna links her with the opera diva. As Stiva Oblonsky and Vronsky wait together at the railroad station, Vronsky asks, "Well, are we to give a supper for the *diva* next Sunday?" (54; pt. 1, ch. 17). On the pretext of inquiring about this supper, Vronsky stops in at the Oblonsky home that evening, catching sight of Anna on the staircase. The opera diva is the decoy. Anna is the true object of desire for both Vronsky and the reader.

Students may be interested to know that an early variant of Princess Betsy's reception in part 2—originally the opening chapter of the novel—makes a direct reference to Giuseppe Verdi's opera *La traviata*, which remains a suggestive subtext to Tolstoy's novel. Comparing the Italian opera to the Russian novel in a class discussion may yield some of the following observations. *La traviata* tells the story of a demimondaine and her lover, a young man whose sister's social prospects may be ruined by their relationship. But Tolstoy rewrote the *Traviata* story by engaging with Verdi's themes in a manner more consonant with literary realism. *La traviata* does not trace the actual consequences of violating society's strictures, as does *Anna Karenina*, since Violetta gives up her lover Alfredo at his father's request. Verdi presents Alfredo's urging of Violetta to give herself to him as the outpouring of sincere love, whereas Tolstoy equates Vronsky's pursuit of Anna more sinisterly with the pleasures of the hunt and with the destruction of his favorite mare. Anna, too, is far more self-interested than Violetta. She does not content herself with an intimate boudoir death scene and makes few concessions to the well-being of any family. *La traviata* preserves the sanctity of the bourgeois family and does not jeopardize the marital prospects of Alfredo's sister. Although the family as an institution is under constant siege in Tolstoy's novel, *Anna Karenina* similarly allows the narrative of family life to overwhelm the narrative of passion, as the Levin-Kitty story line triumphs over the Anna-Vronsky line and outlives it in part 8. Note that Tolstoy ultimately decided to mention explicitly a different opera in his opening chapter, when Stiva Oblonsky makes a reference to "Il mio tesoro," a well-known tenor aria from Mozart's opera *Don Giovanni*. The Don Juan legend as treated by Mozart poses questions about morality and divine retribution that are not applicable to the essentially social premises by which Verdi's opera judges Violetta's wrongdoing.

Is Anna's death operatic? Certainly, she takes her life with the desire to make a grand gesture that will produce a lasting effect. Her suicide writes her out of the gradual, novelistic deterioration of love and beauty that she fears above all else. And yet it seems incongruous that one of the most dramatic suicides in world literature occurs when the heroine jumps awkwardly under a slow-moving freight train at a country station. Anna's death merges operatic denouement with novelistic nuance.

Tragedy

Tragedy is the dramatic mode most frequently associated with Anna's story, and tragic interpretations emphasize the moral issues posed by Tolstoy as well as his heroine's unrealized spiritual potential. New York's *Eclectic* magazine of 1886 typifies these views, pronouncing the novel "the greatest of all social tragedies, the fall of a pure and high-minded woman, who is introduced to us as a model of her sex, a good wife and devoted mother, before the power of an illicit passion" (qtd. in Knowles, *Tolstoy* 347). The tragic view of *Anna Karenina* is the most given to extracting pedagogical utility from the text through an insistence on seriousness, meaning, life lessons, and the like. Such an approach is by no means incompatible with Tolstoy's own fondness for teaching and moralizing. Still, students should be encouraged to question the tragic reading of Anna as potentially reductive.

Students can identify many aspects of *Anna Karenina* that support the tragic interpretive paradigm: Anna's passionate nature and the fundamental incompatibility between her and Karenin, the terrible choice she must make between lover and son, the surrounding social environment that cruelly punishes her for abjuring convenient hypocrisy, her long struggle and eventual defeat. The timing in the novel—for example, that Anna's communications do not reach Vronsky in time to prevent her suicide—also suggests tragedy: events unfold in a fateful manner that human will cannot control.

Classical tragedy features a noble protagonist who is undone by a tragic flaw or because the gods so ordain. Modern tragedy tends to emphasize environmental forces and maintains that ordinary characters can still be tragic. Anna Karenina would seem to fit the criteria for a tragic heroine in either case. Still, some critics have denied Tolstoy's novel and its heroine any kind of tragic stature. The publicist P. N. Tkachov lambasted Tolstoy in 1875 for his pretensions to seriousness: "it is quite natural and not at all surprising that such an empty woman as Anna Karenina should have violated with Vronsky the rights of her highly-placed but rather boring and wooden husband. But what is surprising and even unnatural is that the [consummation] should be painted by the author as some tragic event" (qtd. in Knowles, *Tolstoy* 258).

Students can situate the tragic viewpoint inside rather than outside the novel, however, by examining Anna's own perception of events. After the affair with Vronsky has begun, Princess Betsy makes a trenchant observation to Anna: "You see a thing may be looked at tragically and turned to a torment, or looked at quite simply, and even gaily. Perhaps you are inclined to take things too tragically" (272; pt. 3, ch. 17). Anna does indeed pitch her story toward the upper part of the generic hierarchy, into the heady air of tragedy and grand opera. Her suicidal despair is marked by distorted perceptions of other people and decreasing contact with anything outside her interior experience. She invents hurtful scenes between herself and Vronsky and writes cruel speeches for him in her imagination, "and she did not forgive him for them any more than if he had really said them" (679; pt. 7, ch. 26). Anna's insistence on seeing life in such self-dramatizing terms may actually be the most tragic aspect of *Anna Karenina*.

Melodrama

While Anna sees her life in tragic terms, more than a few critics and readers have relegated her story to the more debased realm of melodrama, refusing to take her or her plight seriously. The populist critic A. M. Skabichevsky expressed outrage in 1875 that "this melodramatic nonsense written in the spirit of French novels of a bygone age is lavished upon the banal love affair of a society fop and the wife of a Petersburg civil servant" (qtd. in Knowles, *Tolstoy* 269). It is possible that Tolstoy intentionally portrayed Anna as behaving melodramatically? In other words, Anna might aim for tragedy but falls short of the mark, generically speaking. In this vein, Gary Saul Morson discusses Anna's story in terms of her narrative narcissism, emphasizing the novelistic fatalism and foreshadowing that Anna uses to structure her story ("Anna Karenina's Omens"). This fatalism leads to a lack of responsibility on Anna's part concerning her life plot, which she mistakenly perceives as art. For Morson, the greatest difference between Anna and Tolstoy's other characters is her sense of the structured nature of time, expressed in generic terms as Romantic novel or melodrama. Why, for example, does she not agree to a divorce when Karenin offers to grant one to her? Does she create more trouble for herself than necessary out of a compulsion to adhere to a particular generic paradigm?

Tolstoy's novel may also intentionally evoke melodrama at certain points, as just one in a series of literary modes that manage to coexist within the plastic, omnibus structure of a large novel. As A. V. Stankevich shrewdly observed, Tolstoy's novel would have been quite different had it ended with Anna's death, following her childbirth fever and reconciliation with Karenin. Such an ending would have shown the reader a "pitiful Anna, in a late but complete repentance and in death paying for her conscious and unconscious guilt," and this Anna "would have retained her moral, albeit sad, beauty not only in Vronsky's memory but also in Karenin's and the readers' " (qtd. in Knowles, *Tolstoy* 300). Perhaps so. But Tolstoy chose not to end his heroine's story in such unambiguous and generic terms. Stankevich himself felt that a melodramatic deathbed scene would have been incompatible with Anna's character as Tolstoy wrote her and would have sidestepped the difficult questions that the novel poses.

It is also possible to consider melodrama in different terms, not as a degraded form of tragedy or realism but, as Peter Brooks does in his study *The Melodramatic Imagination* (1976), as a response to the challenges of a secular, post-Enlightenment society. Melodrama offered a way to dramatize social and cultural anxieties about institutions such as marriage and about aspects of identity such as class. From this perspective, Anna's death restores the established social order while also subversively raising the image of its overthrow, just as melodrama should.

Farce

Below melodrama on the generic hierarchy lies farce, a dramatic mode that re-lies on highly improbable elements of plot and character to comic effect. Farce is a consummately vernacular dramatic form in that it mocks the higher theatri-cal genres. Students may at first be nonplussed by the proposed connection be-tween such a serious novel as *Anna Karenina* and farce, but there are historical precedents for seeing farcical elements in the work. The critic Tkachov, for ex-ample, found astonishing the fact that Tolstoy "discovers tragedy in Vronsky's relations not only with Anna but with his mare Frou-Frou too" (qtd. in Knowles, *Tolstoy* 259).

Tolstoy's earliest intentions for *Anna Karenina* reveal a leaning toward the lower dramatic genres. The original opening to the novel bears the intriguing title "Molodets-Baba," which may be roughly translated as an inelegant ap-praisal on the order of "What a gal!" This working title, which evokes operetta and variety theater, fits Tolstoy's early conception of Anna, who was planned as overweight, vulgar, and coquettish (Eikhenbaum, *Tolstoi in the Seventies*, pt. 3). Anna's husband, Karenin, makes a direct connection between farce and social circumstance when his position as deceived husband evokes Jacques Offen-bach's popular operetta *La belle Hélène* (1864), a burlesque about the Trojan War that celebrates Paris's success in deceiving Helen of Troy's husband, Menelaus (254–55; pt. 3, ch. 13). It enrages Karenin that his life is both theatri-cally derivative and generically trivial.

Other passages in *Anna Karenina* similarly gesture at the heroine's lower generic origins. During the first opera-house scene, Vronsky regales Princess Betsy with the adventures of two officers of his regiment. The mysterious veiled woman the officers spy in a passing sleigh turns out to be the pregnant wife of an apoplectic titular councilor. Vronsky clearly relishes the farcelike silliness of the episode, which seems to offer an implicit, generically debased prefiguring of his love affair with Anna. Vronsky's remarks about his own generic prefer-ences are extremely suggestive: "Where do I come from? [. . .] from the *Theater Bouffe.* I have been there a hundred times, and always with fresh plea-sure. Excellent! I know it's a disgrace, but at the opera I go to sleep, while at the *Bouffe* I stay until the last minute enjoying it" (124; pt. 2, ch. 6). The nineteenth-century opéra bouffe, an outgrowth of the 1860s fashion for operetta, was known for parodic reenactments of lyric or epic mythological themes and show-cased fetchingly dressed female performers. Vronsky's dramatic tastes create an alternative generic context for Tolstoy's heroine and suggest a more satirical perspective on the novel's famous love story.

Tolstoy's novel stages spectacular public events such as the Moscow ball, the steeplechase, Levin's wedding to Kitty, and the provincial nobility elections, but it also asserts that more intimate episodes are no less theatrical in their under-lying dramatic structure. Theater is both a cognitive, hermeneutic tool and a metaphor for human consciousness. Approaching *Anna Karenina* in terms of theater and genre encourages students to read Tolstoy's novel not reductively for moral and theme but in terms of specifically artistic interpretive paradigms. The goal of teaching this way is to help students recognize the diverse generic markers the novel identifies with its heroine. The simultaneous presence of seemingly incompatible generic elements results in the productively ambiguous and endlessly fascinating literary subject that is Anna.

NOTE

This article contains revised material from my book *The Literary Lorgnette: Attending Opera in Imperial Russia.*

The Wedding Bell, the Death Knell, and Philosophy's Spell: Tolstoy's Sense of an Ending

Svetlana Evdokimova

A death, a murder, a birth, a suicide, a marriage, a return, a departure—these are all familiar ways of ending a fictional narrative. Whether a narrative ends in death or marriage largely depends on its genre. Genre shapes our expectations of closure and limits the author's options for the ending. Without fully subscribing to Northrop Frye's rigid taxonomy, it is safe to say that tragedy usually ends in death or murder, a comedy or romance often ends in marriage, while the epic and picaresque tend to end with a return or a departure. But *Anna Karenina* ends with the philosophical and religious ruminations of a man who is not even the title character of the novel. Moreover, while most readers are likely to remember Anna's death under the train wheels, they find it difficult to recollect the details of the novel's ending, including the entire part 8, which focuses on Levin's spiritual quest. This ending is not memorable and is far from climactic, because by part 8 Anna is already dead and Levin and Kitty are already married.

Most of my students are intrigued by the fact that the novel does not conclude with Anna's suicide. Conventional expectations lead them to anticipate that *Anna Karenina* will be the story of Anna and, therefore, will end with the resolution of her fate (whatever it might be). But the novel goes on. Its ending likewise bewildered many of Tolstoy's contemporaries, who complained that *Anna Karenina* was two novels rather than one. Motivated by political objections to Tolstoy's presentation of the Serbian crisis and by his own sense of the novel's unity, Tolstoy's publisher, N. M. Katkov, cut off serial publication of the novel at the end of part 7. Like Katkov, although for very different reasons, Hollywood directors considered Levin's final reflections at the end of the novel to be expendable. Apart from the multitude of other distortions, the Greta Garbo film leaves out part 8 entirely, while the Vivien Leigh version also stops with Anna's suicide. The students' uneasiness about part 8 is therefore fully grounded in the initial reception of *Anna Karenina* and further echoed and reinforced by Hollywood's readings of the novel (see Lanoux, this volume).

There is another problem with the way the novel ends. It opens with its celebrated omniscient pronouncement "All happy families resemble one another, but each unhappy family is unhappy in its own way," but by the end it seems to suggest that the opposite is true. Anna's life follows the pattern of so many other stories of adultery that end in death or suicide. In this sense, her unhappy family resembles other unhappy families. It is not unique. By contrast, Tolstoy seems determined to show that family happiness takes many unexpected forms: "Levin had been married three months. He was happy, but in quite a different way from what he had expected" (436; pt. 5, ch. 14). In the final part, Tolstoy shows that Levin's family life is "happy in its own way": "And though he was a happy and healthy family man, Levin was several times so near to suicide that he hid a cord he had lest he should hang himself, and he feared to carry a gun lest he should shoot himself" (714; pt. 8, ch. 9). This happy man's life clearly has a story of its own.

Does the novel then deny its own premises (and promises)? To what extent is Levin's plot line, especially his search for the meaning of life at the end of the novel, artificial or organic to the novel as a whole? The answer, I believe, largely depends on how the novel is taught.

How Many Novels Does Anna Karenina Contain?

How does part 8 shape our sense of the novel as a whole? Is there any inner logic in Tolstoy's ending the novel as he did? The difficulty in answering these questions stems from the generic confusion that the novel creates. In this essay, I suggest two main strategies for dealing with students' bewilderment at or disappointment with the novel's closure. These are consideration of the parallelism and contrast in Anna's and Levin's lives and discussion of Anna Karenina's generic peculiarities.

One way to explain the novel's ending would be to adopt the traditional strategy used by those who argue for the novel's unity, that is, to demonstrate the inner links between Anna's and Levin's plot lines (see Jahn, this volume; Todd, this volume). Since the parallelism of the two plot lines is the chief structural principle of the novel, we might expect the plots to end in contrasting ways that would illuminate each other. If Levin's story is supposed to provide counterpoint to Anna's, then one would anticipate that, since Anna's ends in suicide, Levin's should end in the opposite of this, in an affirmation of life.

Accordingly, I ask my students to compare the lives of Anna and Levin and consider the novel's two endings in tandem. It is no coincidence that both endings—Anna's and Levin's—evoke suicide. Both address the characters' attempts to make sense of their lives. Tolstoy writes about Anna, "She saw it clearly in the piercing light which now revealed to her the meaning of life and of human relations" (690; pt. 7, ch. 30). "But now I say that I know the meaning of my life," echoes Levin in the end of the novel (721; pt. 8, ch. 12). While trying to comprehend their existence, both characters defamiliarize the world around them. Consider Anna's inner monologue: "Why are those young men in the next carriage shouting? Why are they talking and laughing? It's all untrue, all lies, all deception, all evil! . . ." (693; pt. 7, ch. 31). Compare it with Levin's reflections: "'Why is all this being done?' he wondered. 'Why am I standing here, obliging them to work? Why do they all make such efforts and try to show me their zeal? [. . .] What is it all for?' " (718; pt. 8, ch. 12). Both Anna and Levin claim that the meaning of life revealed to them is universal. These are Anna's final conclusions: "It's the same with me [. . .] and with all the people that live away there by the Volga [. . .] and everywhere and always" (691; pt. 7. ch. 30). Her delusion is echoed in Levin's epiphany: "And not I alone but every one—the whole world—only understands that completely. [. . .] I and millions of men who lived centuries ago and those who are living now [. . .] we all agree on that one thing" (720; pt. 8, ch. 12).

Despite these parallels, Levin's crisis ends with the very opposite of Anna's withdrawal from life: Levin finds a new sense of endurance and perseverance. These opposing outcomes, Tolstoy seems to suggest, stem from Anna's and Levin's contrasting understandings of the meaning of life. Whereas Anna comes to see life as hatred and struggle ("Oh yes! What Yashvin said: the struggle for existence and hatred are the only things that unite people" [689; pt. 7, ch. 30]), love of God is what gives life meaning for Levin ("to live for God, for the soul" [721; pt. 8, ch. 12]). Ironically, in giving herself up to passion, Anna becomes a slave to reason and to Yashvin's rationalistic philosophy: "'Reason has been given to man to enable him to escape from his troubles' [. . .]. These words seemed to answer Anna's thought. [. . .] 'Yes, it troubles me very much, and reason was given us to enable us to escape; therefore I must escape!'" (693; pt. 7, ch. 31). By contrast, Levin refuses to live by reason alone: "Was it by reason that I attained to the knowledge that I must love my neighbor and not throttle him? [. . .] Reason has discovered the struggle for existence and the law that I must throttle all those who hinder the satisfaction of my desires. That is the deduction reason makes. But the law of loving others could not be discovered by reason, because it is unreasonable" (722; pt. 7, ch. 12).

According to a comparative analysis of Anna's and Levin's roles in the novel, *Anna Karenina* should end only when the parallels and contrasts between the two characters are fully completed. But this explanation still does not properly address the problem of part 8. Why is Levin's fate not better integrated into Anna's plot? Can the complex structure of the novel be fully explained by the parallelism of the two plot lines?

To be sure, part 8 is not a traditional epilogue used to tie up loose ends. Readers certainly need to know what happened to Vronsky after he found Anna's mangled body stretched out on a table, but do they learn anything fundamentally new about Levin's domestic life in part 8? The marriage of hero and heroine occurs rather early in the novel (in part 5) and Levin's accommodation to domestic life is also described in part 5 and the beginning of part 6. These sections show Tolstoy's apotheosis of the prosaic in human life: Kitty's hustle and bustle around the house, the newlyweds' petty jealousies and charming quarrels, the nursing of the dying Nicholas, Kitty's pregnancy, the jam cooking with Agatha Mikhaylovna, and other domestic activities. The final chapters of *Anna Karenina* do not add much either to the novel's depiction of Kitty and Levin's family bliss or to its glorification of day-to-day existence. Certainly, if Tolstoy's task was merely to contrast the dangers of romance with the virtues of marriage and family life, Tolstoy could have stopped his narrative much earlier. Neither Levin's fears about his wife and son during the storm nor his rapture over the bathing of little Mitya described in part 8 convey anything new to the readers, who already know that Levin has learned to appreciate the prosaic aspect of life and that he is able to experience joy and pride "when the baby sneezed" (651; pt. 7, ch. 16).

Tolstoy does more than merely contrast Anna and Levin by means of a simplistic binary opposition. Thus, part 8 opens with material that seems not to belong, such as the lengthy discussion of the Serbian war, of the Russian volunteers, and of the scholastic pursuits of Koznyshev, a minor and not particularly attractive character in the novel. Coming after the memorable description of Anna's suicide, this material has a truly jarring effect. But is it extraneous? In order to understand how these discussions figure into the larger design of the novel, we must consider the issue of *Anna Karenina*'s genre.

The Sense of an Ending and the Sense of Genre

I continue the discussion by inviting students to examine the generic assumptions they hold. What does it mean to close a novel? It may be useful to refer students to literary criticism that deals specifically with the issues of closure and genre, such as the works of Mikhail Bakhtin, Frank Kermode, Barbara H. Smith, Marianna Torgovnick, and D. A. Miller.

Since some students even declare that Anna's tragedy is fully convincing, whereas Levin's life and quest are contrived, it is important to make them aware of the role played by their expectations about literary genres in this response. Why do they accept something rather uncommon—Anna's tragic end—as natural and probable and dismiss as something artificial and contrived the more probable, day-to-day existence of a married man and his typical (at least for an intellectual) quest for truth and meaning? It is clear that they are dissatisfied with the way the novel ends not because the ending violates their sense of probability but because it fails to provide an aesthetically pleasing resolution to the novel, which they identify as the story of Anna. Their perplexity is therefore directly connected with certain assumptions they have about how stories about adulterous women should resolve.

As a rule, students can fairly quickly link Anna's tragic end to other novels of adultery, such as *Madame Bovary* or *The Awakening* (Kate Chopin), and to stories of passionate romantic love going back to the myth of Tristan and Iseult. Comparing Anna's fate with that of other adulterous heroines deepens students' understanding of Tolstoy's portrayal of Anna but, at the same time, draws attention to the fact that the ending of *Anna Karenina* is problematic. If the aim of *Anna Karenina* were to resolve an adulterous woman's fate, then closure could have been achieved by ending the novel with part 7. But Tolstoy doesn't do this.

Certainly one should not simplify *Madame Bovary* by assuming that Gustave Flaubert's ending merely represents the resolution of Emma's fate. As Vladimir Nabokov puts it in his discussion of traditional conclusions or nonconclusions, "*Madame Bovary* is finished not only because Emma has killed herself, but because Homais has at last got his decoration [. . .] *Anna Karenin* is finished not only because Anna has been crushed by a backing freight train but because Lyovin has found his God" (Pushkin, *Eugene Onegin* 3: 311). It is still important to remember that neither *Madame Bovary* nor Chopin's *The Awakening* has any character even remotely similar to Levin in terms of his prominence in the novel and his relation to or, more precisely, almost complete lack of relation to the adulterous heroine. The character of Levin suggests that *Anna Karenina* is not a conventional novel of adultery. What is it?

By describing how *Anna Karenina* evolved from the story of an adulterous woman to a novel with a more complex structure, instructors can help students appreciate this novel's generic ambiguity, a facet it shares with many other great Russian novels of the nineteenth century (see Armstrong, this volume). The ending may be discussed not only in view of the novel's literary evolution but also as an expression of Tolstoy's uncertainty about literary genres. Note his frequently quoted pronouncement about how Russian prose works defy generic norms: "From Gogol's *Dead Souls* to Dostoevski's *House of the Dead*, in the recent period of Russian literature there is not a single artistic prose work rising at all above mediocrity, which quite fits into the form of a novel, epic, or story" (War 1366; "Some Words about *War and Peace*").

If students have some background not only in Tolstoy but in nineteenth-century Russian literature in general, it is useful to discuss other Russian novels with controversial and unorthodox endings. When traditional generic definitions do not apply and genres deviate from their canonical forms, as often happens in Russian literature, we can expect unconventional endings, which are sometimes frustrating, sometimes delightful, but inevitably controversial. Russian literature offers many endings that are not really endings. Not only does *Eugene Onegin* not end "properly," with a marriage or death, but it also shifts the reader's attention away from the title character and focuses almost completely on Tatyana. *Dead Souls* strives for an ending in a tantalizing and agonizing way, but its author, Nikolai Gogol, is never able to fulfill the promise and risks losing the reader's interest as part 2 unfolds. This is precisely why Bakhtin claims that "the tragedy of Gogol is to a very real extent the tragedy of a genre" (*Dialogic Imagination* 28). *War and Peace*, which has been said to end arbitrarily, overwhelms the reader with two epilogues instead of one. It is helpful to see these anomalous endings in the larger context of the generic uncertainty of the nineteenth-century Russian novel.

Anna Karenina's *Other Genres*

Finally, in our attempt to make sense of the ending of the novel, I invite students to consider the various genres that *Anna Karenina* evokes. Bakhtin's ideas about genre and the generic ambiguity of the novel can be fruitfully used to provide a framework for discussion of *Anna Karenina*'s genres. Among the genres apparently drawn on are the society novel, the novel of adultery, and the bildungsroman. But none of these seems relevant to the ending. As mentioned above, the novel of adultery in *Anna Karenina* reaches its closure with Anna's death in part 7. Similarly, the bildungsroman within *Anna Karenina*—Kitty's story—resolves and reaches its closure once Kitty has undergone complete social integration through marriage and the birth of her child, events occurring before part 8.

Since part 8 exceeds the boundaries of these genres, we ask whether it evokes any other genres. It has been justly observed that the novels of Tolstoy, like those of Dostoevsky, explore metaphysical and moral dilemmas that the Western reader is more likely to associate with classical tragedy or with the dialogues of Plato. Indeed, if we view *Anna Karenina* not only as a novel of adultery and a bildungsroman but also as a Platonic dialogue of sorts, then the ontological questions raised in the end of the novel do not seem out of place.

Critics have acknowledged Tolstoy's indebtedness to Plato's philosophy (for a detailed analysis of the restaurant scene in *Anna Karenina*, see Orwin, *Tolstoy's Art*; Orwin, this volume; Gutkin). Tolstoy's novel, however, is not limited to the Platonic theme that comes to the surface in such scenes as Stiva and Levin's "symposium" in the restaurant or Levin's thoughts about the righteous peasant named Plato at the end of the novel (pt. 8, ch. 11). It is important to stress not only the thematic and conceptual relation of *Anna Karenina* to Plato's texts— that is, Plato's and Tolstoy's ideas on the nature of love—but also the novel's generic indebtedness to Platonic dialogues. The novel as a whole may be viewed as a Platonic dialogue on the nature of love, with each character embodying and reenacting a particular view of love. It is not coincidental that the novel abounds in dialogues on love. Tolstoy's novelistic version of Plato's *Symposium* raises very similar issues: the nature of love, the meaning of life, the idea of gradual development through a spiritual quest and learning (the Greek concept of *paideia*). The novel also provides various definitions of love and raises various questions about it, although, like Plato's *Symposium*, it does so not in direct speeches but rather through various "images, actions, situations" (750). The Platonic dialogue is thus one of the genres "novelized" by Tolstoy and given a "different resonance," for, as Bakhtin argues, "in the presence of the novel, all other genres somehow have a different resonance. A lengthy battle for the novelization of the other genres began, a battle to draw them into a zone of contact with reality" (*Dialogic Imagination* 39).

Using Plato's Socratic method, Tolstoy presents Levin's life and spiritual quest as an emblem of the Platonic *paideia*. Students may be referred here to Levin's initial misunderstanding of the nature of Platonic love as revealed in his conversation with Stiva in the restaurant. Although many definitions of love are given throughout the novel, it is only at the very end, in chapter 11 of part 8, that Levin arrives at the meaning of life and the meaning of love closest to the one expressed by Socrates in the *Symposium*, that is, the inseparability of the spiritual and the physical in love. Tolstoy, however, makes Levin arrive at this truth not through philosophical arguments but through the experience of life.

Once again, the Socratic argument is transposed into a different genre, into the realm of the novel. Thus, Tolstoy stresses the importance of intuition and personal experience as opposed to the merely logical arguments of philosophical dialogues. Levin discovers the same truth or a truth similar to the one that Diotima teaches Socrates, but in a different way. In Diotima's teaching of the ascent and gradual evolving of the physical into the spiritual, the crucial role is played by a correct guide who should help the lover discover the truth. Levin's teacher is life itself—with all its everyday experiences and accidental occurrences: "Life itself has given me the answer, in my knowledge of what is good and what is bad" (722; pt. 8, ch. 12). Incidentally, the name of Socrates's teacher, the priestess Diotima, means "honor the god"; it is echoed in the name of the peasant Theodore (that is, "gift of God"), who tells Levin about the righteous peasant Plato. The novel ends with Levin's assertion of his will and freedom to choose the good way.

Levin's spiritual quest fails to resolve the multiple threads of the novel and cannot be viewed as the novel's teleological end point. But it is a resolution of the novel's Platonic dialogue. *Anna Karenina* ends with an epiphany consolidating Levin's religious beliefs and crystallizing many of the novel's primary philosophical concerns. The ending thus becomes an ironic reversal of the opening, for Levin's happy family life is happy in its own way and has a story of its own, but its story—unlike Anna's—is undramatic and therefore must be narrated in a different genre.

While the character of Anna endows the novel with tragic overtones, the Levin plot line weaves into the novel a philosophical discourse in the tradition of Plato's dialogues. It is the rudiment of the Platonic dialogue and its "novelization" that lies at the core of the Levin plot line and its resolution in the end of the novel. Thus, whether we view generic ambiguity as a feature special to Russian literature or as an indispensable feature of the novel as a genre, as Bakhtin argues, it is clear that *Anna Karenina* does not permit generic monologue. By disentangling multiple generic voices in it, we can tie together its loose ends.

The Opening of *Anna Karenina*

Kate Holland

Where does *Anna Karenina* begin? With the novel's epigraph? With its aphoristic first line? Or with the paragraph that follows, where the narrative begins? This is the question I pose to the students as we begin our study of Tolstoy's novel. It is a question that will remain central to our reading of the novel.

I ask students what strikes them about the tone. How does Tolstoy grab our attention? The apodictic biblical epigraph, "Vengeance is mine; I will repay," made even more strident by the upper-case letters, which emphasize the threat, is backed up by the first sentence, which seems to lay out the rules for the observation and categorization of the novelistic subject: "All happy families resemble one another, but each unhappy family is unhappy in its own way" (1; pt.1, ch.1).

Yet as we move from the novel's frame into its subject, narrative authority seems to give way to confusion: "Everything was upset in the Oblonskys' house." Immediately we come across the problem that will form the narrative kernel of *Anna Karenina*: adultery. "The wife had discovered an intrigue between her husband and their former French governess, and declared that she would not continue to live under the same roof as him."

Having entered the action, we are ready for the events that will conspire to bring the novel to its tragic close. Yet how did we get there? How does Tolstoy prime us, in the first few lines, for our role as readers of his novel? How can the beginning of a novel provide clues for reading what follows?

Our first task is to determine the speaker of the epigraph and of the first line. We note the quotation marks around the epigraph. Where is it from, what does it mean, and how does it relate to the text that follows? How does its position, at the head of the novel, affect its authority? A student recognizes it as a biblical quotation, and so we surmise that it is God who is speaking. Or could it be God's literary analogue, the creator of this literary universe, Tolstoy?

Like other authors who make use of an epigraph, Tolstoy uses another text to comment on his own. In the process, does he make that statement his? The position of the epigraph, after the title but before the main body of the text, seems to claim equal standing with that text: commenting on it but also competing with it. Would the students read the line "Vengeance is mine; I will repay" differently if it were in its biblical context? What assumptions do they bring to their reading of a novel? Would they read the line differently if it were attributed to God than if it were attributed to Tolstoy? What effect does the lack of attribution have on the authority of the statement? Does that lack increase or decrease its authority?

A handout with the sources of the epigraph reveals its complex origins. The New Testament source, Romans 12.19, reads, "Dearly beloved, avenge not yourselves, but *rather* give place unto wrath: for it is written, Vengeance *is* mine; I will repay, saith the Lord."

But Romans 12.19 is itself a quotation: Paul paraphrases the word of God conveyed through Moses in Deuteronomy 32.35. God's voice, refracted through Moses, warns the Israelites of God's wrath, which will result if they continue to pray to false gods: "To me *belongeth* vengeance, and recompense; their foot shall slide in *due* time: for the day of their calamity *is* at hand, and the things that shall come across them make haste."

Boris Eikhenbaum reveals that Tolstoy originally took the biblical quotation from Arthur Schopenhauer's *The World as Will and Idea*, translating straight from the German in an early draft of the novel, only later correcting it according to the Church Slavonic Bible (*Tolstoi in the Seventies* 195–204). Why did Tolstoy use the quotation from Schopenhauer? Why did he then change the epigraph to the quotation from Romans rather than to the Deuteronomy original, or to an almost identical verse from Hebrews 10.30? I ask the students what differences in semantic emphasis they find in the Old and New Testament variants.

As we move from the biblical epigraph to the opening line, does the narrative voice change? If Tolstoy transcribes the words of God in the novel's epigraph, what of his own apodictic tone of biblical precept in the novel's opening sentence? Is he imitating God, laying claim to the role of judge over his fictional universe? The syntactic structure of the epigraph, a sentence split into two clauses of roughly equal length, is replicated in the first line, though the epigraph's logical progression—the speaker, having laid claim to vengeance, promises to repay it—is muddled in the novel's first sentence by a contrast. The first sentence maintains the structural harmony of the biblical epigraph, but in its second clause that harmony is already beginning to fall away, preparing the ground for the following paragraph, where novelistic disorder takes over from biblical order.

The novel's aphoristic first line seems to invite a neat reduction of the novel to the illustration of a formula. The second half of the sentence introduces the "unhappy family" of the next paragraph, the Oblonskys. The cause of their unhappiness, Stiva's adultery, and his wife's punishment, her declaration that she cannot live under the same roof with him, bring together both the theme of the epigraph, transgression and retribution, and the unhappy family of the aphorism, thus leading us from the frame into the realm of the novel proper: the effect of adultery on a series of families. How else can we view the sequence of epigraph, first line, and succeeding paragraph? The progression from divine law to authorial generalization, which offers the security of categorization if not the absolute determinacy of divinely orchestrated law, to the disorder of the Oblonsky household is a descending hierarchy of authority accompanied by a descending hierarchy of subject matter. As we go from the divine to the sordid and prosaic, we enter the novel.

Reading the novel's beginning retroactively, even after only a few pages, complicates this straightforward transition from God to the messy prosaic world of the novel. The aphorism's model can be seen by attentive students as disintegrating long before the novel's end. The first sentence, which seems to draw out the differing threads of this novel of adultery, is soon contradicted by the novel as a whole: the unhappy families—Anna and Karenin, Stiva and Dolly—are unhappy for the same reason, the adultery of one partner. Furthermore, far more space is devoted to portraying the unhappiness of the standard happy family, Kitty and Levin, than is devoted to their happiness, and this unhappiness often derives from jealousy associated with adultery: Levin's suspicions concerning Vasenka Veslovsky's attentions and Kitty's unhappiness because, first, Levin is not a virgin and, second, he visits Anna. The happiness of Kitty and Levin is qualitatively different from that of the old Prince and Princess Shcherbatsky. Thus we can see that every premise of that first aphoristic sentence is contradicted by the progression of the novel. Does the breakdown of the aphorism signal authorial incompetence, Tolstoy's failure to adhere to the rules Tolstoy set himself? How do the students see this breakdown of paradigm and template at the opening of the novel? Does the erosion of the authority of the aphorism also diminish the authority of the epigraph's message? Or is the divine authority of the epigraph protected from the unstable, human, chaotic element of the novel, which includes its narrative voice, by the boundary of the text itself? Does the epigraph lie outside the text or within it?

As we read on, we continue to return to the question of the epigraph. When teaching *Anna Karenina* through its opening, one inevitably runs up against the problem of finding a way to guide students through the maze of critical literature dealing with the novel's epigraph and its relation to the question of Anna's adultery and her treatment in the novel. Some important examples of this literature can be found in the Norton Critical Edition (Dostoevsky; Gromeka; Eikhenbaum), but I also introduce other readings, those of Viktor Shklovsky (*Lev Tolstoy*), D. H. Lawrence (*Phoenix*), Robert Louis Jackson ("On the Ambivalent

Beginning"), Judith Armstrong (*Unsaid* Anna), Amy Mandelker (*Framing*), and Dragan Kujundžić. As we move from the epigraph to the critical readings and back to the novel, we examine how critics tend to locate the epigraph each in a different source and thus give it a particular semantic emphasis, which in turn they see reflected in the novel. Critics have traditionally fallen into two camps: those who see the epigraph's roots in Old Testament vengeance and those who see in its Pauline context a different inflection. M. S. Gromeka emphasizes the idea of divine judgment and vengeance suggested by the Deuteronomy quotation and sees Anna as punished for her adulterous transgressions, while Fyodor Dostoevsky accentuates the Pauline emphasis on the divine rather than human nature of that vengeance, thus suggesting a reading of the novel according to the dictates of New Testament morality, an emphasis that Jackson sees reflected in the novel's opening (Gromeka [in Tolstoy, Anna Karenina]; Dostoevsky, *Polnoe sobranie* 25: 186–90; Jackson, "On the Ambivalent Beginning" 345–52). Shklovsky takes the emphasis on divine judgment one step further, seeing Anna as the victim of society and Tolstoy as indicting that society for its usurpation of that judgment (436). Locating the source of the epigraph in Schopenhauer, Eikhenbaum reads Anna's fate in terms of Schopenhauerian ethics (*Tolstoi in the Seventies* 195–204). Mandelker and Kujundžić see Tolstoy as exploiting textual echoes from the epigraph's different sources and creating a tension among them, a tension mainly between Old and New Testament morality, which Tony Tanner suggests is an important dynamic in the novel of adultery and in *Anna Karenina* in particular (Mandelker, *Framing* 44–47; Kujundžić 65–68; Tanner 12–13). Mandelker also points out the frequent citation of the quotation in English novels (read by Tolstoy), where cuckolded husbands are encouraged to forgive their adulterous wives (45).

As we discuss the critical debate, I ask the students what they believe to be the true source of the epigraph and how important, or indeed possible, they believe it is to determine that source. Tolstoy truncates the quotation from Romans, removing the words "Thus saith the Lord." We know it is a quotation, but by whom it is spoken and what the context is remain unclear. Do the previous contexts interact? Could Tolstoy be invoking all the previous utterances at different times during his novel? A Pauline interpretation of the epigraph seems to apply in the situation of Karenin, whose desire for vengeance against his wife for her adultery is converted into the forgiveness he extends to her when she is dying in childbirth. But as Karenin falls deeper into religious dogma, he moves away from forgiveness. If Anna's death suggests punishment for adultery and Old Testament morality, why do Stiva Oblonsky and Betsy Tverskaya go unpunished for the same crime? Quick to suggest a particular interpretation of the epigraph, Tolstoy is as quick to violate it. Is the epigraph really a clue to reading the novel, or is it a narrative stooge? A sphinx? Tolstoy's last laugh on us?

To untangle the web of meanings surrounding the epigraph I return to my earlier question: What happens to the meaning and authority of a biblical quotation when it enters the messy, chaotic world of the different human discourses that make up a novel? To discuss the question of authoritative discourse in a novelistic context, I introduce Mikhail Bakhtin's concept of "absolute language" as developed by Gary Saul Morson (*Hidden* 5–36). In his reading of Tolstoy, Morson describes absolute language as discourse that refuses to be paraphrased, insisting on its authority, and that refuses to enter into dialogue with other statements. The prime example of such discourse is the biblical commandment. It brooks no opposition and countenances no historical excuses. It is the antithesis of the language of the novel, which, for Bakhtin, is always colored by the identity of the speaker and the social and historical context of its utterance. Like Tolstoy's epigraph, absolute language obscures or denies its authorship, thus avoiding the irony of origins, the possibility that if the context of an utterance, its speaker, the hidden motivation behind the utterance, were revealed, the authority of the utterance could be weakened. What happens to absolute language when it is placed in a novel? And what happens to a novel that seems to rest on an instance of absolute language?

As we read further, I ask the students to look out for references to the epigraph and echoes of the absolute language of the novel's opening. We find the epigraph's message restated many times by different characters: in particular by Annushka, Anna's maid; by Princess Varvara Oblonskaya; and by Koznyshev. Annushka's reference to the idea of divine rather than human judgment is uttered to Dolly while Dolly is visiting Anna and Vronsky at Vozdvizhenskoe: "Is it for us to judge?" (559; pt. 6, ch. 19). The maid's refusal to judge is contrasted to Dolly's dismay at being overshadowed by Anna's smart new maid and discomfort at hearing Annushka speak her mind. What effect does it have on the sense of moral authority when absolute language is recast in the words of an uneducated servant? Why does Tolstoy choose to have the message of his epigraph articulated partially and weakly by an unreliable witness at a moment when the authoritative viewpoint, in this case Dolly, is belabored by other concerns?

Similarly we see Princess Varvara's insistence that "It is for God to judge them, not for us" (562; pt. 6, ch. 20) in the context of her lack of authority. Dolly, here fulfilling the role of moral barometer and narrative viewpoint, dislikes and distrusts Varvara, suspecting her of using Anna's position as social outcast in order to find an advantage for herself. Koznyshev's statement that "It is not for us to judge, Countess" (704; pt. 8, ch. 4) can be seen as a refusal to engage with thorny moral problems beyond an abstract intellectual level. Moreover Tolstoy has Koznyshev articulate the words of the epigraph when his authority is at its weakest: after the failure of his book.

Thus we trace the message of the epigraph as it is colored by each particular context in which it appears, losing its absolute quality as it departs further from the original words of God and is restated by a variety of characters. The epigraph becomes increasingly problematic, complicated by the chaotic world of human interactions and discourses that form Tolstoy's novelistic subject.

I return to the question, Where does the novel begin? The students begin to sense the complexity of the novelistic frame as a meeting point of extratextual, intertextual, and intratextual discourses. The original authority of the word of God becomes more distant, less absolute. But it is not forgotten. The word of God brings a possibility of universal moral law to the novel, even as that law becomes a product of novelistic discourse; issues forth from the mouths of characters with limited authority; and is affected by particular social, historical, human contexts.

Thus, the opening of the novel is highly unstable, passing a moral code through a variety of filters that seem either to mock or to violate it. I suggest that the violations may be part of Tolstoy's novelistic mission, and I use this issue to discuss the nature of the realist novel.

As we enter *Anna Karenina*, we immediately sense a tension between the divine order of the epigraph and the disordered life of post-Fall human beings as embodied in the first paragraph by Stiva Oblonsky. The novelist, embarking on his task, must turn his attention not to a divine order or to the partial order of the happy families of the first sentence but to the world of difference and disorder, the unhappy families, those who break the paradigm. At the very outset it is those who don't fit who are seen to be the novelist's subject, through the direct movement from the unhappy families of the aphorism to the fictionalized unhappy family of Stiva Oblonsky. Just as Tolstoy's use of the biblical epigraph and its thematization in the novel demonstrate the instability of any universal and divine moral order in his novelistic universe, so the collapse of the structural order of the aphorism in the novel that follows illustrates the infection of order by the human, novelistic, chaotic element.

Yet perhaps it is this very tension between divine order and human disorder, between absolute language and novelistic discourse, between intertextual and intratextual relationships—a tension that enters the narrative voice at the opening of *Anna Karenina*—that characterizes the realist novel's troubled and complex relation to the world that it purports to represent.

The Night Journey:
Anna Karenina's Return to Saint Petersburg

Robert Louis Jackson

> [Dante's] dramatic situations are not lapses from his sub-
> ject; they are his moral subject given in images of action.
> [. . .] The "scenes" in Hell are the true demonstrations of
> the nature of error. They *are* "experience"—and as such
> properly contain the clues to all general ideas.
> —Irma Brandeis, *The Ladder of Vision:*
> *A Study of Dante's Comedy*

Anna's night journey to Saint Petersburg (pt. 1, ch. 29) is one of the great tran-
sitional moments in her drama (Wasiolek, *Tolstoy's Major Fiction* 134–36;
Gustafson 302–09; Mandelker, *Framing* 130–40). Her experience dramatizes a
state of intense moral and psychological conflict in which a powerful passion
crashes through a barrier of will and conscience. Tolstoy's account of this internal experience is remarkable for its representation of Anna's crisis in epic terms.
The battle engages her entire being, physical, psychological, moral, and spiritual, drawing in her immediate surroundings and nature in the broadest sense
of the term.

In Tolstoy's view, we are never separate from the world around us. We are inextricably a part of reality: we relate to it consciously and unconsciously; it participates in our moods, choices, and decisions. There is the fatality of individual
human character, to be sure, but chance and circumstance, playing at its edges,
ever seeking an entrance, probe and test our defenses, our strengths and weaknesses, our uncertainties and ambiguities, thus measuring what we are and
defining our ever shifting margins of freedom. We are free but within limits.
Tolstoy's art and vision are based on this recognition.

Anna is free and therefore responsible. Yet as this scene discloses almost
from its first line, she is increasingly ravaged by the opposite pulls of her nature:
overflowing energy and moral awareness, a sense both for what is right and
good and for what she feels is good for her. In this respect, she embodies the
human dilemma of all people at all times. One thing is certain: for Tolstoy, actions have consequences.

Anna's journey into the night begins with the words "Well, that's all over,
thank God!" (91; pt. 1, ch. 29).[1] Anna is referring to her encounter with Vronsky
in Moscow.

Two thoughts come to mind with respect to this exclamation: first, nothing is
ever completely over or finished, least of all when a passion or obsession is involved. Where temptation and moral conflict are concerned, the moment of

imagined freedom is often the moment of greatest vulnerability and danger. Such is the case with Raskolnikov in Fyodor Dostoevsky's *Crime and Punishment* when, after his nightmare, he says to himself, "Thank God, it's only a dream!" and, a short while later, exclaims, "Freedom, freedom! He is free from that spell . . . from the temptation."[2] Yet he is not free, as his fervent prayer for help attests: "Lord! . . . Show me my way, and I'll renounce this cursed . . . dream of mine" (50, 51; pt. 1, ch. 5). God helps those who help themselves.

Anna thanks God a second time at the end of the first paragraph: "Thank God, to-morrow I shall see Serezha and Alexey Alexandrovich again, and my good and accustomed life will go on as of old" (91). Here, again, her feeling of release or freedom from the passion that has taken root in her is deceptive. She has not reflected seriously on her real feelings for Vronsky, on her actions in Moscow, or on what lies beneath her "good and accustomed life."

Every aspect of ourselves, even the slightest gesture, Tolstoy believes, belongs to a unity of self. Anna is playing a cunning game with herself. The narrator mentions her "deft [lovkii] little hands" as they reach into her red bag. "Lovkii" here may be variously translated as "deft, dexterous, agile," but the word may also suggest "cunning." Anna's deft hands (in this scene her hands are very expressive of her feelings) at this moment suggest something of her evasive state of mind, her inability to face her feelings squarely. These same deft hands take out from her bag "a paper-knife and an English novel,"[3] both of which will play a role in her inner drama.

She settles down and tries to read the novel . . . But to grasp fully her slow descent into a state of profound, if momentary, mental and physical turmoil, one must take into account not only what is on her mind, or just beneath its surface, but also the somewhat eerie and disorienting environment in which she finds herself: surroundings that seem at once to impress themselves on her inner world and, increasingly, to express what is going on in that world.

The "semi-light" or "semi-darkness" (the narrator uses both phrases) of the train compartment (91; pt. 1, ch. 29) mimics a marginal world of consciousness, one precariously balanced between reality and dream. The invalid and two other women in the compartment; the noise of the train and the bustle of people passing through; the muffled conductor on his way through the train, covered with snow on one side; the maid Annushka, with her broad hands and a hole in one of her gloves; the snatches of conversation; the movement of the cars; the erratic changes in heat and cold in the compartment; and the talk of "an awful snow-storm [. . .] raging outside"—all this not only distracts Anna but also enters into her anxious mental state. As though to underscore the unsettling impact of her surroundings, the narrator reiterates:

> And so it went on and on: the same jolting and knocking, the same beating of the snow on the window-pane, the same rapid changes from steam-

ing heat to cold, and back again to heat, the gleam of the same faces through the semi-darkness, and the same voices—but at last Anna began to read and to follow what she read.   (91)

"My good and accustomed life will go on as of old," Anna had remarked complacently as she settled down in her seat. However, the unsettling experience of the train and the railroad itself, of this invention of modern industrial capitalism tearing into and tearing up the old agricultural and patriarchal way of life of Russia—an essential ingredient in Tolstoy's conception of the tragedy of Anna in general—portends a different outcome.[4]

Seated in the semidarkness of the compartment, Anna tries to make her way into the uncut pages of an English novel. "At first she could not read" ("Pervoe vremia ei ne chitalos'" [*Polnoe sobranie* 18: 106]), and only later "began to read and to follow what she read" (92; "stala chitat' i ponimat' chitaemoe").[5] Anna is not actively reading, or only a part of her is reading. (For discussion of Anna as a reader, see Sloane, this volume.) Her attention is drawn to what is going on around her. Finally, however, "she read and understood, but it was unpleasant to read." Anna wants to live. "She was too eager to live herself" ("Ei slishkom samoi khotelos' zhit'"). This phrase in Russian (*ei khotelos'*), an impersonal reflexive form of the verb "to want" that is used four times (Gustafson 305), not only underscores Anna's desire but also suggests a drive to live that is almost outside her. "But there was nothing to be done, so she forced herself to read, while fingering [perebiraia] the smooth little paper-knife" (92).

The paper knife first appears as a utility tool that cuts a path into the romantically engaging English novel. The instrument, however, fits Anna's hands, as it were, lending itself to her deep psychic needs and desires. Her restless fingering of the paper knife speaks of her frustrated desire to make her way into a novel or romance of her own life. "She was too eager to live herself. [. . .] But there was nothing to be done."

What she desires arouses in her a feeling of shame. The question of shame comes up in connection with the English novel and its hero. "The hero of the novel had nearly attained to his English happiness of a baronetcy and an estate, and Anna wanted to go off to the estate with him, when suddenly she felt that he must have been ashamed, and that she was ashamed of the same thing,—but what was he ashamed of? 'What am I ashamed of?'" asks Anna, opening up a dialogue with herself (92). Tolstoy, master of the interior monologue—so often consisting of a dialectic of inner voices disclosing and advancing conflict—opens the processes of Anna's troubled consciousness and conscience.

She conflates the hero and heroine in the English novel with herself and Vronsky. She challenges herself over her shame; indignant, she asks herself, "What am I ashamed of?" "She put down her book, leaned back, and clasped the paper-knife tightly in both hands. There was nothing to be ashamed of," comes the answer. Appropriately, this declaration of her freedom from shame directly follows the observation that she was clasping the paper knife tightly in both hands—an advance beyond merely fingering it.

The paper knife in Anna's hands now seems to give expression not only to her restlessness and impatience but also to her will to self-empowerment. The gripping hands point to the destructive character of her passion (Wasiolek, *Tolstoy's Major Fiction* 135). What is implicit here is not only the defiance of social convention but the destruction of family life as a consequence of arbitrarily making her way out of family life and entering another novel or romance of adultery. The pen knife as metaphor unites Anna's physical and mental action of reading, the narrative action of the English novel, and her overpowering will to life—a will that in the nature of things must involve the cutting of bonds. ·

On the note of no shame, Anna sorts through ("perebrala" [*Polnoe sobranie* 18: 107]) her Moscow recollections. "They were all good and pleasant." Tolstoy's use of the verb *perebrat'*—earlier used in its imperfective form to describe Anna fingering or toying with the paper knife but now used in the related sense of sorting out or sifting through recollections—is not accidental. Anna undergoes a process of remembering, or more tangibly working her way toward, the source of her restless feelings and desires: her passionate attraction to Vronsky.

The Anna who has just expressed her freedom from shame now recalls her "good and pleasant" Moscow stay.

> She recalled the ball and Vronsky and his humble, enamoured gaze, and their relations with one another; there was nothing to be ashamed of. And yet at that very point of her recollections when she remembered Vronsky, the feeling of shame grew stronger and some inner voice seemed to say to her, "warm, very warm, hot!" "Well, what of it?" she finally said to herself with decision, changing her position on the seat.   (92)

Increasingly Tolstoy suggests the interaction of heat in the compartment and erotic heat in Anna's consciousness. The heat on the train seems to prompt her words and passion as she moves closer to the source of her alternating feelings of shame and defiance. Again Tolstoy, master psychologist, points to the subtle interplay of the objective and subjective worlds, of the physiological and psychological. He also points to the sometimes imperceptible pressures that external experience or phenomena, at critical moments and in the way of chance, may have on the subtle oscillations of an inner conflict.

"Warm, very warm, hot": to this conventional phrase that in the ubiquitous guessing game announces that the player is getting closer and closer to the truth, that is, closer to guessing some place, object, or phenomenon; to this inner voice Anna, resolutely shifting in her seat, answers with a phrase that suggests that she knows very well what the matter is about but doesn't care: "Nu, chto zhe?"(*Polnoe sobranie* 18: 107)—an expression in Russian that may be translated as, "Well, so what?" or "Well, what of it!"

The guessing-game words do not prelude a disclosure. They constitute the disclosure: erotic heat, passion. ("Hot" here is a translation of the Russian *go-riachii*, a word that may also be translated as "burning" or "passionate.")

Anna's "Well, so what?" or "What of it?" both concedes the reality of her erotic interest and defiantly embraces it. And yet with a degree of uncertainty Anna still asks herself at this point, "What does this mean? Am I really afraid to look straight at it?" And again, as though taking a good look at the matter, she responds again, "Well, what of it?" She then discloses what is on her mind: "Is it possible that there exists, or could exist, between me and this officer-boy any relations differing from those with other acquaintances?" She smiles "disdainfully and again took up her novel; but now she absolutely could not understand what she was reading" (92). The narrative of her own life has blotted out the fictional world of reading. A relationship between a married woman and an officer boy strikes her as incongruous. Yet incongruities lie at the root of life. Anna herself wishes to relive her youth.

She asks whether sexual relations exist or could exist between her and Vronsky. The use of the present tense in the first part of the phrase suggests that an erotic relationship already exists between her and Vronsky, that is, she clearly has experienced an erotic attraction to him.

She smiles disdainfully at the idea, yet thoughts, emotions, questions, and answers follow rapidly on each other in her mind. Her smile dissolves almost instantly into another kind of feeling, an awareness that marks a resolution of her internal dialogue. This new feeling is accompanied by a gesture with the paper knife: "She passed her paper-knife over the window-pane, then pressed its cold smooth surface against her cheek and almost laughed aloud, suddenly overcome with unreasoning joy" (92).

The paper knife, which at first served a concrete function as a paper cutter, then served figuratively as an embodiment of her restless desire to open a way to a romance of her own, then made manifest the destructive implications of her passion and will to self-empowerment, now in an organic way conveys to Anna the heat of her passion. Whether the warmth of her cheeks is the flush of shameful erotic awareness, the warmth of her body, or both—Tolstoy indeed is pointing again to the responsiveness of two temperatures to each other—the message is clear.

The testing of the cold blade against the warmth of her cheeks signals the moment when the heat of passion, the object of passion, and the acceptance of passion merge in Anna's consciousness. Anna embraces her shame, and shame becomes shameless. Her loud but suppressed cry of almost primitive joy preludes her breaking through the barrier of her inner sense of what is good or right (all that motivates her sense of shame) to her egoistic sense of what she feels is good for her. Ethical reality is momentarily lost in an aesthetic or sensual reality. The ideal unity between the good and the beautiful is sundered when the pull of passion triumphs.

The focus here is not primarily on the penknife as a phallic object or image. Tolstoy recognizes the universal sign and its significance in the realm of the

subconscious. He is not concerned with sexual imaging, however, but with relationships. He is interested, in this final appearance of the pen knife, in the way
it mediates the relation between mind and body, between the sensuous and
sensual, between the storm outside and the storm within; he is concerned with
depicting that moment when sexuality, suffusing Anna's whole being and consciousness, makes its age-old claims. It is the sublimation of the sexual object, of
phallic imaging, not its actualization or realization in explicit imaginative terms
that gives this episode its power.

Anna's deliriums, her hallucinations, or what we might for convenience's sake
call her nightmare, follow on her recognition and her joyful acceptance of her
sexuality, her shame, her passion for Vronsky. Her passion is the focal point of
her nightmare, but the nightmare itself centers on the conflict this passion
arouses in her, with her inner awareness of the consequences of her passion for
Vronsky. What we are witness to are the convulsions of conscience. The emotional climax of those convulsions is both a vicarious experience of sexuality and
a premonition of death—a premonition linked with her encounter with Vronsky
at the railroad station and her troubled reaction to the death of the guard.

There is, finally, the biological link that Tolstoy establishes between the pro-
creative sexual instinct and death: he alludes to it, for example, in "Father
Sergius" (1891). In the temptation scene of that story, the beautiful widow
Makovkina calls out to Father Sergius in his cell, "For God's sake! Oh, come to
me! I am dying, oh!" A moment earlier Sergius formulated the temptation he is
prey to with an image that shares with Makovkina's words a common subtext: "a
solitary couch is a coffin" (*Great Short Works* 524, 518). In the deepest biological sense, then, Tolstoy perceives the sexual drive as beyond good and evil; it
serves the laws of nature, the ineluctable rhythms of life and death. Procreation, not pleasure, governs sexuality, Tolstoy insists in *Anna Karenina* (for a
discussion of this episode, see Jackson, "Father Sergius" 471). Yet in the same
breath he recognizes that his beloved Anna, like every human being, moves
freely about within the iron triangle of desire, conscience, and the law of life.

Anna's struggle for and against her passion—her nightmare is about this
struggle—is complex. It is presided over by a living conscience; it is marked by
what Anna's sister-in-law Dolly Oblonsky calls Anna's way of looking at things
"too gloomy" ("slishkom mrachno" [*Polnoe sobranie* 19: 216]; 579; pt. 6, ch. 24)
and by what Princess Betsy (a person wholly disinclined to meditate on moral
issues) with irony calls Anna's inclination "to take things too tragically" (272; pt.
3, ch. 17). This complexity, Anna's whole nature, one that includes a fully awakened sexuality, manifests itself in her delirious inner turmoil. In respect of this
deep and essentially tragic nature, Anna is much the opposite of her brother,
Stephen Oblonsky (his dalliance with a former French governess is a focus of
attention at the beginning of the novel), a person of good heart but shallow nature, a man in whom the erotic drive is also powerful but, unlike in Anna, transparent and trivial.

Anna's experience of joy quickly passes into an experience of disorientation, delirium, and terror. Tolstoy conveys the implications of her distress in lines of extraordinary artistic and psychological power and depth:

> She felt that her nerves were being stretched like strings drawn tighter and tighter round pegs. She felt her eyes opening wider, her fingers and toes nervously moving, and something inside her stopping her breath, and all the forms and sounds in the swaying semi-darkness around struck her with unusual vividness. Momentary doubts kept occurring in her mind as to whether the train was moving forwards or backwards, or standing still. Was it Annushka who was sitting beside her, or a stranger? "And am I here, myself? Am I myself or another?" She was afraid of giving way to this oblivion [zabyt'ë]. Something seemed to draw her to it, but she could at will yield to it or resist. To get over it she rose, threw off her wrap, and took off the cape of her coat. She came to her senses for a moment, and knew that the lean peasant in the nankin coat with a button missing who had come into the compartment was the carriage stoker and was looking at the thermometer, and that the wind and snow rushed in when he opened the door; but afterwards everything again became confused. . . .   (92–93)[6]

The transition in Anna to a new perception of herself and life, the overcoming of moral resistance in herself to her involvement with Vronsky, takes on the form of violent and chaotic sensations that seize her entire being. The implications of her passion are traumatic. She experiences her choice in the form of an almost delirious disorientation. The storm of sensory experience around her, like the furious wind and snow that bursts into the train in the wake of the peasant-stoker who has come to check the thermometer, not only symbolizes her disorientation but also contributes to her inner turmoil.

In all this chaos of dying and birth, it would seem that Anna is at the mercy of an implacable determinism, at the mercy of elements, internal and external, driving her into a new world of judgment and experience. Yet the elements that participate in this upheaval (and chance plays a role here) express both her elemental breakthrough to a new state of consciousness and her conflict and resistance. Anna is not a victim. She is conscious of her freedom throughout (Browning 329). "She was afraid of giving way to this oblivion. Something seemed to draw her to it, but she could at will yield to it or resist ("i ona po proizvolu mogla otdavat'sia emu i vozderzhivat'sia" [*Polnoe sobranie* 18: 108]).

I have translated Tolstoy's "po proizvolu" as "at will." *Proizvol* has roughly three distinct though related meanings in Russian: one's own choice, desire; self-will (*svoevolie*); arbitrariness. Tolstoy's use of this phrase is marked by calculated ambiguity. In the context, Anna can freely choose to yield to oblivion (*zabyt'ë*) or to resist it. Yet the phrase also suggests that yielding to oblivion involves a certain anarchic self-will. If, as we read the passage silently or out loud, we take in as a unity the first semantic unit—"ona po proizvolu mogla otda-vat'sia emu"—we become aware of the meaning of *proizvol* as "self-will" or "arbitrariness" (we might translate thus: "out of self-will she could yield to [oblivion]"). As we read on, however and take in the phrase "i vozderzhivat'sia" ("or resist"), thereby forming a new and larger semantic unit, our understanding of the word *proizvol* reverts to the idea of "at will," that is, to the idea of freedom to choose.

Using the Russian phrase *po proizvolu* with its variant meanings to convey Anna's thought processes, Tolstoy encapsulates the conflicting pulls in her, strains that find expression, as we have noted, in such strange sensations as "whether the train was moving forwards or backwards" or in her wondering who was sitting beside her or whether she was herself or somebody else. Anna fears giving way to this oblivion, that is, to the condition of a person who has lost a sense of her whereabouts or relation to what is going on around or in her. The Russian word for oblivion also evokes the terror of forgetting that she is married.

Anna, then, still possesses moral freedom, though this freedom (as with all freedom) is not unconditional, not absolute.[7] It is manifested in her awareness that she can yield to or resist the forces drawing her into the abyss, but it is also—her moral consciousness, her agonizing choice—the storm she experiences, her disorientation, her terror.

"But afterwards everything again became confused. . . ." ("no potom opiat' *vse smeshalos´* . . ." [*Polnoe sobranie* 18: 108; emphasis mine]): these words form the gateway to the dramatic and ominous climax of Anna's nightmare. The first time the narrator uses the phrase "vse smeshalos'" ("everything was confused") is in the second paragraph of *Anna Karenina*: "Everything was [in confusion] in the Oblonsky's household" (1; "Vse smeshalos' v dome Oblonskikh" [3]). The painful dismemberment of the family (the body, the body of the family household; on the symbolic plane, the church and its congregation) constitutes the subtext of the opening two paragraphs of the novel, which introduce, as we have noted, the infidelity of Stephen Oblonsky and its familial consequences.[8] Not without reason do the words "everything was in confusion" prelude the ominous ending of Anna's hallucinations, one marked by a sense of almost apocalyptic chaos, dismemberment and destruction.

> Everything was in confusion. . . . The peasant in the long coat started gnawing at something on the wall; the old woman began stretching her legs the whole length of the carriage and filled it with a black cloud; then something squeaked and clattered in a dreadful manner, as if some one were being torn to pieces; then a blinding red light appeared, and at last everything was hidden by a wall. Anna felt as if she had fallen through the floor. But all this did not seem dreadful, but gay. The voice of a man wrapped up and covered with snow shouted something just above her ear. She rose and came to herself [. . .].   (93)

These lines—the images of the black cloud and the red fire, the dreadful screech and clatter, the sense of somebody "being torn to pieces," and the wall (death) blanking out everything—clearly point back to the terrible accident at the railroad station (58–59; pt. 1, ch. 18), an accident that so morbidly affected Anna ("It is a bad omen" [60]) precisely in the context of her nascent interest in Vronsky. In this accident a muffled guard, on the tracks, is caught unawares and crushed by a train. The same lines depicting Anna's hallucination also point forward to the "darkness" ("mrak" [*Polnoe sobranie* 19: 348]) of her state of mind before her suicide and to her dismemberment at a railroad station (695; pt. 7, ch. 31). Her death is closely linked with the unraveling of her relationship with Vronsky and with the destruction of the family.

Death images dominate the climax of Anna's hallucinations. Every detail in Tolstoy's art carries meaning. The mysterious old lady ("starushka" [*Sobranie* 8: 116]) of Anna's hallucination "began stretching her legs the whole length of the carriage." The Russian phrase "protiagivat' nogi"—to stretch out, to extend one's legs (forward), also may mean, colloquially, "to turn up one's toes," that is, to die. Stretched out the full length of the railroad carriage, the old lady lies as in a coffin. The symbolic message of the old woman of Anna's hallucination and of the black cloud is death.

Tolstoy's image of the old woman is probably an allusion to Baba the Bony-Legged One, the notorious sorceress of Slavic mythology. Baba Yaga, as she is known, lives in a forest in a hut that stands on chicken legs; it is surrounded by a fence of human bones and skull heads. She likes to eat people and is, consequently, continually trying to stuff them into her oven. Vladimir Ia. Propp suggests that the reason Baba Yaga's head, body, and legs fill the hut is not because she is large but because—appropriate to her role as guardian of the realm of death—she lives in a coffin (70–71). The old woman of Anna's hallucination echoes the fat woman who at the beginning of part 1, chapter 29, talks about the heat as she wraps up her legs. The railroad carriage is of course coffin-shaped, and, as we have noted, the railroad in *Anna Karenina* (as in Tolstoy's later work "The Kreutzer Sonata") is, both as symbol and social phenomenon, an embodiment of death and destruction.

Anna instinctively comprehends the images of death in her dream, but their full message does not reach her in her conscious state. After a massive inner conflict over her passion, she falls. Figuratively speaking, she dies; her death, however, is also rebirth, but in a fallen state . . .

Her recognition of her desire for transgression begins with "unreasoning joy" and is quickly replaced by feelings of terror; in turn, her terror, at the end, abruptly is replaced by an unnatural sense of gaiety. This strange levity would seem simultaneously to symbolize both her denial of and delight in her fall. "But all this [experience of falling] did not seem dreadful, but gay." The account of her night journey ends on not a falling but a rising note. Her state of mind seems artificially illuminated, like the station platform.

The train arrives at a station. Anna steps out onto the platform where the whistling wind disputes with her over whether she should go out of the door of the carriage or whether it, the wind, should go in. "And this too struck her as gay" (93). She steps out into the fresh air: the wind whistles gaily "and tried to seize and carry her off." We have here a final reminder of what Anna's internal storm has accomplished and of the euphoric feelings it has paradoxically engendered in her. She has arrived at a new station in her life. "With enjoyment she drew in full breaths of the snowy, frosty air as she stood beside her carriage looking round at the platform and the lighted station." Does she, like Raskolnikov after his nightmare, feel inwardly free of her temptation and obsession? Whatever the answer, her meeting with Vronsky on the same station platform only moments later makes it clear that she is not at all free. "Her face beamed with a joy and admiration she could not repress" (94; pt. 1, ch. 30).

What connection, we may ask in conclusion, is there between the beginning of chapter 29—"Well, that's all over, thank God!"—and its end? We can, indeed, say at the end of the chapter that everything is over: not her relations with Vronsky, however, but her "good and accustomed life," a life that until now has taken a routine and familiar course. That particular chapter in the novel of her life has come to an end. A new chapter will open, just as a new one has begun for Vronsky, a man who, unlike Anna, is not inclined to view things tragically. This new drama, involving Anna, Vronsky, Karenin, and her son Serezha, among many others, will be not routine or simple in character but fatefully complicated; it will bring Anna into conflict with society and herself; it will finally lead her to the realization that one cannot get away from oneself (689; pt. 7, ch. 30).

For the moment, however, "all this did not seem dreadful, but gay," remarks the narrator immediately after her fall. We have a hint of the future in the line that follows this remark: "The voice of a man wrapped up and covered with snow shouted something just above her ear" (93). What this man, a conductor or trainman, literally shouts into her ear is not of significance to us; what this same cloaked man, clearly a fate figure in the novel, shouts into her unhearing ear she will learn in the final moments of her life, when "the candle, by the light of which she had been reading that book filled with anxieties, deceptions, grief, and evil, flared up with a brighter light than before, lit up for her all that had before been dark, flickered, began to grow dim, and went out for ever" (695: pt. 7, ch. 31)

NOTES

An earlier version of this essay was published under the title "Anna Karenina's Return to St. Petersburg," *Life and Text: Essays in Honour of Geir Kjetsaa on the Occasion of His Sixtieth Birthday*, ed. Erik Egeberg et al. (Oslo: Meddelelser, 1997), 159–68.

[1]My quotations from the Maude translation of *Anna Karenina* are occasionally emended for the purposes of closer analysis of the text.

[2]We have here an interesting version of Dostoevsky's use of the indirect narrative

style, one that in this instance underscores Raskolnikov's distance from the reality of his inner, unrecognized inclinations.

[3]"Razreznoi nozhik"—a little paper knife or paper cutter (*nozhik* is a diminutive for *nozh* ["knife"]), used for slitting uncut pages.

[4]For an analysis of Anna's meeting with Vronsky at the railroad station and the role of the railroad in Tolstoy's ideological design of *Anna Karenina*, see my "Chance and Design."

[5]The use of impersonal or passive constructions (*chitalos´, chitaemoe*) in the Russian original accents the passive character of Anna's reading, her distraction or detachment.

[6]*Zabyt´ë* ("oblivion") is linked etymologically with *zabyt´* ("to forget"); it may refer to a half-conscious state, oblivion, a drowsy state, or a moment of distraction or separation from surroundings, as when in excitement people lose track of their whereabouts or of what is going on around them.

[7]Tolstoy broadly develops this idea in his historical-philosophical discourse in the second epilogue of *War and Peace*.

[8]The dismemberment of Anna at the end of the novel is only the last act of this tragedy, just as the disfigured corpse of the guard at the Moscow railroad station is the first harbinger of Anna's death. See the discussion of the importance of the first and second paragraph of the novel in my article "On the Ambivalent Beginning."

Anna's Dreams

Thomas Barran

Although for decades Sigmund Freud has drawn fire from literary critics, ideologists, and even psychologists, college students can benefit from the study of his ideas, since they provide the foundation for the psychoanalytic approach to literary criticism over the last century. Applying the Freudian method of dream interpretation to *Anna Karenina* accomplishes two things at once: it familiarizes students with an early and important component of Freud's psychoanalytic theory, and it encourages them to probe more deeply into Tolstoy's text.

The pre-Freudian dreamers in *Anna Karenina*—Anna herself, Stiva Oblonsky, and Alexey Vronsky—share the belief that dreams have meaning, and that the dreaming mind is doing more than merely discarding accumulated impressions of the previous day or randomly firing its neurons. These characters react seriously and emotionally to their dreams. They meditate on them and work hard to recall their details, although they lack the sophisticated methods of analysis and interpretation that the various schools of twentieth-century psychology have given us. Tolstoy marks the importance of dreams in his novel with prominent placement and recurrence, with vivid accounts of his characters' emotional reactions to them, and with his uncanny mimesis of actual dreaming in the descriptions of his characters' nocturnal visions. He involves readers, willingly or involuntarily, in the task of deciphering these baffling mental events. Since Freud employs many of the techniques of literary hermeneutics in his *Interpretation of Dreams* (1900), he provides a systematic and productive way of extracting meaning from the dreams in *Anna Karenina*, whether or not one accepts its results. Of course, instructors must emphasize that the dreamers are characters in a novel, not patients undergoing analysis. Instructors should also caution students to suspend judgment about the final validity of any one interpretation and to keep in mind as well that Tolstoy predated Freud. It helps to tell students that Freud himself described dream images as overdetermined and multivalent.

Instructors can encourage ambitious students to read *The Interpretation of Dreams*, one of Freud's more accessible works, but others in the class can benefit from a summary of Freud's theory of dreaming, such as the one that follows. Freud assumed that the content of a dream invariably contained a representation, usually disguised, of a wish fulfillment and that the wish could be identified from the remembered parts of the dream either by an analysis of the mental associations the dreamer provides or by an interpretation of the dream's images—the notorious "Freudian symbols." According to this theory, dreaming takes place on two levels, each of which produces a different type of content: the unconscious wishes that stimulate the dream comprise the "latent content," while the "manifest content" consists of the conscious material the dreamer witnesses subjectively while asleep and remembers after awakening. The manifest content actually originates in the latent content but acquires its peculiar character from the way in which the mind disguises material that might prove threatening to the dreamer's psychological stability if experienced directly.

In the process by which latent content becomes manifest, which Freud calls the "dream work," the mind transforms the unconscious meaning of the dream by means of displacement and condensation. Displacement isolates a part of a whole idea or, conversely, supplies a whole context when only a part has latent significance; or it replaces one idea with another to which it is linked by associations. Condensation assembles unrelated dream material by semantic compression, so that a dream image in the manifest content can carry multiple meanings or a human presence can have several identities at once. The work of displacement clearly resembles the production in language of such rhetorical figures as metonymy and metaphor, while the process of condensation has much in common with the creation of literary symbolism.

An explanation of Freud's theory of dreaming, accompanied perhaps by some examples of interpretation, will prepare the class for an examination of the heroine's nocturnal visions. Once Anna consummates her affair with Vronsky, she has a dream that recurs almost every night:

> She dreamt that both [Karenin and Vronsky] at once were her husbands, and lavished their caresses on her. Alexey Alexandrovich wept, kissing her hands, saying: "How beautiful it is now!" and Alexey Vronsky was there too, and he also was her husband. And she was surprised that formerly this had seemed impossible to her, and laughingly explained to them how much simpler it really was, and that they were both now contented and happy. But this dream weighed on her like a nightmare, and she woke from it filled with horror.   (136; pt. 2, ch. 2)

Students may explain this dream by citing Freud's contention that all dreams contain wish-fulfillment fantasies and arguing that Anna's sleeping mind imagines the desired resolution of the terrible conflict between her love for Vronsky and the demands of her marriage. Others might mention her earlier triumph in Moscow—effecting the reconciliation of Stiva with his wife Dolly, who had discovered his affair with their French governess. In her dream, Anna applies her powers of persuasion to another adulterous situation and fulfills her need for approval by winning the gratitude and affection of the two men she has reconciled. Some might mention another kind of wish fulfillment, that of her desire to exert control and impose her will on the people around her, which she typically represses in order to maintain the passive attitude that her times and social milieu demanded of women. In her dream she appears as the bearer of superior wisdom, making peace between two weak and childish men and bringing peace, harmony, and beauty to the scene.

The instructor should point out that Anna would hardly awaken with such horror if the dream did not carry more threatening content than is apparent.

How does she interpret her dream? What disturbing wishes lurk in her unconscious, sending their traces into the condensed images of the manifest scene? Here, encouraging free association could elicit interesting explanations from the class: for example, given her tendency toward hasty self-accusation, Anna may infer that her sexual urges are abnormally strong, because she wants to have two men at once. Or she may be disgusted by the explicit physicality with which both Vronsky and Karenin "lavish their caresses on her," for now both are her husbands and can possess her sexually—a grotesque possibility when one considers that Karenin is old enough to be her father, while numerous places in the novel attest to a maternal component in her passion for Vronsky.

Here the teacher has an opportunity to explain that Freud's theory of the Oedipus complex applies to women as well. In her dream, Anna directs most of her seductive energies toward Karenin, who responds more demonstrably, while Vronsky appears in an afterthought (he was there, he was her husband too). In Tolstoy's descriptions of him, Karenin emerges as a less than attractive sexual partner, but as the embodiment of religious law and civic respectability he assumes paternal, even patriarchal, qualities. Numerous scenes in the novel demonstrate his significance as a father surrogate in Anna's psyche, and while we primarily overhear Anna tell Vronsky of her loathing toward Karenin, we must remember that she enjoyed eight years of marital intimacy with him before she met Vronsky. We must assume she feels, or felt, countervailing emotions of love, adoration, and incestuous desire that contribute to the kind of ambivalence a daughter feels toward her father in the conflicted family romance. This suggestion of incest would explain her horrified reaction to the dreams, for while she may be an adulteress, she still has rigid standards of personal morality, and any emergence of latent incestuous desires would suffice to turn this dream into a nightmare for her.

Anna's other recurring dream, which features an old peasant muttering French phrases while he alternately rummages around in a sack or manipulates some iron, has received much critical attention, both because it belongs to the cluster of railroad motifs so important to the novel and because it defies final explication. It offers an excellent opportunity for students to apply Freud's interpretive method by examining symbols and using free association. Anna describes the dream twice, once before she gives birth to Vronsky's child and once on the morning of the day of her death. In the first variant, she finds the old peasant in her bedroom, bent over and rummaging around in a sack, while he mutters in French, "It must be beaten, the iron, pulverized, kneaded. . . ." (329; pt. 4, ch. 3). Dreaming that she has awakened, she asks her husband's servant Korney to interpret what she has just seen, and he replies that it means she will die in childbirth. Awakening from a dream that contains a prediction of death in childbirth would be terrifying enough, but she describes her terror as beginning with the appearance of the old peasant.

The instructor or a student who has read *The Interpretation of Dreams* could point out that the sack belongs in Freud's category of female genital symbols.

Interestingly, Korney provides an interpretation consistent with Freudian symbolism when he predicts death in childbirth, for the peasant's hands have entered the uterus/sack while he speaks of destroying what it presumably contains. Even considered apart from Anna's pregnancy, the dream still represents the violation and contamination of her genitals by someone filthy and unkempt.

Why does the peasant speak French? A Russian peasant would not know French, but nearly everybody in Anna's social milieu uses it interchangeably with Russian. In certain instances, however, the narrator explicitly states that a character uses French, thereby marking its significance. Vronsky, for example, uses French when he tries to persuade Anna not to risk humiliation and scandal by going to the opera. Karenin, who seems to have the keenest sense of the differences between French and Russian and of the situations in which one would be more appropriate than the other, tells Anna in French that she behaved improperly by not concealing her emotions when she saw Vronsky and Frou-Frou fall at the horse race. When she admits her affair with Vronsky, Karenin writes her a letter dictating the conditions under which they could continue to live together, using French because its formal second person plural does not have the coldness that it does in Russian. French carries the sense of social obligation and duty—even the peasant repeats the phrase "*Il faut*"—"One must." Perhaps this presence of words signifying demands will lead a student to volunteer that Anna's dream predicts her destruction at the hands of a hypocritical and demanding social class that has no more rectitude than a filthy old peasant.

Instructors might ask about the bent-over position of the peasant. In the first version of Anna's dream, the peasant bends over a sack and mutters French words about iron, while in the second variant he bends over the iron *and* over her. What about Anna's physical position in the second dream? The peasant bends over the iron, but he holds it above Anna, so she must be crouched or supine beneath him. If the students can free their associative faculties, they may note the quality of iron's hardness and the obsessive attention the old man devotes to his manipulations and conclude that the picture suggests masturbation or intercourse. Anna emphasizes the peasant's utter indifference to her in the dream: to a woman who is not a willing participant, a man in a state of arousal during a sex act would appear to be so preoccupied with his own pleasure as not to recognize her presence.

Instructors could continue to elicit interpretations from the class, stressing that dreams, like literature, have no final answers. Alternatively, instructors could lead the discussion to a conclusion in the manner that Freud used when persuading his patients that their latent fantasies coincided with his psychological theories. They could begin with the question "Whom or what does the peasant represent?" The peasant is old; so is Karenin, relative to Anna and Vronsky. So are our fathers, relative to us. The peasant speaks French and talks about iron; Karenin reads French books and uses French perhaps more frequently and precisely than any other character. He also has a certain physical rigidity and remains unwilling to compromise; he has an iron will. If the peasant in her dreams represents her husband, Anna is taking a peculiar revenge by reducing him to a filthy peasant. Karenin was not born into a distinguished family, but he rose in his career through talent, education, and a capacity for hard work. By contrast, Anna's family, the Oblonskys, has princely status and can trace its ancestry back to Rurik, the Scandinavian founder of the dynasty that ruled Russia through the sixteenth century.

Instructors could offer a tentative interpretation for Anna's peasant dreams, according to which she lowers her husband's social status while creating a scenario in which he forces himself on her sexually, shapes the material that ultimately destroys her (the iron of the train), and tries to steal Serezha, the child of her womb, the real object he searches for in the uterine sack. Then, continuing in true Freudian manner, instructors could suggest that Anna's husband only masks the real object of her dreaming.

If Anna's nightmares about sexual violation follow the pattern of disguised wish fulfillment that Freud described in his *Interpretation of Dreams*, the latent content of her dreams could represent the desires she felt toward her real father during the oedipal phase of her sexual development. Since these desires must remain unconscious, her mind transforms her father into someone repulsive and filthy, associates him with her despised husband, and turns the incestuous act of love she desires into an impersonal violation, a contamination of her genitals. The wish present in the latent content emerges in the manifest content so successfully disguised that it inspires horror. If her nightmare indeed represents a disguised oedipal wish, its recurrence, combined with her actual marriage to a father substitute, points to unresolved oedipal conflicts in her psyche. Of all the secret desires her dreams exhibit—her wish to exercise her will, her need to dominate her men, her abnormally strong sexual urges—Anna's most powerful and poignant psychological dynamic may be her hunger for the love of her real father, Arkady Oblonsky.

The Moral Education of the Reader

Gina Kovarsky

There are critics who charge that in *Anna Karenina* Tolstoy sacrifices his moral integrity and his aesthetic principles to tendentiousness. In their view, he relinquishes sympathy for Anna in favor of judgment, jeopardizing the truthfulness of his vision. Thus D. H. Lawrence famously chastises his fellow novelist for suppressing "passional inspiration" for the sake of a "didactic purpose"—although Tolstoyan absolutism founders, Lawrence states, because the novel as a genre resists categorical thinking and "knocks all old Leo's teeth out" ("Novel" 180). The philosopher Lev Shestov similarly construes Tolstoy's moralism in *Anna Karenina* as an evasion of all that is vital and authentic in experience and therefore also as a form of self-betrayal. According to Shestov, Tolstoy attempted to forget the insufficiency of absolutes by transforming his fiction into a "sermon" (11). His psychological need to hide from the "insolubility of the tormenting problems of life" even shapes his plot: he destroys his heroine because her questions are too much like his own (69, 72).

The pedagogical approach suggested in this essay offers instructors and students an alternative, less agonistic way to consider how ethics and artistry bear on each other in *Anna Karenina*. While Lawrence and Shestov focus on a conflict within Tolstoy, I dwell instead on how the text transfers the conflict to its readers. When viewed from this angle, didacticism emerges as more deliberately productive of artistic and experiential complexity than Lawrence and Shestov allow. Students working with the analytic tools described below may observe that the author weaves didacticism into the fabric of his narrative, instructing readers each time he involves them in the characters' feelings and actions. As readers focus on textual structures that drive them to participate in the characters' dilemmas, they can recognize the subtlety of Tolstoy's method.

Students typically respond to Tolstoy's moral exercise by debating his perspective on his characters. Some may accuse Tolstoy of imposing his own standards on Anna in portraying her as largely culpable. Others will find that he places the greatest share of the blame for her situation on her milieu. Teachers can validate students' diverging reactions by referring to the history of the novel's reception, suggesting that critics have disagreed about, or been confused by, the author's attitude to his heroine because of contradictory evidence in the text. So great was the critical confusion early on that Tolstoy was driven to clarify his intentions in his well-known letter to Strakhov describing the novel as a "labyrinth of linkages" (*Polnoe sobranie* 62: 268-69). He was not only writing about "things that I like." He was seeking to embody an idea too complex to be conveyed by nonartistic means.

To explore a reading experience is to invoke the phenomenological approach to literature, which "lays full stress on the idea that, in considering a literary work, one must take into account not only the actual text but also, and in equal measure, the actions involved in responding to that text" (Iser, *Implied Reader* 274). The approach proposed here grounds itself in this idea. The teacher anchors part of each class in the close analysis of strategies that shape response, paying special attention to Tolstoy's creation of observer figures and textual mirrors for the reader. Instructors can adapt the suggestions in this essay to their own classroom contexts and levels, from the undergraduate survey course in the nineteenth-century novel to the advanced seminar on Tolstoy or on the theory of literature.

As a guide for classroom work, I describe some of Tolstoy's techniques for presenting the Oblonsky siblings, Stiva and Anna. In establishing a pattern for imitation, the author begins with a relatively simple case—Stiva's—and after baiting us but letting us off the hook, he continues to seduce us, enforces identification with the highly attractive, erring Anna, then dares us to extricate ourselves from her predicament without playing the hypocrite or stifling moral feeling. I concentrate here on the way characters are viewed through part 1, chapter 23 (the ball), but instructors and students can apply the same interpretive strategies to other episodes where represented observers or mirrors for the reader are attracted, even mesmerized, placed on their guard, but also morally implicated through identification. For example, this pattern informs the episode describing Anna's journey to Saint Petersburg (91–97; pt. 1, chs. 29–31), the chapters leading up to and including the steeplechase (168–83; pt. 2, chs. 23–25), and the scene in which Levin meets Anna under her portrait (630–35; pt. 7, chs. 9–10).

Structural, linguistic, and narrative elements that contribute to the text's infectious power reinforce the reader-oriented dynamic. These elements include the depiction of the very responses Tolstoy is hoping to elicit, "expressive syntax" (as Gustafson terms the linguistic and syntactic devices Tolstoy uses to make his characters' experiences contagious for the reader [379]), and the use of point of view. In treating episodes that draw the audience into an ambivalent response to the Oblonsky siblings and to their transgressions, the instructor can simultaneously address the author's complex discourse on art and his use of Platonic and Aristotelian theories of mimesis. Tolstoy manages to turn the aesthetic realm into an object of moral scrutiny, even as he induces readers to acknowledge the power of art's illusions and seductions.

The Reader's Experience of Stiva

As the novel begins, Stiva appears before us as a principal actor in a domestic farce, lamenting his predicament in theatricalized moans (2; pt. 1, ch. 1). To be sure, the author invites us to take stock of the character's moral flaws, but when students are asked how they responded in the opening chapters, they admit to being entertained. They thereby at least partially affirm the primacy of aesthetic over ethical criteria and join ranks with Stiva, who also evaluates his situation in aesthetic categories: he declares that the affair with the governess is "bad" not in moral terms but because there is "something banal, a want of taste, in carrying on with one's governess" (3; pt. 1, ch. 2).

Tolstoy in fact subtly engineers his reader's attraction to, sympathy for, and identification with Stiva Oblonsky. The opening chapters establish Stiva's carefully tended body as a source of pleasure for himself and others (1, 5, 7; pt. 1, chs. 1, 2, 3). With a small step, one may pass from enjoyment of the body to tolerance of the whole person. Indeed, it turns out that almost everyone smiles on recognizing Stiva: "there was something in him—in his handsome and bright appearance, his beaming eyes, black hair and eyebrows, and his pink-and-white complexion, that had a physical effect on those he met, making them feel friendly and cheerful. 'Ah! Stiva Oblonsky! Here he is!' said almost every one he met, smilingly" (13; pt. 1, ch. 5).

Readers may begin to take stock of a dangerously reflexive quality in this reaction but not before yielding to it themselves and not before entering into a conspiratorial tie with the fictional character on the model of Stiva's relationship with his valet Matthew (4; pt. 1, ch. 2).

In the dinner scene at the Angleterre Restaurant (30–39; pt. 1, chs. 10–11), the text returns to the pleasure observers experience in Stiva's company. Levin is drawn to gaze on Oblonsky, who continues to elicit approving smiles. The Russian text brings the audience into the scene by phonetically evoking the sounds involved in Stiva's consumption of the "quivering oysters" (32; pt. 1, ch. 10; in Russian, "shliupaiushchikh ustrits" [*Polnoe sobranie* 18: 39]). As we watch his enjoyment communicating itself to the represented observers, it is made palpable for us in the very texture of the language. Yet the passage ultimately interrupts the implied temptation of the reader by depicting the discomfort and withdrawal of the observing object of seduction.

Tolstoy's threefold strategy—enforcing attraction, creating ambivalent feelings of kinship, and establishing moral distance—works to complicate the reader's ethical experience. We are hard pressed to disown Stiva and Anna or to deny the power of the seductions to which they more or less willingly succumb and that they embody for others. The author compounds the moral complexity by eliciting not only understanding but also compassion for the heroine (e.g., during Anna's visit with her son Serezha [482–88; pt. 5, chs. 29–30]).

The Reader's Experience of Anna

Representing Stiva's lovely, elegant sister, Tolstoy intensifies the seduction while exploring the moral and spiritual costs of Anna's error and the alienating transformations it produces in her character. Meanwhile, as with Stiva, he invites us to analyze each layer of response by portraying observer figures who respond to Anna in the text. Central to his presentation of his heroine is the insistence on her mesmerizing physical effect on others. The text associates Anna with the loss of voluntary control and, in miming suggestibility and the surrender of will, itself becomes an instrument of suggestion. She arrests the observer's attention: Vronsky feels "compelled" to "have another look at her" (56; pt. 1, ch. 18) and finds himself "involuntarily" listening to her voice outside the carriage door. Her smile communicates itself to Vronsky, as her brother's did to Levin and many others: "Vronsky did not take his eyes off her, and kept smiling, *he knew not why*" (57; emphasis added). Yet more is at work than a surrender of control, for the hint of something kindred and the promise of acknowledgment are what compel Vronsky's second look: "he saw in her sweet face as she passed him something specially tender and kind. [. . .] Her bright grey eyes [. . .] rested for a moment on his face as if recognizing him" (56).

Instructors might want to dwell here on the crucial impact of narrative point of view in shaping the reader's response. Throughout the sequence where Anna is introduced (pt. 1, ch. 18), the narration presents her exclusively through the eyes of her admirer—as "Karenina." "Karenina" becomes "Anna" only at the end of the chapter, when she is alone with Oblonsky (60) and the narration allows readers to share the more intimate perspective of Anna's brother. Tolstoy's heroine becomes "Anna" in Vronsky's thinking immediately following the train journey back to Saint Petersburg that intensifies the connection between them (96; pt. 1, ch. 31). But it is only once the affair has been consummated that we hear him address her by her first name ("'Anna! Anna!' he said in a trembling voice. 'Anna, for God's sake! . . .' " [135; pt. 2, ch. 11]). To broaden the context for this discussion, instructors can refer students to Boris Uspensky's treatment of the role of naming in establishing point of view (20–32; Uspensky draws many of his examples from Tolstoy's *War and Peace*).

The narrative connects Anna's hypnotic effect to her "charm" (*prelest´*), a word as ambiguous in Russian as it is in English (Whitcomb). Tolstoy marks it in the novel through repetition, most obviously when he introduces Anna at the ball through Kitty's admiring gaze (72; pt. 1, ch. 22) or when he presents Anna and Vronsky's mutual seduction through Kitty's eyes (76; pt. 1, ch. 23). The repetition of "charming" in the second passage (seven times in one sentence) works hypnotically—like an incantation or magic charm—and in the readers' experience linguistically imitates Anna's effect on Kitty and Vronsky, while the recurrent use of this ambivalent word serves to destabilize the readers' relationship to the heroine. First seduced, then alienated, the readers also learn by seeing themselves in another ("in the mirror of Anna's face" [74]). Point of view once again plays a central role in the readers' moral education, ensuring that judgments make room for understanding.

Tolstoy on Mimesis

In Tolstoy's view, the artist teaches best who imparts a deeply felt experience of moral conflict, succeeding better than a polemicist who presents ready truths. As Tolstoy wrote in 1852, morally effective literary works elicit empathy only if readers "recognize in [a character] as many of their own weaknesses as they do their virtues; the virtues are optional; the weaknesses necessities" (*Polnoe so-*

branie 46: 145). His belief that error-centered didactic strategies elicit identification derives from Aristotelian and neo-Aristotelian theories of tragedy and reflects the same ethos. Indeed, the complex type of understanding afforded readers in the ball scene is a prerequisite for tragic catharsis. With Anna's story, Tolstoy brings us even closer to the heart of the tragic experience as Aristotle defined it in the *Poetics*. As one scholar explains, the "requirement that the character be like ourselves makes possible the *sympatheia*, the emotional identification which is necessary if we are to feel pity or fear" (Aristotle xxiii). Tolstoy reiterated in 1884 that, unless a work of art elicits "imitation" (podrazhatel'nost') by representing through "mimicry" (mimichnost') an error that the artist himself has committed and overcome, the work will fail to act on others (*Polnoe sobranie* 52: 127). His statement suggests that he viewed aesthetic experience as a two-way performance, during which an artist relives and an audience imitatively experiences moral struggle. His remarks show that for him aesthetic practice was closely involved with moral education.

Discussion of the ways Tolstoy models the reader's response may thus serve as a point of entry for instructors wishing to familiarize students not only with the author's thinking on art but also with ideas that have been central to literary theory since classical times. Noticing and keeping track of moments that elicit the contemplation of likenesses can lead students to consider the Aristotelian dimension in Tolstoy's poetics. Tolstoy's extended meditation on mimesis occurs in the portrait scene, where Anna's effect on Levin as mediated by her portrait closely conforms to the Aristotelian model of aesthetic response: he perceives her as fallible and pitiable (Mandelker, *Framing* 47, 113–15 and "Illustrate" 54, 59n2). The episode keeps in focus the moral dimension of aesthetic response by engaging also (somewhat paradoxically) with the Platonic vision of mimesis as dangerous because it is thrice-removed from the real and capable of inducing improper imitation (Plato, *Republic* 140–65 [bk. 3], 421–39 [bk. 10]). Students will recognize this Platonic argument as a reprise of the critique of dangerous aesthetic enchantment that Tolstoy had already begun in the passage describing Anna's reading of a novel on the train. (For more on Plato in Tolstoy, see Orwin, this volume.)

As students will become prepared to conclude, Tolstoy based the infection theory of art he set forth later in *What Is Art?* at least in part on his own experience as a writer. At the same time, the degree to which aesthetic response is subject to analysis in *Anna Karenina* also reveals his anxieties about art's relation to ethics. Thus, when he indirectly explores the mechanics of temptation and seduction as they relate to the aesthetic, he may be said to interrogate the reader's seduction, by art, into a view of life that values pleasure instead of moral work.

An emblematic vignette in the novel's penultimate chapter once again takes up the motif of mimesis. Kitty stages an "experiment" for Levin's benefit in which baby Mitya gives proof of awareness when he recognizes his mother and smiles but frowningly shakes his head at an unfamiliar female face (737; pt. 8, ch. 18). Kitty and Levin delight in the smile of recognition that indicates the baby has recognized "all his own people." Tolstoy has just been representing the deepening understanding in Levin of the way love binds him to other human beings, and in this context the child's recognition of family members carries special meaning. On a metaphoric plane, to recognize one's own people means of course to perceive oneself as connected to the human family. Therefore, the vignette represents as pivotal for human development the very experience that Tolstoy has made central in the moral education of his reader, the recognition of one's own kind (in the text's mirrors and portraits). At the same time, the vignette offers a somewhat disturbing commentary on the perils of constructing a community based on facile notions of identity. After all, society excludes Anna from its midst in part because she fails to conform to its norms. Throughout his novel, not only through the means described above but also through frequent allusions to the New Testament parable of the woman taken in adultery, Tolstoy forces his readers to recognize their similarity to those they might be tempted to judge, and thus to acknowledge the hypocrisy of casting stones.

While performing the analyses proposed above, students can fortify themselves against the temptation to simplify Tolstoy's moral vision in *Anna Karenina*. Although more than one critic has read backward from the late Tolstoy to find simplifying moralism at work in *Anna Karenina*, internal evidence shows that he constructed his novel to impart a sometimes discomfiting experience of ethical complexity. His initial presentation of Stiva sets the pattern for all future scenes where attraction, sympathy, and identification coexist in ambivalent equilibrium with moral judgment. By beginning the novel with Stiva, he begins to break down resistance to Oblonskian tendencies. The moral journey readers undertake leads them to acknowledge their pleasure-loving tendencies and, by extension, to surrender on one level to a vision of human beings as essentially determined and degraded by physical needs and wants. Such conclusions parallel those espoused by Anna during her final carriage ride (688; pt. 7, ch. 29). With another small step, one might accede, as Anna does, to self-loathing and contempt for the species. Yet all the while, Tolstoy guides us into a less deterministic view of the human condition. For him the effort of claiming one's moral freedom begins at the moment when one begins to attend to the ethics of response. Indeed, the process that sharpens self-awareness and moral consciousness is as important as any conclusion toward which he may have wanted to guide his audience. His letter to Strakhov about the impossibility of extracting a thought from its artistic embodiment in a structure of linkages suggests that the lesson of *Anna Karenina* inheres in, and is not separable from, the whole of the novel as the reader moves through it.

I have emphasized the pragmatic function of Tolstoy's reader-oriented cues, but the instructor can also dwell on the metaphoric dimension of the allusions to reading and interpretation that run through the novel. When Anna interprets the scenes of life from her carriage window (684–85; pt. 7, ch. 28; 687–88; pt. 7, ch. 29) or when Levin decides, after beholding the stable pattern of stars in the night sky, to invest the meaning of goodness into every instant (740; pt. 8, ch. 19), we are prompted to envision reading in the broadest sense, as a making sense of the human condition. The allusions to reading constitute a thread that guides us through Tolstoy's labyrinth toward an understanding of life's central task. This task is consistently depicted as the bringing to bear of awareness and conscience to a reading of life's "book" (695; pt. 7, ch. 31).

Students can take the initiative in discovering the patterns of response outlined above. They might keep a diary of their reactions to a character, identifying the point of view through which the narration is filtered in each instance and isolating cues that shape response, including repeated details like the characters' smiles (see Pursglove). The class could be divided into groups, each of which would follow Tolstoy's use of a particular strategy: embedded readers or observers, expressive syntax, shifts in point of view. Alternatively, each group might regularly report on a particular layer of response. A comparison of the finished novel with the author's drafts can yield further insight into his rhetorical intentions. (For those with no knowledge of Russian, Turner provides a useful summary in *A Karenina Companion* [187–204].) The class can delve more deeply into the problem of response by surveying the novel's critical reception (e.g., in Knowles, *Tolstoy*). Instructors might assign supplementary writings on the theory of narrative (Cohn; Uspensky) and reader response (Freund; Suleiman and Crosman; Tompkins) and suggest texts on the theory and practice of rhetorical criticism (Booth; Fish). Like Stanley Fish on Milton's *Paradise Lost*, Gary Saul Morson views didacticism from the point of view of the reader in his essay on Tolstoy's didactic poetics in the *Sebastopol Stories* ("The Reader"), although he comes to different conclusions about moral training in *Anna Karenina* ("Prosaics"). Students will learn a good deal about the reader-oriented dimension in Tolstoy's poetics from Gustafson (esp. 373–91) and gain additional perspectives on the role of embedded readers or observers in *Anna Karenina* from Amy Mandelker (*Framing* and "Illustrate"); Svetlana Evdokimova; and Robert Belknap. Finally, Kathryn Feuer's article situating Stiva against the topos of the dream of life can guide students into a broader understanding of the attractions and dangers of Oblonskyism.

NOTE

My thanks to *Tolstoy Studies Journal* for permission to use portions of my article "Mimesis and Moral Education in *Anna Karenina*."

Tolstoy Sees the Truth but Waits:
The Consequences of Aesthetic Vision in
Anna Karenina

Justin Weir

Tolstoy's *Anna Karenina* is not as overtly about painting as, say, Thomas Mann's *Doctor Faustus* is about music. Nevertheless there are three portraits of Anna in the novel, several scenes where looking is an activity charged with aesthetic and ethical implications, and two highly significant chapters that explicitly examine the artist Mikhaylov's theory of creativity. If we broaden the scope further, we will find seemingly everywhere Tolstoyan lessons about how and what to see. One cannot spend valuable course time on each scene that qualifies as visually aesthetic, however. We seem forced to choose: either introduce the rich but technically specific critical history of ekphrasis (the verbal description of visual art) or work somehow from the text itself. In most undergraduate courses the second, less theoretical, approach is more practical. One can use the text to show how a kind of visual aesthetics—how we judge ourselves, other people, and objects when we look at them—shapes our interpretation of the novel as it influenced Tolstoy's writing of it.[1]

For Tolstoy, the mercurial nature of the visual world makes it a poor model for epistemology; visual perception alone often impedes rather than facilitates accurate knowledge. Vision is generally better adapted for aesthetic truth seeking. By integrating social, moral, and emotional experiences—by using what makes each act of seeing a deeply individual experience—vision can tell us who we are and what our place is in the world. Before analyzing specific instances of this kind of vision in the novel, I ask students to imagine viewing a famous statue from an odd perspective rather than from the front. The statue itself does not change with this shift in perspective, of course, but the unusual appearance of the statue reveals how one's spatial relation to it has changed. For Tolstoy, to put it very simply, self-perception is largely formed by how we see ourselves in relation to the world around us. Thus if an unfamiliar, or defamiliarized, visual experience is not explained by the world's having changed, then it must be we who have changed. Defamiliarized vision is a first step toward altering self-knowledge.

I usually introduce students early on to the critical concept of defamiliarization, *ostranenie* in Russian. *Defamiliarization* is a far-reaching literary term introduced by the Russian formalists, with reference to Tolstoy's narrative practice of rendering habitualized acts of perception in an unfamiliar or strange way so that they may be experienced anew by the reader. Yet this strangeness itself is not what is most important for Tolstoy. The essential point I try to convey to students is that a defamiliarized visual perception always demands further explanation or interpretation.

To walk around the statue to an unusual viewpoint is to follow, metaphorically speaking, in Tolstoy's footsteps as he pursues the truth via narrative strategies of misdirection, deferral, and a kind of patient vigilance, as though he were stalking the truth. First glances and first impressions can be misleading: in general, Tolstoy would have been a devastating critic of the consumer culture of instant gratification. He seems to suggest that the best things in life are either worth waiting for, as Levin waits for Kitty, or worth cultivating, as Levin grows his own food instead of, like Stiva, "stealing rolls" (37; pt. 1, ch. 11).

One could easily have students debate this point in reference to the scene where Vronsky first sees Anna and apparently mistakes for flirtation her recognition of him from his mother's stories (56; pt. 1, ch. 18). Anna, Vronsky, and Golenishchev are mistaken in their appraisal of Mikhaylov's painting, *Pilate's Admonition*; and in a different way even Levin's first impression of Mikhaylov's portrait of Anna is also mistaken. Moreover, the many images that appear in mirrors in the novel, because of their misleading immediacy, are especially untrustworthy—as though Tolstoy believes an image produced so instantly could only be the flickering projection of one's desired self. Curiously enough, psychologists often note that the mind falsifies when it transforms the mirror image, which for mathematical reasons actually appears at half its real size on the glass surface, back into something like its original dimension (Gombrich 279). Visual images in *Anna Karenina*—in mirrors, portraits, and landscapes—confront characters with their own projected fictions.

When Anna wants to reaffirm her identity as a loving mother, for example, she takes out Serezha's portraits. Of course there is nothing odd about a mother admiring her son's image, but Anna sometimes prefers portrait to child. At one point she even hands away her infant daughter in order to look at Serezha's portrait of the same age (and compare it favorably) (489; pt. 5, ch. 31). As she admires the image of Serezha, she reminds herself of a comforting self-image: the loving mother cruelly separated from her child (not an entirely delusional account of herself and her situation). She realizes that aesthetic images have a unique communicative currency: she leaves the pictures of Serezha on the table so that Vronsky will see them and know how upset she is (490). Earlier in the novel, when she contemplates taking Serezha and running away from Karenin, she enters the drawing room and sees the following: "Serezha, dressed all in white, was standing by a table under a looking-glass, and arranging some flowers he had brought" (264; pt. 3, ch. 15). All that would be necessary here is the image of Anna as artist in the mirror's reflection to perfect the implied self-referential composition, which might be titled *Still Life with Child and Looking-Glass*.

It is unlikely that Tolstoy had a particular painting in mind for this scene or for other similar scenes in the novel. The kind of self-referential art that inextricably engages the spectator in the composition of its image and play of mirrors, such as Edouard Manet's *Le bar aux Folies-Bergère* (1881–82), can provide an analogue to Anna's conscious or subconscious manipulation of her own aesthetic image. As she looks at herself, we look at her too and thus become involved in the elaborate staging of her persona, as discussed by, among others, Julie Buckler (in this volume) and Thomas Seifrid. Although Tolstoy was certainly not the first to suggest that the way one looks at an object or person says as much about the subject looking as the object seen, he uses this observation to great effect, both comical and philosophical. Thus in Italy the responses Anna and Vronsky have to Mikhaylov's painting confirm his initial opinion of them, that they are dilettantes. The greater their conviction that Mikhaylov paints well merely on the strength of his technique (which they derive from their feigned attention to the details of the canvas), the easier it is to conclude that they know nothing of genuine art. This comedy is made complete by Vronsky's medieval Italian hat and cloak.

Mikhaylov's *Pilate's Admonition* is a focal point in the novel's debate on visual aesthetics, and students will probably benefit from a few minutes of lecture on this painting. Golenishchev associates Mikhaylov with what he calls the "Ivanov-Strauss-Renan attitude toward Christ and religious art" (424; pt. 5, ch. 9), and *Pilate's Admonition* undoubtedly recalls Alexander Ivanov's *The Appearance of Christ to the People* (1858).

Ivanov and others grouped under the rubric of the historical school in Russian nineteenth-century painting believed that Christ should be portrayed as a real human being. Yet neither the depiction of Christ in Ivanov's painting nor in

Fig. 1. Alexander Ivanov, *The Appearance of Christ to the People.* From *Gosudarstvennaia Tret'iakovskaia Galereia* (1964), courtesy of the Tretiakov Gallery

Fig. 2. Ivan Kramskoi, *Christ in the Wilderness*. From *Gosudarstevnnaia Tret'iakovskaia Galereia* (1970), courtesy of the Tretiakov Gallery

another noteworthy work by Ivan Kramskoi, *Christ in the Wilderness* (1872), would seem especially realistic to the average undergraduate today.

In this context, one might tell students that Tolstoy considered such paintings to be too realistic in their depiction of Christ. Kramskoi actually visited Tolstoy in 1873. His ideas about painting and his plan for a new work that would depict Christ before Pilate were likely models for Tolstoy's characterization of Mikhaylov and *Pilate's Admonition*.

One can show these two paintings by Ivanov and by Kramskoi in the classroom and through their juxtaposition identify a key opposition in the visual aesthetics of *Anna Karenina*. Christ is the center of Kramskoi's painting, just as the face of Christ is in the center of Mikhaylov's painting (429; pt. 5, ch. 11). The viewer is called on to contrast this living human Christ with the utterly barren desert, even as the viewer invariably concludes that the desert supports, complements, and even conforms to Christ's figure: multiple planes of composition intersect in the image of Christ's hands clasped in prayer at the center of the canvas. If Tolstoy encourages the reader of *Anna Karenina* to consider identity as an act of seeing the self in relation to the world, here is a painting that corresponds to that view and perhaps transcends it. Epitomizing the human, Christ appears in stark contrast to the desert; revealing the divine, Christ's body is seemingly in alignment with the angles of the universe.

Ivanov reveals his Christ in a dramatically different way. Most important for the discussion of visual aesthetics in *Anna Karenina* is how this Christ literally appears—at a distance, with the people watching him approach. As viewers of the painting, we are overwhelmed by the viewers in the painting—these figures watch one another recognize Christ as he approaches. Given the drama of this foregrounded visual activity in Ivanov's painting, one immediately sees the significance of Mikhaylov's watching Anna, Vronsky, and Golenishchev as they view *Pilate's Admonition*. He wants them to understand, and in their presence "in an instant his whole picture became alive before his eyes" (430; pt. 5, ch. 11). Like Karenin, who watches Anna watching Vronsky at the racetrack, Mikhaylov ultimately recognizes betrayal in their reactions to what they see. In Ivanov, then, Tolstoy rediscovers the drama of observing the visual event unfold.

One need not go outside the novel to find similarly important scenes of viewing art. Compare Anna, Vronsky, and Golenishchev's viewing of *Pilate's Admonition* with Levin's viewing of Mikhaylov's portrait of Anna. Levin interprets the portrait to be looking down at him "victoriously." Vanquished by the beauty of Anna captured in the portrait (and later by Anna herself), he later feels ashamed to admit to Kitty that he even visited Anna. The situation itself, reminiscent of a postdinner party visit to the brothel, and his stunned conclusion that the portrait was "more beautiful than a living woman should be" (630; pt. 7, ch. 9) compromise his altruistic intentions, and he makes little attempt to justify himself to his wife. Levin's position as observer of the painting and his shame at being caught even looking at it create the guilt of a virtual adulterer (who stands alongside real adulterers, one might add).

In the classroom I try to step back from these involved abstract interpretations by asking students a question long associated with discussions of ekphrasis in scholarly criticism and central to these narrative sequences with Mikhaylov's paintings: Why does an author spend so much time writing about art that cannot actually be seen in a written novel? That question is related to a familiar ontological dilemma associated with ekphrasis: language in the novel cannot capture the visual essence of the portrait, yet the portrait exists only insofar as it is described by the novel's language. This paradox is embedded in the narrative of the novel. Vronsky's reaction to Mikhaylov's portrait of Anna is indicative: "'One needed to know and love her as I love her, to find just that sweetest spiritual expression of hers,' thought Vronsky, though he himself had only learnt to know that 'sweetest spiritual expression' through the portrait. But the expression was so true that it seemed both to him and to others that they had always known it" (434; pt. 5, ch. 13). That is to say, Anna's unrepresentable spiritual essence is revealed by the visual representation, and Vronsky therefore recognizes what he has never seen.

Vronsky's impossible act of visual recognition conforms to Tolstoy's dissatisfaction with traditional empirical epistemology: empirically, you cannot recognize as true what you have never known. Tolstoy was not a romantic, and Vronsky is not born with the imprint of Anna on his soul. The painting simply reveals something so true that it seems as though he had known it all along. To rephrase: Vronsky recognizes the truth of the representation of Anna's expression, not the expression itself. What makes Mikhaylov's mode or method of visual representation so truthful?

Mikhaylov paints, for want of a better term, by negation or subtraction. He tries to eliminate what prevents an image or idea from appearing fully to the viewer; he removes the wrappings:

> He knew that much attention and care were needed not to injure one's work when removing the wrappings that obscure the idea, and that all wrappings must be removed [. . .]. In all he painted and ever had painted he saw defects that were an eyesore to him, the results of carelessness in removing the shell of the idea, which he could not now remedy without spoiling the work as a whole. And in almost all the figures and faces he saw traces of wrappings that had not been entirely removed and that spoilt the picture.   (431; pt. 5, ch. 11)

This idea of removing the wrappings creates a visual metaphor not only for the artistic process but also for more substantial questions of existential truth. In the chapter devoted to the death of Levin's brother Nicholas, the last thing the dying man does is "clutch" at his clothing: "And Levin noticed that all day long the sick man really kept catching at himself as if wishing to pull something off" (458; pt. 5, ch. 21). This narrative sequence follows directly after the chapters devoted to Anna and Vronsky's visit to Italy and to Mikhaylov's studio, thus allowing the original image of wrappings to broaden into a philosophically profound metaphor, an overarching metaphor in Tolstoy's fiction: clothing, furnishings, and material objects in general get in the way of the truth and obscure our seeing it. In later stories, such as "The Death of Ivan Ilych" and "Master and Man," Tolstoy returns to the idea that a main task of illness and death is to strip away the material and egoistic impediments to spiritual salvation (Gustafson 152–53).

It is a remarkable characteristic of *Anna Karenina*, and of Tolstoy's novels in general, that seemingly peripheral subjects such as painting or aesthetic vision become, on closer inspection, crucial to his most cherished ideas. The notion of aesthetic vision emerges, at first, from his curiosity about the vagaries of visual perception—that vision can be deceptive—and subsequently matures into a key metaphor of salvation. This truth is a different sort from that associated with his "absolute language," as Mikhail Bakhtin terms those generalizing, authoritative dicta that one comes across from time to time in the novels and stories.

The truths of Tolstoy's absolute statements often reside in the "negative space" that prepares the reader for an important image or visual composition. Rudolf Arnheim writes that negative spaces—the emptiness created by the chisel that gives shape to the stone—require "sufficient figure quality to be perceivable in their own right" (236). What you cannot visualize in the language of the novel prepares you for what you can visualize. Take the novel's opening, in which the Oblonsky household, and ultimately Stiva on the leather sofa in his study, materialize out of the context of two of Tolstoy's most authoritative statements in the novel—the biblical epigraph and the famous opening line (see Holland, this volume). One could ask students to pause for a moment and visualize those lines. Or the next line, "Everything was upset in the Oblonskys' house," which is somewhat better but still too colloquial to put before the mind's eye. Significantly, that entire second paragraph, while effectively creating a general image of domestic chaos, contains barely any visual detail. It is not until Stiva, with his "plump, well-kept body," appears on the "morocco leather-covered" and "springy" sofa that readers have anything substantial to imagine (1). As Stiva opens his eyes, so do we; but what a difference there is between what he sees and what we see.

Tolstoy's language seems to support Stiva's plump body by placing Stiva's infidelity in the context of the novel's broader ideas; but his indulgent physicality also effaces Tolstoy's language and the absolutism of the epigraph. For there can be no question—this happy man will not really suffer vengeance for this or any other infidelity. The novel's epigraph thus creates an imageless discursive space that prepares for Stiva's bodily appearance. When Stiva first opens his eyes that morning, he is disappointed to find the real world in place of his dream, to find truth instead of fiction. We too are meant to see the truth instead of fiction in *Anna Karenina*, but few readers will share Stiva's disappointment.

NOTE

[1]Instructors interested in further reading on visual aesthetics in *Anna Karenina* should consult Mandelker's insightful study *Framing* Anna Karenina as well as her "Illustrate"; Kovarsky's "Mimesis"; Evdokimova's "Drawing"; and Seifrid's "Gazing." Useful general treatments of ekphrasis are the studies by Murray Krieger and by Mary Ann Caws. Gary Saul Morson discusses narrative perspective in *Anna Karenina* (*Narrative*) and Tolstoy's use of "absolute language" in *War and Peace* (*Hidden*). See also Bayley; Gustafson.

Anna Karenina through Film

Andrea Lanoux

Anna Karenina has inspired over twenty film adaptations around the globe, including seven silent films, a ballet version, several made-for-television miniseries, two Hollywood film classics starring Greta Garbo and Vivien Leigh, plus more recent versions starring Jacqueline Bisset and Sophie Marceau. This wealth of material provides an excellent opportunity for the comparative study of narrative structures and devices in the novel and its various film adaptations. In Russian Literature into Film, an introductory-level course at Connecticut College, students read five Russian literary classics and view their film adaptations, concentrating on the problems of narrator, character, point of view, story (*fabula*), and plot (*siuzhet*),[1] and their presentation in a verbal versus a primarily visual and auditory medium. For basic definitions of these terms, we consult Gerald Prince's *Dictionary of Narratology*; for discussions of basic cinematic devices (such as camera angle and shot) and concepts in film theory (signification, representation, and perception), we turn to the works of Louis Giannetti, of James Monaco, and of David Bordwell and Kristin Thompson. The aim of comparing literary works with their film adaptations is not to ask which is better, the book or the film, or to determine whether an adaptation is faithful to the original. Rather, the primary goal of the course is to introduce students to Russian literature, narrative theory, and film theory. In addition to honing students' analytic skills, the study of literary works and their film versions provides an important point of departure for discussing problems such as high versus popular art forms, the translation of cultural markers from one national context to another, the conceptual process of reading versus the perceptual process of viewing, and different modes of artistic production (such as an individual author's writing for a relatively small, literate audience versus the collective process of filmmaking for a mass, usually profit-oriented industry).

As one of the more complex and understudied problems in literary and film studies, adaptation is an important cultural phenomenon and one that is especially relevant to our own time.[2] Historically, adaptation has enjoyed periods of both acceptance and suspicion as a way of creating original art. Just as the Enlightenment witnessed the creation of new works consciously based on previously existing models, in our time the practice of fusion and sampling in music, the use of prefabricated images in visual art, and the borrowing of ready-made materials in computer art demonstrate that adaptation is an important and common practice in contemporary artistic life. Even decades ago, Russian film theorists such as Sergei Eisenstein and Vsevolod Pudovkin considered collage and pastiche to be fundamental artistic practices for early filmmaking. In addition to these reasons, it is important to study adaptation as a form of interpretation. Students are invited to question the notions of original versus imitation and to articulate the essential elements that make it possible—or impossible—to call the novel and its film adaptations versions of the same work. This last point, the relation between the novel and its film adaptations, leads students to the broader problem of intertextuality.

In the course we treat five pairs of literary works and their film adaptations: Anton Chekhov's *Uncle Vanya*, Ivan Turgenev's *First Love*, Fyodor Dostoevsky's *Notes from Underground*, Tolstoy's *Anna Karenina*, and Boris Pasternak's *Doctor Zhivago*. The course is organized according to specific narrative problems presented by each pair, such as the relation between film and theater (in Louis Malle's *Vanya on Forty-Second Street*), differing presentations of point of view (in Maximillian Schell's *First Love*), a reordering of the plot (in Gary Walkow's *Notes from Underground*), and the translation of cultural markers and use of music to convey poeticity (in David Lean's *Doctor Zhivago*). *Anna Karenina* is a pivotal work in the course for its presentation of a complex set of problems associated with the severe cuts necessitated by compressing an eight-hundred-page novel into a two-hour film. Besides the immense amount of story material omitted, there is the accompanying restriction in points of view presented that inevitably alters the range of possible interpretations. In the course, we view three different film versions of *Anna Karenina*: the entire 1948 version, directed by Julian Duvivier and starring Vivien Leigh; portions of the 1967 Russian adaptation, directed by Aleksandr Zarkhi and starring Tatiana Samoilova; and portions of the 1935 Hollywood version, directed by Clarence Brown and starring Greta Garbo. I show only portions of the last two films, not because the films are less instructive than the 1948 version but because of time constraints; the 1967 and 1935 versions prompt excellent discussion even when viewed in part.

Before viewing the films, we spend two weeks discussing the novel in class. Discussion is focused on the structure and form (narrator, point of view, characterization, and the notorious parallel plots) as well as the thematic and symbolic plane. Students are asked to articulate a relation between the novel's formal features and its themes (such as Tolstoy's presentation of love, both platonic and carnal, in the interplay of the parallel plots). In this manner we analyze some of the more famous passages, including the ball scene, Anna's and Vronsky's dreams, Kitty and Levin's psychic communication (as opposed to Landau's and society's pseudo-psychic communication), Levin's mowing, and the highly cinematic steeplechase scene. In-class discussion is enhanced by contributions to an online threaded discussion board accessible through the course Web site.[3]

After discussing the novel, students view the 1948 film version of *Anna Karenina* outside class. I have chosen to have them see this version in its entirety because of its fairly obvious use of cinematic techniques (such as lighting, shot composition, and voiceovers) to portray the emotions and highly subjective experiences that Tolstoy often conveys through the technique of internal monologue. Two of the most notable are Duvivier's extensive use of the long shot to convey emotional distance (in scenes between Anna and her husband) and his use of dramatic lighting and music to convey sensuality (in scenes between Anna and Vronsky). The film opens and closes by establishing a direct relation to Tolstoy's text with still shots of pages from the novel: "All happy families resemble one another, every unhappy family is unhappy after its own fashion" and "the light by which she had been reading the book of life . . . went out forever" (1; pt. 1, ch. 1; 695; pt. 7, ch. 31).[4] Yet the film deviates from Tolstoy's text in a number of significant ways. In several instances, important plot points that are conveyed over the course of many pages of the novel are conflated into a single scene (such as Levin's proposal to Kitty at a salon and her rejection of the proposal as Vronsky stands nearby). The 1948 version tells the story almost exclusively from Anna's point of view, with the Levin-Kitty plot line pushed far into the background. This feature brings us back to a discussion of the relation between the parallel plots as presented in the novel. With primarily Anna's story and point of view presented in the film, how are we to reinterpret the story of Tolstoy's novel, which is so essentially structured around the interconnection between the parallel plot lines and themes?

In an effort to promote sympathy with Anna and to simplify the plot, the 1948 film introduces several major changes in the plot (such as presenting Anna's child with Vronsky as stillborn). The reason for Anna's affair with Vronsky is explained unambiguously in a scene where Anna is rejected by both her husband and son. In another instance of plot modification, Kitty shows up brazenly at Levin's estate, picking up the undeveloped plot line just in time to contrast, in a series of quick intercuts, her marriage to Levin with Anna and Vronsky's elopement. While many symbols from the novel are retained (such as the irritating knuckle cracking, the blizzard, the train, the horse symbolism, and the mysterious French-speaking peasant), the lack of discussion of the major themes that are amplified by the novel's structure often leaves them hollow or unrecognizable as symbols. This adaptation is the story of a tragic love affair that, like most other film versions, ends with Anna's death.

The 1967 Russian film version provides a striking contrast by restoring the Kitty-Levin plot line, complete with the figure skating and chalk scenes. We view the first twenty-five minutes of the film in class (to the ball), plus the steeplechase and Levin's mowing scenes. These segments provide enough material to discuss point of view, for unlike the 1948 version, this adaptation shows all the main characters' points of view. The 1967 film employs a different repertoire of shots and devices to convey emotional turmoil, such as repeated tracking shots in which actors follow a moving camera through a corridor. Like the 1948 film, the Russian adaptation retains some of Tolstoy's symbolic structure, albeit often to hyperbolic and humorous degrees. For example, the Russian version features a candle (or entire candelabra) in many scenes involving Anna—a visual presentation of Tolstoy's metaphor for the "light" by which she is reading the book of life. During the steeplechase, the director indulges in a series of quick intercuts between Anna and Frou-Frou—an overstated technique that never fails to evoke laughter in class. Such techniques can be read as typical Soviet heavy-handedness (to ensure that art is accessible to everyone and contains no ambiguity regarding what symbols mean) or simply as less successful instances of translating elements from the novel to the screen. The film has many successful renderings as well, such as the spinning camera at the ball and the swell of peasants' song tracking over Levin's mowing. Students are invited to question whether a symbol can be interpreted as having the same meaning (or the same potential meaning) in the film as in Tolstoy's novel and to support their claims with evidence.

The 1935 Hollywood version of *Anna Karenina* is similarly entertaining and instructive with its use of stereotypes, melodrama, slapstick humor, and seemingly gratuitous alterations of plot. The first ten minutes of this ninety-five-minute film consist of scenes found nowhere in the novel. The movie opens with a shot of an enormous platter of black caviar being devoured by imperial officers by the spoonful; among them is Vronsky, dressed in white, while all the others are dressed in black. An officer barbarously sinks his teeth into a hand-held turkey leg; others dance with Gypsy women and sing Russian folk songs. Cut to a long buffet table lined with young officers engrossed in a drinking game. Vronsky remains standing while the others fall (he is a real Russian man: he can hold his liquor); then he grabs a full bottle of vodka, stumbles over to Stiva, and says, "Now we can settle down and do some drinking." Fade out to two male servants whipping Stiva and Vronsky in the bathhouse . . .

Students immediately see that this film is a far cry from Tolstoy's novel. Anna (yet somehow always Garbo) is presented in the most sympathetic light and free from blame: her liaison with Vronsky is only to escape a tyrant husband, and reference to an illegitimate child is conspicuously absent. The ending presents yet another gratuitous departure from the novel: Vronsky sits drinking with Yashvin, mentioning how during his last meeting with Anna he did not give her "the sympathy and a kind word" that she wanted; rather he "hardened his heart," and for this he can never forgive himself. Yashvin reassures him that "she's forgotten, and she's forgiven," as the camera pans to a picture of Garbo's smiling face. Dramatic music, the end.

But are these deviations in plot really gratuitous? They demonstrate the aesthetic sensibility of the Hollywood industry in the 1930s at the height of the Russian émigré community in Paris and Hollywood's love affair with culture *à la Russe*. Gary Saul Morson justly observes that the Garbo film "celebrates Romantic love in its most extreme, most cliched form: that is its ideology" ("Brooding Stiva" 57). This film, widely regarded as a classic of American cinema, also opens up a discussion of high versus popular art forms. Students are asked to consider whether there is an essential (i.e., a formal) difference between high art and popular or whether the difference is primarily one of perception and reception. In his 1984 book *Distinction: A Social Critique of the Judgement of Taste*, Pierre Bourdieu suggests that the difference between the two is on one level formal, with high art's aiming to "distinguish" itself from existing forms while popular art employs recognizable patterns. At the same time, he argues that the ability to distinguish between high and popular art is a learned skill and one closely associated with social class (4, 26–28, 32–33).

Several other recent and easy-to-find film adaptations of *Anna Karenina* could be used to explore further the questions of high versus popular culture. The 1985 made-for-television version starring Jacqueline Bisset and Christopher Reeve opens with a text explaining that adultery in nineteenth-century Russia was punishable for women and divorce was a condemned practice. Such basic cultural information was clearly deemed necessary by the filmmakers to heighten the drama for an audience having a fifty-percent divorce rate. Another recent adaptation, the 1997 version starring Sophie Marceau and Sean Bean, aspires at once to be an upscale blockbuster and an art film. Its artistic pretensions—as reflected in its inclusion of Tolstoy himself in the narrative, its effort to deviate from traditional models of *Anna Karenina* adaptations by introducing new scenes, and its ample helping of sex—have been both positively and negatively received. Every available film version of *Anna Karenina* has something to offer, by making apparent some of the better hidden devices of literary and cinematic storytelling and by helping students better articulate relations between content and form.

NOTES

[1]The distinction between *fabula* and *siuzhet* as theorized by the Russian formalists has found resonance in both narratology and film theory and for this reason can be helpful to students studying narrative structures of literature and film.

[2]The problem of adaptation is beginning to receive more attention by literary scholars. Irina Makoveeva analyzes the film versions of *Anna Karenina* starring Garbo (1935), Leigh (1948), Samoilova (1967), and Merceau (1997) as examples of *kinolubok*, illustration, interpretation-commentary, and interpretation-analogy. Gary Saul Morson ("Brooding Stiva") discusses the Garbo and Masterpiece Theatre versions, juxtaposing his remarks about the films with insightful analysis of the novel.

[3]The URL is camel2.conncoll.edu/is/CSOLL/Russian.157.description.html. The Web design is by David Lavoie.

[4]I give here the translation presented in the film.

APPENDIX: FILMS FOR COMPARATIVE STUDY

Anna Karenina. Dir. Vladimir Gardin. Perf. Mariia Germanova, Vladimir Shaternikov, and Mikhail Tamarov. Russkaia Zolotaia Seriia, 1914 [silent].

———. Dir. J. Gordon Edwards. Perf. Betty Nansen, Edward José, and Richard Thorton II. Fox Film, 1915 [silent].

———. Dir. Márton Garas. Perf. Irén Varsányi, Desider Kertesz, and Emil Fenyvessy. Hungria Filmgyr, 1918.

Love (Anna Karenina). Dir. Edmund Goulding. Perf. Greta Garbo, John Gilbert, and Brandon Hurst. MGM, 1927 [silent].

Anna Karenina. Dir. Clarence Brown. Perf. Greta Garbo, Frederic March, and Basil Rathbone. MGM, 1935.

————. Dir. Julien Duvivier. Perf. Vivien Leigh, Kieron Moore, and Ralph Richardson. London Film; Twentieth Century Fox, 1948.

————. Dir. Rudolph Cartier. Perf. Claire Bloom, Sean Connery, and Marius Goring. BBC, 1961 [made for television].

————. Dir. Aleksandr Zarkhi. Perf. Tatiana Samoilova, Nikolai Gritsenko, and Vasilii Lanovoi. Mosfil'm; Camacico-Prodis, 1967.

————. Dir. Margarita Pilikhina. Perf. Maia Plisetskaia, Aleksandr Godunov, Vladimir Tikhonov, and the Bolshoi Ballet. Mosfil'm, 1974 [ballet].

————. Dir. Basil Coleman. Perf. Nicola Pagett, Stuart Wilson, and Eric Porter. BBC, 1977 [television miniseries in ten parts].

————. Dir. Simon Langton. Perf. Jacqueline Bisset, Christopher Reeve, and Paul Scofield. Colgems; Rastar, 1985 [made for television].

Anna Karenina (Anna Karènine). Dir. Bernard Rose. Perf. Sophie Marceau, Sean Bean, Alfred Molina, and James Fox. Icon Entertainment Intl.; Warner Brothers, 1997.

Anna Karenina. Dir. David Blair. Perf. Helen McCrory, Kevin McKidd, Stephen Dillane, Douglas Henshall, and Paloma Baeza. Company Pictures, 2000 [television miniseries in four parts].

Diadia Vania (Uncle Vanya). Dir. Andrei Konchalovskii. Perf. Innokentii Smoktunovskii, Sergei Bondarchuk, Vladimir Zel'din, Irina Kupchenko, and Irina Miroshnichenko. Mosfil'm, 1970.

Doctor Zhivago. Dir. David Lean. Perf. Omar Sharif, Julie Christie, Geraldine Chaplin, Rod Steiger, and Alec Guinness. MGM, 1965.

First Love. Dir. Maximilian Schell. Perf. John Moulder Brown, Maximilian Schell, Dominique Sanda, and Valentina Cortese. Alfa Seitz UMC Pictures, 1970.

Notes from Underground. Dir. Gary Walkow. Perf. Henry Czerny and Sheryl Lee. Walkow/Gruber Pictures and Renegade Films, 1995.

Uncle Vanya. Dir. Stuart Burge. Perf. Laurence Olivier, Max Adrian, Lewis Casson, Fay Compton, Rosemary Harris, Robert Lang, Joan Plowright, Michael Redgrave, and Sybil Thorndike. British Home Entertainment, 1962.

Vanya on Forty-Second Street. Dir. Louis Malle. Perf. Julianne Moore, Brooke Smith, George Gaynes, Jerry Mayer, Phoebe Brand, Lynn Cohen, Larry Pine, Wallace Shawn, and Andrei Gregory. Columbia TriStar, 1994.

Note: The *Internet Movie Database* lists the following rare film versions of *Anna Karenina*: Germany, 1910 [silent]; Russia, 1911 [silent]; France, 1911 [silent]; Italy, 1917 [silent]; Germany, dir. Frederic Zelnik, 1919; France, 1934; India, 1952; Soviet Union, dir. Tatiana Lukashevich, 1953; Argentina, 1956; Arabic, 1961; Soviet Union, 1971; and Italy, dir. Sandro Bolchi, 1974 [made for television].

Using Reader-Response Journals in Teaching *Anna Karenina*

Jason Merrill

Leo Tolstoy's diaries and journals, which occupy thirteen of the ninety volumes of his collected works (*Polnoe sobranie*), clearly played an important role in his intellectual growth. Early in his career, Tolstoy discovered that writing in a journal can make one a better reader and writer. Students reading *Anna Karenina* may be inspired by his example. While reading Catherine the Great's *Instruction* in March 1847, he wrote, "since I've generally made it a rule when reading any serious work to think about it and copy out any remarkable thoughts from it, I'll write down my opinion here about the first six chapters of this remarkable work" (*Tolstoy's Diaries* 4). Within a month he was convinced that this practice would help him develop as a thinker and writer: "I have never kept a diary before, because I could never see the benefit of it. But now that I am concerned with the development of my own facilities, I shall be able to judge from a diary the progress of that development" (5). Tolstoy used his journals and notebooks as a place to write down ideas as they appeared, without concern for spelling, grammar, or structure. As Boris Eikhenbaum notes, Tolstoy's journals function as a creative laboratory, where his "devices are prepared and the general foundations of his poetics are thought out" (*Young Tolstoi* 46).

In class I explain to my students that, in fact, Tolstoy did not keep a diary or journal during the writing of *Anna Karenina*. In its place the novel became a record of the author's spiritual and intellectual development during the years of its writing; we can thus consider the novel "a surrogate diar[y]" (*Tolstoy's Diaries* 7). *Anna Karenina* is long, with distinct plots and developing characters; it has almost as many interpretations as readers. Keeping a daily journal encourages students, at each stage of the reading, to confront their increasingly complex feelings about Tolstoy's work, help them navigate this large book, and provide them with a diary experience that seems suitably Tolstoyan.

Recent research on reading and writing suggests that using a variety of writing assignments is the best means of encouraging and assessing student progress in literature courses. John C. Bean's *Engaging Ideas* provides models for a large range of writing assignments that can be tailored to fit the goals of each lesson and the needs of each group of students. Regardless of subject, Bean emphasizes that in order to develop thoughts effectively, students need to write as frequently as possible in an informal setting where ideas, not form, have priority. Tolstoy, too, felt that the early stages of writing should be done "without thinking about the right place for the thoughts or their correctness of expression" (*Tolstoy's Diaries* 51). Keeping a reader's journal, then, is a type of writing exercise that is being promoted by current pedagogical experts, and it was also practiced and valued by Tolstoy himself.

In my undergraduate literature classes, I ask students to respond to each day's reading in a journal entry, which they complete before class, either on a loose piece of paper or in a bound notebook. They are encouraged to complete their entry while the text is still fresh in their minds. This assignment can prepare the class for the next discussion, especially if students are required to note specific passages in the text that will be the focus in class. The assignment can also be used to initiate or stimulate class discussion. For suggestions on grading journals, providing feedback for them, and using them effectively, even in large lecture classes, I recommend Bean (98–117), Toby Fulwiler, and Donna Perry.

There are several options available for instructors desiring to use technology to expedite this exchange of ideas. The simplest is e-mail; students can e-mail their journals to instructors, who can return them electronically with comments. With a course mailing list, e-mail makes it easy for students to distribute their journals to all their classmates, and they can receive feedback just as easily.

Two Web-based options keep the discussion in one central location. First is a threaded messaging bulletin board, to which students post journal entries and also view their peers' responses. They can contribute to the board at any time, and their comments can be organized by topic and saved; this method leaves an accessible record of the entire semester's discussion. Second is a live chat room, which better reproduces the feel of a class discussion, because students can post ideas and see responses in real time. Chat room discussion, however, is not archived, and all students must be logged on simultaneously to participate.

The journal entries assigned depend on the variables of the class. The simplest type of journal assignment, freewriting, does not pose a question but asks students to write about their initial response, what struck them most about a particular section, or about a theme or character they thought played an important role. These assignments capture their immediate reactions, not influenced by class discussion. To avoid digressions unrelated to the novel, I ask students to support their opinions with evidence from the text.

In these open-ended assignments students may explore aspects of the novel that are personally significant to them, or they may state whether they liked the assigned pages or not and explain why. Some compare *Anna Karenina* with other works they have read; others bring up their own life experiences, often incidents or people close to them. They frequently use such personal "evidence" to argue for or against Tolstoy's positions. Once they are engaged with an issue of personal interest, comments from the instructor can easily push them further toward their own reading of the text.

Freewriting journals also serve as a barometer for the instructor as to how the students are reading and interpreting the text and what problems they are encountering. Journals often contain questions about the reading, about details that instructors take for granted but that can be unclear to students: "Why is there chalk on the table where Levin and Kitty are sitting?" "Why does Levin stand in church?" Such questions make these journals unpredictable (yet fascinating) reading. Because each student in the class comes to the text with different experiences of life and literature, the journals will certainly teach the instructor something new about *Anna Karenina* as well as about the students.

While some students enjoy the freedom to choose topics, others prefer to have topics assigned. One aim of specific questions on the reading is to guide students and help them explore aspects of the novel that they might otherwise miss. They can be asked to comment on the abundant symbolism of Anna's train ride from Moscow to Saint Petersburg (91–95; pt. 1, chs. 29–30) or of the steeplechase (179–83; pt. 2, ch. 25; 188–94; pt. 2, chs. 28–29). It is interesting to ask them why Tolstoy includes scenes that some critics have found superfluous, for example: "Why does Vronsky dabble in art and visit the painter Mikhaylov (417–35; pt. 5, chs. 7–13)?" "Why do Varenka and Koznyshev go mushroom picking (509–13; pt. 6, chs. 4–5)?" Questions can be used to direct students to thematic links, for example: "Compare Levin at his brother's death (453–59; pt. 5, ch. 20) and at the birth of his child (642–51; pt. 7, chs. 14–16)."

Another type of journal question asks students to trace parallels between the novel's two plot lines. "What is the expressed attitude toward the countryside and the peasants? (part 3)." "Tolstoy brings Anna and Vronsky close to death: Why does he save them? Are Levin's experiences with death similar to theirs? (part 4)." "At the end of part 5 Anna and Vronsky leave for the country. Why? How will their experience in the country compare with that of Kitty and Levin? (part 5)." "Compare Levin and Vronsky as country farmers and as elected officials (part 6)." At any point it is useful to ask students if the characters or their attitudes toward the characters are changing, as their sympathies oscillate during their reading of the novel.

Once we have finished the novel, students are asked to consider the novel as a whole. An example of a good warm-up question for an essay exam or a paper is, "In response to critics who said the novel was really two separate stories, Tolstoy insisted there was 'an inner continuity' (754) that unifies the novel. So why is the novel simply called *Anna Karenina*? Who do you feel is right, Tolstoy or his critics? Be sure to use evidence from the text." Or, "Now that you have read the novel, reconsider the epigraph. Who is speaking? On whom was vengeance exacted and why?" You can also ask students to discuss one or more of the novel's major themes: country versus city, peasants, children, death, family, God and religion, adultery and marriage, falsehood, love and passion, work, trains, Tolstoy's style, or one particular character. In my experience students enjoy discussing God, religion, adultery, and trains, but they are bored by Levin, the peasants, and work. I also include a few general questions on their experience with the novel; I might ask them to explain the meaning of this work to a friend who has not read it or ask them if they would recommend it to a friend for summer reading and why.

To take advantage of the resources in the Norton edition of *Anna Karenina*, I have students read one of the critical articles on the novel and summarize and critique it in their journals; we discuss the results in class. Or, without assigning the actual articles, I use quotes from them to pose my journal questions—for example, "Merezhkovsky argues that Tolstoy possessed 'insight into the flesh' (770). What do you think he means? Do you agree? Does Tolstoy possess this gift more than other writers you have read?" If students have studied Dostoevsky, you can ask them to predict how Dostoevsky reacted to *Anna Karenina* and then have them compare their predictions with the selection of Dostoevsky's reaction (757–61), or you can summarize it in class.

Choices for such questions are not limited to the Norton edition. Almost any provocative statement about *Anna Karenina* to which students can react will make an effective journal question. D. H. Lawrence, Georg Lukács, Thomas Mann (see Adelman 123–34) and Vladimir Nabokov (137–236) are some of the critics and writers whose words should generate much response.

Students are impressed by the wide range of authors and critics who have reacted to *Anna Karenina*, many of whom they have studied in other contexts and never expected to encounter in this course. They are relieved to see that many of these famous figures wrestled with the same problems and questions of interpretation they face. This type of journal assignment not only exposes students to other opinions on the novel but also shows them that ideas, instead of existing in a vacuum, interact continually with other ideas from different eras and thinkers.

To appeal to students who learn from more creative exercises, I depart from exegetical types of questions to questions such as "Conduct an imaginary interview with Tolstoy. Write the three questions you would most like to ask him and the answers you feel he would give (use the letters in the Norton edition [743–54] for examples of Tolstoy's nonfiction voice)." "Describe Oblonsky. Do you know anyone like him?" "How would you define realism? Does *Anna Karenina* fit your definition?"

Many students remain unsatisfied with the ending, especially Anna's fate, and productive exercises for the last day that we discuss the novel can focus on the ending. I hand out Garrison Keillor's "Sequel," in which Anna is alone and living in New York City, while Vronsky (her husband) and her children are living at other places in the United States. Students can be invited to write their own continuation of the novel, on the premise that Anna does not throw herself under the train. They can then share their endings with small groups or the class as a whole. They often feel that Tolstoy is too harsh with Anna, that she deserves, if not happiness, at least a chance to live longer and rebuild her life. They often are also frustrated with Levin and Kitty's marriage and feel that Tolstoy makes it too idealized and unrealistic. In their sequels, students often have Kitty or Levin engage in an adulterous affair and experience what Vronsky and Anna go through. They express little sympathy for Levin and his search for truth. More than one sequel has focused on Anna's two children and their subsequent fate. Writing their own ending to the novel forces students to consider their response to the course of events in the novel. They enjoy the position of ultimate power that the author occupies.

Because "the process of writing drives thinking" (Bean 98), our students need to write as often as possible. Unlike traditional research papers, journals reflect the process of learning, not its product, and they therefore make an excellent complement to the more formal paper. They also become an additional source of interaction between teacher and student. Journals of freewriting and assigned questions encourage students to consider the text and their reactions to it very closely. By using this approach, students may come to a better understanding of *Anna Karenina* and to its author's artistic method as well.

Mapping *Anna Karenina*:
A Creative Approach to
Understanding the Novel

Mary Laurita

One very effective and creative way to explore *Anna Karenina* is to map out various sections of the novel. "Mind mapping," a term coined by Tony Buzan and Barry Buzan, is a graphic technique that can be used as an aid in any decision-making process, as a means to more effective note taking, as a mnemonic device, or as a way to organize and make sense of a complicated literary text. It is an expression of nonlinear thinking. A mind map is composed of key words or symbols that are connected to one another by lines (horizontal, vertical, or curved) and that range over the length and width of a page, a space on a blackboard, or a computer screen.

My idea of using this kind of mapping as a key to a better understanding of *Anna Karenina* arose from a need to give my undergraduate students some method of organizing the many characters, events, and themes encountered in the first two parts of the novel. Since a vast majority of the students taking my introductory-level undergraduate literature course traditionally have had very little or no experience with Russian language or culture, they often focus on keeping track of the numerous characters (with their often confusing Russian first names, patronymics, and last names) rather than on important events, themes, and relationships. As a result, much is overlooked. If students are to remain sufficiently engaged in reading *Anna Karenina* to its conclusion, it is essential that they grasp as much as possible about each character, relationship, event, and theme during the novel's opening sections. I therefore introduce mind mapping early in our reading of the novel.

To complete an in-class mapping exercise, students should be given a clear explanation of how to create a mind map, a focus for their map, and questions to guide them through the process. Optimally, they should work in groups of three or four. They will need sufficient blackboard space or large pieces of paper on which to draw and colored chalk or magic markers, since colors stimulate memory and creativity (Buzan and Buzan 98). Ideally, the exercise should take two-thirds of a given class period, leaving time for general examination and analysis of the maps. It is important to bring out the maps' common points, note their differences, and discuss any useful discoveries made by students as they worked through the mapping process.

In my experience, mapping out sections of *Anna Karenina* enhances students' understanding of the novel in several ways. First, during the process of creating a mind map, they must physically write out words or draw images representing essential themes, characters, character traits, and events. The act of extracting textual material and transferring it to an empty space on a board or a piece of paper enables them to focus on words, ideas, and images in ways that are not possible during a more straightforward reading and discussion of the text. This exercise allows students to respond to the text in a creative and personal way. Second, since memory works by an activation process that spreads from word to associated word (80), the more students engage themselves in the process of mind mapping, the more they begin to remember about the text itself. The experience of being able to see connections more easily, without constantly referring to the printed page, gives them the confidence to engage more actively in the creative process of free association. Third, doing this mapping in groups is a form of collaborative learning that requires verbal interaction. Students tend to become more animated as their mind maps gain in complexity and as they begin to discover previously hidden textual connections. In sum, while creating a mind map, students are required to interact with the text and with one another in ways that are not possible in more traditional lecture formats. The class is engaged visually, orally, aurally, and tactually.

As students read through the rest of the novel, they can be required to work on, and refine, their initial maps or create new ones. They thus continue the process of analyzing and thinking about *Anna Karenina* in this nonlinear, associative way. Working at home, they can draw their maps either by hand or using a computer program, such as *Inspiration* (www.inspiration.com) or *MindManager* (www.mindjet.com).

No matter how complex later maps become, it is essential that the first mind map be produced in as unstructured and unrestricted an environment as possible. The purpose of this particular exercise is to get students thinking about a text, in this case *Anna Karenina*, in a new, more creative, and ultimately more productive way. They should be encouraged to work quickly and to put down whatever connections come to mind. Accuracy in spelling and consistency of colors, line notation, key words, and so on are not crucial at this stage. The mind maps produced during this initial attempt are not intended to present a definitive interpretation of *Anna Karenina*. Rather, they are intended to stimulate further discussion, commentary, and ideally more maps. The two that accompany this essay reflect this initial stage. Produced under the circumstances described above, they have been left in their original state and, as a result, may exhibit some inconsistencies and lack of refinement.

It is important to give the students a focus for their maps. I have found that concentrating on specific groupings of characters—according to gender or occupation, for example—works well. As students attempt to group characters and find connections among them, topics of discussion generally surface. Since a goal of my course is to give students a greater understanding of nineteenth-century Russian culture through the reading of great works of Russian literature, when we read *Anna Karenina* I focus on such topics as the relation between the individual and society, the developing concept of self, and the position of women in society.

Creating a map using the novel's female characters, for example, can bring the developing characters of Anna and Kitty into sharp focus (see fig. 1) and in the process allow students to speculate on Tolstoy's perceptions about women,

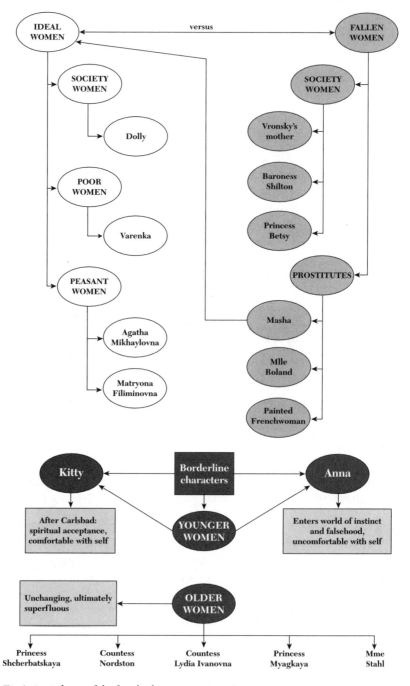

Fig. 1. A mind map of the female characters in *Anna Karenina*

about female virtue ("Who, according to Tolstoy, is an ideal woman?"), about sexual morality, about social position, about motherhood.

Although both Anna and Kitty belong to the same stratum of society, it is difficult to place them in any one category, especially as each of the categories falls somewhere along the continuum between the ideal and the fallen woman. Examining these two women, the choices they make, and why they make them can lead nicely into a discussion of what exactly constitutes Anna's fall. A map of the novel's female characters can help students see beyond the superficial reason, the relationship with Vronsky, to deeper reasons, which have more to do with Anna's personality, the constraints placed on her by the society in which she lives, her family origins, and the loveless relationship with her husband. Finally, mapping out all the female characters that appear in *Anna Karenina* calls attention to the fact that even minor characters can play a critical role in the overall structure of the novel. For example, the peasant nurses, Matryona Filiminovna and Agatha Mikhaylovna, serve as important maternal figures. At the other end of the spectrum, Tolstoy gives us the characters of Mlle Roland, the Oblonskys' former governess and Stiva's mistress, and the "painted Frenchwoman," a prostitute with whom Stiva has a passing acquaintance (30), as examples of women enmeshed in the purely physical world of base instinct. Characters such as Nicholas Levin's mistress, Masha; Vronsky's mother; and the Baroness Shilton fall between these two extremes. Although all are minor characters, their situations and views on life must be considered when discussing the complex problem of Anna's moral dilemma.

Another suggestion for an effective mapping exercise is to have students consider the characters who appear in the first two parts of the novel. By the end of part 2, all the major characters and plot lines have been introduced: Kitty has refused Levin, Vronsky has dropped Kitty, Anna has become Vronsky's mistress, and Vronsky has begun to compromise his brilliant career under the influence of his passion for Anna. I highly recommend that students also map out the relationships that exist among characters and attach some kind of identifying marker to each relationship, using either symbols or key words (see fig. 2).

The mind map that results will reveal important information about the main characters and their positions in Tolstoy's novelistic world. First, although Levin judges himself harshly, he is generally surrounded by good people who wish him well. There are a few notable exceptions—namely, his brother Nicholas, Princess Shcherbatskaya, and Countess Nordston. However, the first is ill and in need of Levin's love, understanding, and compassion, and the other two turn out to be misguided or mean-spirited. In addition, extrapolating from the mind map, we can see that Levin's idealization of Kitty, peasants, and nature (the country) indicate that Levin not only exists in the practical, physical world but has some kind of higher, spiritual life as well.

Like Levin, Anna is surrounded, at least in the beginning of the novel, by people who love and respect her and wish her well. In particular, her relationship with her son and the way in which she relates to others, especially Stiva,

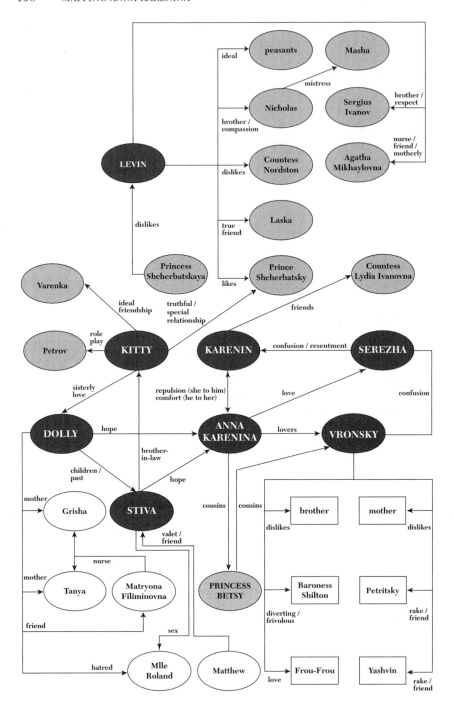

Fig. 2. A mind map of the main characters and their relationships in parts 1 and 2 of *Anna Karenina*

Dolly, and Kitty, suggest that she has an inner strength and peace that set her apart from other members of her society. Paradoxically, her relationship with her husband is cold and unnatural. It is not surprising that this relationship is the fracture point for her comfortable life. As the mind map illustrates (see fig. 2), Anna is drawn to people like Alexey Vronsky and Princess Betsy, who exert a morally destabilizing influence over her previously irreproachable life. With the exception of Anna, Vronsky is surrounded by people who like but do not love him, who are morally suspect and celebrate this fact, who have no spiritual life, and whom he does not particularly like himself, for example, his mother and brother.

Finally, Kitty, like Levin, is surrounded by people who wish her well and whom she respects, loves, and admires. The notable exception is Vronsky. However, his influence over her is brief and eventually negated by the stronger, positive relationships in her life, especially the relationship with her father. Although by the end of part 2 Kitty and Levin have not yet experienced that special Tolstoyan moment of mutual recognition, love, and understanding that they will experience later, the mind map clearly suggests that they belong to the same world and share many of the same values: they are surrounded by many of the same well-intentioned people; they both feel compassion and respect for those in need; they tend to idealize certain people in their lives; and, most important, they are directly connected to each other by a strong, instinctual feeling of comfort and well-being.

The process of creating mind maps aids students in understanding and discovering for themselves how characters relate to one another and how each fits into the larger scheme of the novel. Mapping works particularly well with *Anna Karenina*, because of the complex structure of the novel and the juxtaposition of the stories of Anna and Constantine Levin. This exercise helps students discover for themselves the hidden connections between these two characters and their accompanying plot lines. It can also help them discern the novel's underlying themes and overall design.

Additionally, these maps can become part of a successful study plan, enhancing note-taking and study skills. In my experience with *Anna Karenina*, after introducing mapping into my syllabus, I noted that students' attitude toward reading the novel improved. Their command over the material increased, as did the level of class participation, the quality of in-class discussions, and the creativity shown in devising paper topics. Most important, perhaps, I learned a great deal about the creative ways in which my students were thinking about *Anna Karenina*.

On a Scavenger Hunt in Tolstoy's Labyrinth of Linkages

Liza Knapp

Tolstoy offered an insight into how *Anna Karenina* should be read in a letter he wrote to his friend Nikolai Strakhov in the spring of 1876, while he was at work on the novel. He declares, "If I wanted to say in words all that I had in mind to express by my novel, I should have to write the same novel which I wrote all over again." He explains why this is so:

> In everything, almost everything, that I have written, I was guided by the need to gather together interrelated thoughts in order to express myself; but every thought expressed separately by words loses its meaning and is terribly degraded by being taken out by itself from that linking in which it is found. The linking itself is brought about not by thought (I think), but by something else, and to express the basis of that linking immediately in words is in no way possible; it can only be done indirectly by describing with words, images, acts, situations. (*Polnoe sobranie* 62: 269; my trans.)

Annoyed at "nearsighted critics" and their assumptions about *Anna Karenina*, Tolstoy envisions a different approach to the novel: "we need people who would show the senselessness of seeking out separate ideas in a work of art and who would continually guide readers in that endless labyrinth of linkages which the essence of art consists of, and to the laws which serve as basis for that linking" (269).

These statements, providing us with what may well be Tolstoy's artistic credo of the time, offer some suggestions about how to approach *Anna Karenina*.[1] In introducing students to the novel, instructors may regard their task as that of guide through the Tolstoyan labyrinth, but a guide who trains others to navigate on their own. Taking to heart Tolstoy's clear premise that ideas should not be extracted from the text, instructors will seek means of encouraging students to look carefully at ideas and images in their context and to examine the fabric of the text.

To help students in my undergraduate classes discern the Tolstoyan linkings, I use an exercise that is probably best described as a textual scavenger hunt. Students are given a list of particular items that recur in the novel. The list includes different kinds of things—images, themes, events, literary devices. (See the appendix to this essay.) They are asked to find multiple examples of a number of these items as they read the novel. They consider each example in its context and then look for possible patterns that emerge, for linkages among different examples as well as for apparent lack of connection and for randomness. It is possible that the Tolstoyan labyrinth is not constructed according to a neat system, that it may contain some red herrings.

Students may find it interesting to note that many readers have complained of *Anna Karenina*'s lack of unity: the novel contains two disparate plots, and there is a proliferation of superfluous information. A reader such as Henry James was not able or willing to discern the labyrinth; he dismissed Tolstoy's novels as "large loose baggy monsters" with questionable artistic merit or meaning.[2] Responding to one of his readers, who suggested that the novel lacked "architectonics," Tolstoy himself asserted its presence but noted that "[t]he vaults are thrown up in such a way that one cannot notice where the link is. [. . .] The unity in the structure is created not by action and not by relationships between the characters, but by an inner continuity" (Anna Karenina 754). Many critical works on *Anna Karenina* offer valuable insight into the structure of the novel and into how motifs, themes, and symbols are linked together to provide some of this structure (see Al'tman; Gustafson; Mandelker, *Framing*; Schultze; Stenbock-Fermor; see Goscilo, this volume).

The scavenger-hunt exercise helps readers notice the hidden architectonics and appreciate the intricate, glorious structure created by these linkings. A hunt through the Tolstoyan labyrinth reveals that whatever lifelike, prosaic randomness the novel appears to represent is clearly part of Tolstoy's deep artistic design. In this regard, the exercise works equally well no matter what ultimate view a reader takes of *Anna Karenina*—that *Anna Karenina* imitates the apparent randomness and prosaicism of life; that *Anna Karenina* shows human life governed by determinism, fatality, or divine providence; or that *Anna Karenina* shows Tolstoy struggling (as he did in *War and Peace*) to represent the tension between providence and freedom, all the while wondering whether human life makes any sense at all.

Because the process of culling examples from the text threatens to defy the very principles Tolstoy himself outlined when he wrote of the danger of degrading an idea by taking it out of its context and trying to express it directly in words, it is important to make sure that students do not go about this exercise in a reductive way. Instead of extracting meaning or an idea from the text, they should look deeper into the context and attempt to see the network of words, images, acts, and situations that Tolstoy uses to express a particular idea, which, in turn, is bound to be inextricably linked to other ideas.

To illustrate how this scavenger hunt may be used to uncover layers of meaning in the labyrinth of *Anna Karenina*, I focus on cows and horses. Although the list of items that my students hunt for includes formal devices (similes, examples of authoritative language, inner monologue and related forms of narrative), the scavenger hunt is most naturally suited for tracing the thematic motifs (like bears, stars, teeth, and French influence) that play a central role in the novel. This exercise may be used to engage in thematic "textual practices" that "suffer from" what Naomi Schor (after Gaston Bachelard) terms an "Ariadne complex," because by tracing themes they produce a reading "that cling[s] to the Ariadne's thread ('fil conducteur')" (3). Given that Tolstoy himself referred to *Anna Karenina* as a labyrinth, the search for an Ariadne's thread seems apt.

Cows and horses work well for various reasons. Students will have no trouble identifying them in the daily life depicted in the novel. They will soon notice, however, that these cows and horses seem also to have a symbolic function. Students who have read Eliot's *Middlemarch, Madame Bovary* (two works with which *Anna Karenina* is often compared), or any number of other novels will be familiar with how authors use bovine and equine motifs to convey both subliminal and direct messages to the reader (on cows and horses in *Madame Bovary*, see Nelles 55–60). Jonathan Culler has suggested that the "proliferation" of bovine elements in *Madame Bovary*, especially encoded in names, is a signal that Flaubert was practicing not realism but rather what Culler dubs "vealism" (7). Culler suggests that this vealism undermines the representational quality of language. It is a manifestation of Flaubert's anxiety about the limits of language, an anxiety that figures prominently in *Madame Bovary*. By studying how Tolstoy uses horses and cows, students may likewise come to conclusions about the nature, limits, and special characteristics of his realism as well as about his anxiety about what words can and cannot express.

A good place to begin scavenging for the meaning of horses in *Anna Karenina* is the episode that shows Vronsky's treatment of his racehorse Frou-Frou, who dies because of the way Vronsky rides her in the steeplechase. From Tolstoy's time on, readers have noted that there is something marked and unnatural in Tolstoy's inviting the reader to consider Frou-Frou as a substitute for Anna, so that what happens to the horse becomes a possible allegory for what is in store for the woman. This effect is heightened by the fact that the steeplechase occurs right after Anna has informed Vronsky that she is pregnant with his child. Whether Frou-Frou's destruction is regarded as a prophecy (prefiguring Anna's fate) or as a cautionary tale (warning her of what might happen, given Vronsky's character, if she does not act), or whether the accident is viewed simply as a red herring designed to fool the reader into making connections that are not really there, will depend on how the book as a whole is interpreted.

Because *Anna Karenina* is a "labyrinth of linkages," where different bits of the text are linked to others in mysterious ways, Frou-Frou's death because of Vronsky's "own fault" (179–83; pt. 2, ch. 25) can be juxtaposed with Levin's care for Pava, his prize milk cow, after she has given birth. (After Kitty refuses his offer of marriage, Levin returns to his estate, where, as many students note, he appears to sublimate his feelings for Kitty by caring for his cow.) In Tolstoy's labyrinth, Vronsky's equine passion is contrasted with Levin's bovine affinities, which were a prominent feature of Levin's character even in the early drafts of the novel. Tragic events at a steeplechase are contrasted with tender moments in a cowshed. Levin's relations with Pava are described earlier (86–87; pt. 1, ch. 26), but students usually see the modal significance of these relations only in retrospect, after Tolstoy has described Vronsky's relations with Frou-Frou in part 2. As early readers noticed with some dismay, much as Tolstoy presents Frou-Frou as a surrogate for Anna, he invites us to see Levin's relations with Pava as an allegory for his future relations with Kitty.

Will Kitty follow in Pava's hoofprints? Is Kitty more than a milk cow? Is a milk cow the most a Tolstoyan woman can be? In Tolstoy's work, a high premium is placed on maternal breast-feeding, so that a mother nursing her young is the apotheosis of womanhood. At two critical moments toward the end of the novel, when Anna comes in desperation to Dolly's house just before committing suicide and when a recently suicidal Levin is contemplating matters of life and death, Kitty is bent on one thing: giving milk to her child. Does Levin's glorification of his milk cow show that Tolstoy was ever the disciple of Jean-Jacques Rousseau, who proclaimed in *Emile* that the problems of the world would evaporate if women would content themselves with (nothing more than) nursing their young (46)? Although posing these questions directly may amount to degrading Tolstoy's work, they do echo in his labyrinth of linkages.

In part 3, when students come across the cows mentioned in the descriptions of Dolly's life in the country, these animals are less obviously significant. They appear to be more real and less sacred, but they too play their role in the Tolstoyan labyrinth. It turns out that among the numerous things that Oblonsky neglected when he attempted to prepare the estate for his family was repairing the fences. As a result, the cattle, including an aggressive, butting bull, are loose in the garden. Of the nine milk cows, none is producing milk. The references to cows in chapter 7 do not stand out in the description of all the troubles that Dolly has as she settles in for the summer. The chaos on the estate (despite or because of Oblonsky's setting things up for his family) is linked to the mess in the Oblonsky household in Moscow at the opening of the novel: students can discuss the ways in which sexual issues are invariably related to the domestic— even to the bovine—sphere.

The cows who fail to produce milk for the Oblonsky children are the bearers of an important Tolstoyan idea. Tolstoy uses the motif of children suffering from a lack of milk to signal that their parents are failing them. Thus, in part 4, chapter 19, the infant Annie goes hungry until, thanks to Karenin's intervention, the wet nurse is examined and found not to be producing the necessary milk. Milk is also not provided for the Oblonsky children in the opening scenes of the novel, when their mother takes to her bedroom and neglects her household duties after discovering Stiva's adultery. Many other things go wrong as well: the cook quits, the children hurt themselves on a make-believe train ride, one child is fed spoiled broth and gets sick. But when Dolly finally emerges from her bedroom, "drowning her [wifely] grief" in the "daily cares" of motherhood, her first act is maternal. She asks, "Has the milk been sent for?" (12–13; pt. 1, ch. 4).

When Levin visits Dolly and the children, he offers to lend Dolly milk cows. His offer is natural, given his success as a dairy farmer. But his desire to provide milk for the children takes on further significance; it is a natural extension of his loving care of Pava's calf, which he watches over as if it were his own. His offer to Dolly prefigures his more active, fatherly care for her children after he is married to Kitty.

In a revealing exchange between Dolly and Levin, during which she rebuffs his offer of the loan of cows, she looks askance at his positivist attitude to cattle farming, whereby the cow becomes a "machine for the transformation of fodder into milk" (244; pt. 3, ch. 9). In her simpler view, her cows Spotty and White-flake would start producing milk properly if the cook stopped giving the family's leftovers to the laundress's cow. These leftovers rightfully belong to Spotty and Whiteflake. Dolly wants what belongs to her family to stay in her family. The family is better off that way.

Once students become familiar with how Tolstoy expresses his ideas, they can readily see that through Dolly he is indirectly commenting on Oblonsky's behavior. Clearly the family would be better off if Oblonsky would stop wasting his seed and the family's money outside the family, on the former French governess and later on the ballerina Chibisova. In their context in the Tolstoyan labyrinth, Dolly's convictions on the subject of animal husbandry (which boil down to the basic question of how to get Spotty and Whiteflake to produce enough milk to feed her children) reveal to us, indirectly, an important truth about her husband's behavior.

As the novel progresses, more and more associations come into play each time a horse or cow appears on the scene. Horses figure prominently throughout part 6, and they play an important role in the juxtaposition of life on Levin's estate and life on Vronsky's estate (see Knapp, "Estates"). Much of *Anna Karenina* is built on the contrast between how Levin and Kitty live their lives and how Vronsky and Anna live theirs. In part 6, Vronsky's stinginess with the feed he gives to the horses of his visitors is contrasted with the generosity at Levin's stables. Similarly, Levin's reluctance to let the overweight Veslovsky ride his prize horse tells us that Levin has what Vladimir Mayakovsky would later call "the proper attitude toward horses." For Tolstoy, having the proper attitude toward horses is an indicator of a person's moral worth. He took horses seriously, as his story "Kholstomer" ("Strider"), which is told from the point of view of a horse, demonstrates.

When Anna is seen riding at Vozdvizhenskoe, this seemingly innocent, if indulgent, activity brings with it a whole network of implications. The British debate over whether it was fitting for English gentlewomen to ride horses figures in the novels of George Eliot and Mary Elizabeth Braddon, both of whom were read by Tolstoy at Yasnaya Polyana. When Anna on the train in part 1 reads of how "Lady Mary rode to the hounds," "she wanted to do it herself" (92; pt. 1, ch. 29). But this and other desires inspired by her English novel are frustrated. (Mandelker discusses Anna's desires to emulate the "English happiness" in her reading [*Framing* 133–35].) Now Anna, who has broken free of the constraints of her former life, is on horseback herself.

Dolly at first is taken aback at the sight of Anna on horseback: it does not seem proper. We are told that "in Dolly's mind the idea of horse-riding for women was connected with youthful coquetry, which in her opinion was unsuitable to a woman in Anna's position" (553; pt. 6, ch. 17).[3] Dolly, however, arrives at Vozdvizhenskoe ready to accept and embrace Anna and the choices she has made in attempting to be happy. Dolly thus reconciles herself to the sight of Anna on horseback, against her better judgment.

Yet in the murky depths of the Tolstoyan labyrinth, Anna's riding horseback is another indicator of her engaging in sex but rejecting maternity. This idea is encoded on many levels. It was a commonly held belief that riding horseback was dangerous to unborn fetuses, a fact that readers of *Middlemarch* are likely to remember. The headstrong Rosamond Lydgate ignores her physician-husband's warnings, rides horseback, and miscarries their baby. Riding horses, thus, is not something practiced by women who devote their bodies to motherhood; it is for women who seek pleasures other than motherhood. The contrast between the image of Anna on horseback at Vozdvizhenskoe and what is going on meanwhile at Pokrovskoe is telling: at Pokrovskoe, where motherhood and pregnancy are sacred, everyone, especially Levin, does everything possible to ensure the safety of the baby in Kitty's womb. Levin tells her "with a meaning look" that "it is not good for you to be standing" (501; pt. 6, ch. 1); as they walk together, he tells her to "lean more on me," avoids "places where she might take a false step," and "interrupt[s] the conversation to rebuke her for making too quick a movement while stepping over a branch," confessing: "In my heart I wish for nothing more, except that you shouldn't stumble" (506–08; pt. 6, ch. 3). So the sight of Anna on horseback suggests an emblem of her rejection of motherhood. In fact, later that evening she informs Dolly that she is practicing a form of birth control that was introduced to her by a doctor after the birth of Annie. This news shocks Dolly, who is somewhat repulsed by Anna from this point on. What Anna tells her in words—that she will have sex but no more babies—has already been communicated subliminally by the image of Anna on horseback.

Tolstoyan reality, for all its aura of verisimilitude, has its own kind of fourth dimension, thanks to the labyrinth of linkages. In *Anna Karenina*, a horse is a horse, but it is also something more. The same is true of cows. Do we end up with Flaubert's vealism or an ism of another species?

To help students make sense of Tolstoy's cows and horses—and to appreciate the nature of his departure from realism—instructors may introduce them to Richard Gustafson's arguments about Tolstoy's emblematic realism. Gustafson maintains that Tolstoy sought to "transform the nature of realism." He argues that the human reality reflected in his works is of a different order from the reality associated with realism, which presents a deterministic and materialistic view of human existence. Gustafson explains that reality in Tolstoy's understanding is imbued with the divine presence; "the world is the embodiment and revelation of spiritual truth" (203). Gustafson draws attention to Tolstoy's related penchant for thinking allegorically and interpreting life allegorically. For Tolstoy, that divine presence and spiritual truth are embodied in the real world means that what human beings do in that world—at every moment—has significance. Every encounter with a horse or cow is telling.

In attempting to use thematic threads to interpret *Anna Karenina*, instructors may also want to highlight the fact that Tolstoy wrote this novel during a period in which he was searching for answers to spiritual questions. For many readers, *Anna Karenina* reflects the tension he felt between his yearning for faith in divine providence and his despair at the thought that human life (reality) might be ultimately meaningless. This tension shows up in the poetics of the novel and makes this novel qualitatively different from his other works, as Boris Eikhenbaum has suggested (*Tolstoi in the Seventies* 148–62). One manifestation of this difference is the novel's elaborate network of symbolism, in which the real world and its metaphoric realm interact, together forming a labyrinth. *Anna Karenina* depends on an "endless labyrinth of linkings" that at times reassures us that real life can be meaningful (especially if we treat horses and cows properly). At other times this same labyrinth of linkings threatens to engulf its contents in an infinite abyss or to become a machine bent on destroying Anna.

NOTES

[1]For a portion of this letter, see Tolstoy, Anna Karenina 750.

[2]"[B]ut what do such large loose baggy monsters, with their queer elements of the accidental and the arbitrary, artistically *mean*?" (515).

[3]Dolly's response here is linked in the labyrinth to the fact that, in her attempt to bring Kitty and Levin together again in Part 3, Dolly wanted Levin, to his embarrassment, to bring a sidesaddle so that Kitty would be able to ride.

APPENDIX: PRACTICAL SUGGESTIONS FOR A SCAVENGER HUNT

Before we begin reading *Anna Karenina*, I hand out instructions and a list of items to be found in the text. Students report their findings in writing at regular intervals, according to a schedule. Their written work is supplemented by class discussion of the scavenger-hunt material. They need not find all items, but for each item a number of examples (three or four) should be found, so that they have enough data to begin to see patterns—or the lack thereof. They are encouraged to include figurative as well as literal appearances of an item. (Thus, in seeking out bears in the text, they could report and comment on references to the constellation Ursa Major, the fairy tale of the three bears, and references to bear hunting. In seeking out teeth, they could report a simile about extracting an aching tooth as well as mention of a character's actual teeth.) They are asked to discuss each example and then comment on any patterns they discover.

This type of exercise has potential for collaborative, group, or pair work and for the use of electronic technology: students might e-mail their results to the instructor or to their fellow students; findings might be amalgamated and posted on a course Web site, with the result a guide to the labyrinth of *Anna Karenina*.

A Sample List of Items to Be Found in *Anna Karenina*

a. extended similes or metaphors
b. cattle
c. horses
d. bears
e. generalizing or categorical statements
f. inner monologues
g. teeth
h. English imports (ideas, products, people)
i. commentary on the nature of language. Examples would be references to any of the following: the inadequacy of words to express human thought or feeling, difficulties resulting from confusion over the meaning of words, the notion that language is an arbitrary system of signs, the idea that language has become debased.
j. a painting, drawing, sculpture; any work of art
k. sweet food
l. body language
m. an incident where a peasant (or servant) judges, teaches, criticizes, or advises a member of the gentry
n. a seemingly random event, object, or circumstance that takes on symbolic significance and is regarded as an omen
o. dreams
p. iron
q. the French language, customs, or people
r. stars, planets
s. money trouble (overspending, debt, not being able to make ends meet)
t. an example of free indirect discourse
u. body parts
v. candles and candlelight
w. books and reading
x. lies or falsehoods
y. direct or indirect references to the woman question
z. women's clothing

NOTES ON CONTRIBUTORS

Judith Armstrong is senior associate of the Department of Germanic Studies and Russian at the University of Melbourne. She is the author of *The Novel of Adultery* (Macmillan, 1976), *The Unsaid* Anna Karenina (Macmillan, 1988), and *The Christesen Romance* (Melbourne UP, 1996).

Thomas Barran, professor of Russian at Brooklyn College, City University of New York, is the author of numerous articles on eighteenth- and nineteenth-century Russia and of *Russia Reads Rousseau: 1762–1825* (Northwestern UP, 2002).

Julie A. Buckler is Harris K. Weston Associate Professor of Slavic Languages and Literatures at Harvard University. She works in Russian literature, urban cultural studies and semiotics, gender studies, and the performing arts. She is the author of *The Literary Lorgnette: Attending Opera in Imperial Russia* (Stanford UP, 2000), "Her Final Debut: The Kadmina Legend in Russian Literature" (1998), and "Novelistic Figuration, Narrative Metaphor: Western and Russian Models of the Prima Donna" (1998). Her forthcoming book is *Mapping St. Petersburg*.

Manucher Dareshuri, assistant professor at Chestnut Hill College, specializes in economics and global politics. He is the author of "Tax Policy and Plan to Economic Development" and "Multinationals and Mismanagement of Technology" in the *Management International Review* and is currently researching cultural problems involved in the transfer of technology to less developed countries as well as economic aspects of the 1979 revolution in Iran.

Caryl Emerson is A. Watson Armour III University Professor of Slavic Languages and Literatures and professor of comparative literature at Princeton University. Her most recent books are *The Life of Musorgsky* (Cambridge UP, 1999), *Critical Essays on Mikhail Bakhtin* (Hall, 1999), and *The First Hundred Years of Mikhail Bakhtin* (Princeton UP, 1997).

Svetlana Evdokimova, associate professor of Slavic languages at Brown University, is the author of *Pushkin's Historical Imagination* (Yale UP, 1999). She has also published extensively in nineteenth- and twentieth-century Russian literature, history, and culture—in particular on Pushkin, Tolstoy, and Chekhov.

Helena Goscilo is UCIS Professor of Slavic at the University of Pittsburgh. Among her most recent publications are *Dehexing Sex* (U of Michigan P, 1996), *The Explosive World of Tatyana N. Tolstaya's Fiction* (Sharpe, 1996), *Russia—Women—Culture* (edited with Beth Holmgren; Indiana UP, 1996); *Russian Culture of the 1990s* (spec. issue of *Studies in Twentieth-Century Literature*, 2000). She is a leading translator and editor of contemporary Russian authors.

Kate Holland, a doctoral candidate in the Department of Slavic Languages and Literatures, Yale University, is writing her dissertation on Dostoevsky's conception of the novelistic as an aesthetic and ethical category. She is the author of "'The Fictional Filter: 'Krotkaja' and the *Diary of a Writer*" (2000).

Robert Louis Jackson is B. E. Bensinger Professor Emeritus of Slavic Languages and Literatures at Yale University. He has written several books on Dostoevsky, and articles on Pushkin, Gogol, Tolstoy, Turgenev, Chekhov, Solzhenitsyn, and other Russian writers of the nineteenth and twentieth centuries. He is doing research on Chekhov's prose and Goethe's *Elective Affinities* (*Die Wahlverwandtschaften*).

Gary R. Jahn, professor of Slavic languages at the University of Minnesota, is the editor of *Tolstoy's* The Death of Ivan Ilych: *A Critical Companion* (Northwestern UP, 1999) and the author of *Leo Tolstoy's* The Death of Ivan Ilich: *An Interpretation* (Macmillan, 1993). He has published widely in Tolstoy studies, most recently "On the Style of a Story for the People" (1998) and "Brother or Other: Tolstoy's Equivocal Surrender to the Concept of Brotherhood" (1996).

Mary Helen Kashuba, SSJ, DML, professor of French and Russian at Chestnut Hill College, has published articles on French and Russian literature and drama. She is also a specialist in the fields of women's education and global studies and the author of *Tradition and Risk: Chestnut Hill College, 1924–1999* (Donning, 1999).

Liza Knapp, associate professor in the Department of Slavic Languages and Literatures at the University of California, Berkeley, wrote *The Metaphysics of Inertia* (Northwestern UP, 1996) and edited *Dostoevsky's* The Idiot: *A Critical Companion* (Northwestern UP, 1998). She has published articles on Tolstoy, Chekhov, Gogol, and Tsvetaeva.

Gina Kovarsky, an instructor in the Department of Foreign Languages and in the International Studies Program at Virginia Commonwealth University, is a specialist in nineteenth-century Russian and European literatures. She has published "Musical Metapoesis and Metaphysics in *War and Peace*" (2000) and "Mimesis and Moral Education in *Anna Karenina*" (1995–96).

Andrea Lanoux, assistant professor in the Department of Slavic Studies at Connecticut College, has published articles on Russian women's writing and literary canon formation, including "Nadezhda Sokhanskaia" (1999) and "Formirovanie literaturnogo kanona russkogo romantizma" (2001). She is currently editing a volume on gender and national identity in Russian culture.

Mary Laurita is an assistant dean in the College of Arts and Sciences at Washington University. Her fields are nineteenth- and twentieth-century Russian literature, the arts in Russia, and intercultural and global studies. Her most recent publication is "The Vrubel'-Demon Entanglement: The Creation of a Symbolist Myth" (1999).

Amy Mandelker is associate professor of comparative literature at the Graduate Center, City University of New York. Her articles on Tolstoy, Russian and European literatures, and literary theory have appeared in *PMLA, Comparative Literature, Novel, Tolstoy Studies Journal*, and *Slavic and East European Journal*. She is the author of *Framing* Anna Karenina: *Tolstoy, the Woman Question, and the Victorian Novel* (Ohio State UP, 1993), coeditor (with Elizabeth Powers) of *Pilgrim Souls: An Anthology of Spiritual Autobiographies* (Simon, 1999), and editor of *Bakhtin in Contexts: Across the Disciplines* (Northwestern UP, 1996).

Jason Merrill is assistant professor of Russian at Michigan State University. His articles on Fedor Sologub's dramas have appeared in *Elementa, Russkaia Literatura* (Saint Petersburg), and *Slavic and East European Journal*. He has also published *Russian Folktales: A Student Reader* (Focus, 2000).

Gary Saul Morson is Frances Hooper Professor of the Arts and Humanities, Charles Deering McCormick Professor of Teaching Excellence, and professor of Slavic languages at Northwestern University. His *Narrative and Freedom: The Shadows of Time* (Yale UP, 1994) received the René Wellek Prize from the American Comparative Literature Association. Under the name Alicia Chudo, he published *And Quiet Flows the Vodka: The Curmudgeon's Guide to Russian Literature and Culture* (Northwestern UP, 2000).

Harriet Murav, who holds a joint appointment in the Departments of Slavic Languages and Literatures and Comparative Literature at the University of Illinois, Urbana, is a specialist on nineteenth- and twentieth-century Russian literature and Russian-Jewish cultural interactions. Her *Russia's Legal Fictions* (U of Michigan, 1998) won MLA's Aldo and Jeanne Scaglione Prize for best book in Slavic studies. She is also the author of *Holy Foolishness: Dostoevsky's Novels and the Poetics of Cultural Critique* (Stanford UP, 1992) and is currently engaged in a book-length study of Avraam Uri Kovner.

Donna Orwin is associate professor in the Department of Slavic Languages and Literatures at the University of Toronto. She is the editor of *Tolstoy Studies Journal*, editor of *The Cambridge Companion to Tolstoy* (Cambridge UP, 2002), and author of *Tolstoy's Art and Thought, 1847–1880* (Princeton UP, 1993).

David A. Sloane, associate professor in the Department of German, Russian and Asian Languages and Literatures at Tufts University, specializes in the fields of nineteenth-century Russian prose, poetry, and language pedagogy. He is the author of *Aleksandr Blok and the Dynamics of the Lyric Cycle* (Slavica, 1988), "Pushkin's Legacy in *Anna Karenina*" (1991), and "The Poetry in *War and Peace*" (1996).

William M. Todd III is Harvard College Professor and Harry Tuchman Levin Professor of Literature at Harvard University. He is the author of *The Familiar Letter as a Literary Genre in the Age of Pushkin* (Princeton UP, 1976) and *Fiction and Society in the Age of Pushkin: Ideology, Institutions, Narrative* (Harvard UP, 1986). He is the editor of *Literature and Society in Imperial Russia* (Stanford UP, 1978) and *Sovremennoe amerikanskoe pushkinovedenie* (Saint Petersburg, 1999). His current project treats serialization of the nineteenth-century Russian novel.

Justin Weir, assistant professor in the Department of Slavic Languages and Literatures at Harvard University, is coeditor and cotranslator (with Timothy Langen) of *Eight Twentieth-Century Russian Plays* (Northwestern UP, 2000). He is the author of *The Author as Hero: Self and Tradition in Bulgakov, Pasternak, and Nabokov* (Northwestern UP, 2002).

SURVEY PARTICIPANTS

Judith Armstrong, *University of Melbourne*
Thomas Barran, *Brooklyn College, City University of New York*
John Bartle, *Hamilton College*
Elizabeth Beaujour, *Hunter College and Graduate Center, City University of New York*
David Bethea, *University of Wisconsin, Madison*
Karen Black, *Millersville University*
Elizabeth Blake, *Ohio State University, Columbus*
Julie A. Buckler, *Harvard University*
Julie Cassiday, *Williams College*
Caryl Emerson, *Princeton University*
Svetlana Evdokimova, *Brown University*
Melissa Frazier, *Sarah Lawrence College*
Helena Goscilo, *University of Pittsburgh, Pittsburgh*
Robert Louis Jackson, *Yale University*
Gary Jahn, *University of Minnesota, Twin Cities*
Kelly Herold, *Grinnell College*
Peter Hodgson, *University of California, Los Angeles*
Kate Holland, *Yale University*
Mary Helen Kashuba, *Chestnut Hill College*
Michael Katz, *Middlebury College*
Gina Kovarsky, *Virginia Commonwealth University*
Andrea Lanoux, *Connecticut College*
Mary Laurita, *University of South Alabama*
Hugh McLean, *University of California, Berkeley*
Jason Merrill, *Michigan State University*
Robin Feuer Miller, *Brandeis University*
Gary Saul Morson, *Northwestern University*
Harriet Murav, *University of Illinois, Urbana*
Donna Orwin, *University of Toronto, Mississauga*
Stephen Parker, *University of Kansas*
Daniel Rancour-Laferriere, *University of California, Davis*
Debra Ratner, *Albany Adult School*
Sydney Schultze, *University of Louisville*
David A. Sloane, *Tufts University*
William M. Todd III, *Harvard University*
C. J. G. Turner, *University of British Columbia*
Irena Ustinova, *East Carolina University*
Irina Vayl, *Institute of the Theory of Literature*
Justin Weir, *Harvard University*

WORKS CITED

Adelman, Gary. Anna Karenina: *The Bitterness of Ecstasy.* Twayne's Masterwork Series. Boston: Twayne, 1990.

Allen, Elizabeth Cheresh, and Gary Saul Morson, eds. *Freedom and Responsibility in Russian Literature: Essays in Honor of Robert Louis Jackson.* New Haven: Yale UP, 1995.

Al'tman, M. S. *U L'va Tolstogo.* Tula: Priokskoe, 1980.

Aristotle. *On Poetry and Style.* Trans. and introd. G. M. A. Grube. Lib. of Liberal Arts. Indianapolis: Bobbs, 1958.

Armstrong, Judith. *The Novel of Adultery.* New York: Barnes, 1976.

———. *The Unsaid* Anna Karenina. New York: St. Martin's, 1988.

Arnheim, Rudolf. *Art and Visual Perception: A Psychology of the Creative Eye: The New Version.* Berkeley: U of California P, 1974.

Avseenko, V. G. "Po povodu novogo romana grafa L. N. Tolstogo." *Russkii vestnik* 5 (1875): 400–20.

Babaev, E. G. *Lev Tolstoi i russkaia zhurnalistika ego èpokhi.* Moscow: Moskovskii U, 1978.

Baehr, Stephen. "The Troika and the Train: Dialogues between Tradition and Technology in Nineteenth-Century Russian Literature." *Issues in Russian Literature before 1917: Proceedings from the III International Congress on Soviet and East European Studies.* Ed. Douglas Clayton and R. C. Elwood. Columbus: Slavica, 1989. 85–106.

Bakhtin, Mikhail. *The Dialogic Imagination: Four Essays by M. M. Bakhtin.* Ed. Michael Holquist. Trans. Caryl Emerson and Holquist. Austin: U of Texas P, 1981.

———. *Lektsii po istorii zarubezhnoi literatury: Antichnost´, srednie veka (v zapisi V. A. Mirskoi).* Ed. I. V. Kliuevaia and L. M. Lisunovaia. Saransk: Mordovskii U, 1999.

———. "Preface to Volume 13: *Resurrection* [by Tolstoy]." Trans. Caryl Emerson. *Rethinking Bakhtin: Extensions and Challenges.* Ed. Gary Saul Morson and Emerson. Evanston: Northwestern UP, 1989. 237–57.

———. *Problems of Dostoevsky's Poetics.* Trans. and ed. Caryl Emerson. Introd. Wayne C. Booth. Minneapolis: U of Minnesota P, 1984.

———. *Rabelais and His World.* Trans. Helene Iswolsky. Bloomington: Indiana UP, 1984.

Barnes, Julian. *Flaubert's Parrot.* London: Cape, 1984.

Bayley, John. *Tolstoy and the Novel.* Chicago: U of Chicago P, 1988.

Bean, John C. *Engaging Ideas: The Professor's Guide to Integrating Writing, Critical Thinking, and Active Learning in the Classroom.* San Francisco: Jossey-Bass, 1996.

Belknap, Robert. "Tolstoy's Prince Who Resembles a Cucumber." Allen and Morson 153–58.

Benson, Ruth Crego. *Women in Tolstoy: The Ideal and the Erotic*. Urbana: U of Illinois P, 1973.

Bethea, David M. *The Shape of Apocalypse in Modern Russian Fiction*. Princeton: Princeton UP, 1989.

Bloom, Harold, ed. *Leo Tolstoy*. Bloom's Major Novelists. Broomall: Chelsea, 2002.

———, ed. *Leo Tolstoy's* Anna Karenina. Introd. Bloom. New York: Chelsea, 1987.

Blumberg, Edwina Jannie. "Tolstoy and the English Novel: A Note on *Middlemarch* and *Anna Karenina*." W. Jones, *Tolstoi* 93–104.

Booth, Wayne C. *The Company We Keep: An Ethics of Fiction*. Berkeley: U of California P, 1988.

Bordwell, David, and Kristin Thompson. *Film Art: An Introduction*. 6th ed. New York: McGraw, 2001.

Bourdieu, Pierre. *Distinction: A Social Critique of the Judgement of Taste*. Trans. Richard Nice. Cambridge: Harvard UP, 1984.

Bronfen, Elisabeth. *Over Her Dead Body: Configurations of Femininity, Death, and the Aesthetic*. New York: Routledge, 1992.

Brooks, Jeffrey. *When Russia Learned to Read: Literacy and Popular Literature, 1861–1917*. Princeton: Princeton UP, 1985.

Brooks, Peter. *The Melodramatic Imagination: Balzac, Henry James, Melodrama, and the Mode of Excess*. New Haven: Yale UP, 1976.

Browning, Gary L. "The Death of Anna Karenina: Anna's Share of the Blame." *Slavic and East European Journal* 30 (1986): 327–39.

Brun, M. "Razvod." *Èntsiklopedicheskii slovar'*. Ed. I. E. Andreevskii. Vol. 26. Saint Petersburg: Brokgauz, 1894. 131–36.

Buckler, Julie. *The Literary Lorgnette: Attending Opera in Imperial Russia*. Stanford: Stanford UP, 2000.

Buzan, Tony, and Barry Buzan. *The Mind Map Book*. New York: Plume, 1996.

Carmichael, Joel. "On Retranslating a Russian Classic." Tolstoy, *Anna Karenina* [Carmichael] 869–73.

Caws, Mary Ann. *Reading Frames in Modern Fiction*. Princeton: Princeton UP, 1985.

Chernyshevsky, Nikolai. *What Is to Be Done?* Trans. Michael R. Katz. Ithaca: Cornell UP, 1989.

Christian, Richard F. *Tolstoy: A Critical Introduction*. Cambridge: Cambridge UP, 1969.

Cohn, Dorrit. *Transparent Minds: Narrative Modes for Presenting Consciousness in Fiction*. Princeton: Princeton UP, 1978.

Cover, Robert. "The Supreme Court 1982 Term. Forward: Nomos and Narrative." *Harvard Law Review* 97.4 (1983): 4–68.

Culler, Jonathan. "The Uses of *Madame Bovary*." *Flaubert and Postmodernism*. Ed. Naomi Schor and Henry F. Majewski. Lincoln: U of Nebraska P, 1980. 1–12.

Diderot, d'Alembert. "Luxury." Diderot et al. 203–33.

Diderot, d'Alembert, et al. *Encyclopedia*. Trans. Nelly S. Hoyt and Thomas Cassirer. New York: Bobbs, 1965.

Dostoevsky, Fyodor. *Crime and Punishment*. Trans. Jessie Coulson. Ed. George Gibian. Rev. ed. Norton Critical Ed. New York: Norton, 1975.

————. *The Idiot*. Trans. Alan Myers. Oxford: Oxford UP, 1992.

————. *Polnoe sobranie sochinenii*. 30 vols. Ed. V. G. Bazanov et al. Leningrad: Nauka, 1972–90.

————. *A Writer's Diary*. 2 vols. Trans. Kenneth Lantz. Evanston: Northwestern UP, 1994.

Eaton, Henry. "Marx and the Russians." *Journal of the History of Ideas* 41 (1981): 89–112.

Edwards, Anne. *Sonya: The Life of Countess Tolstoy*. New York: Simon, 1981.

Eikhenbaum, Boris. *Tolstoi in the Seventies*. Trans. Albert Kaspin. Ann Arbor: Ardis, 1982.

————. *Tolstoi in the Sixties*. Trans. Duffield White. Ann Arbor: Ardis, 1982.

————. *The Young Tolstoi*. Trans. Gary Kern. Ann Arbor: Ardis, 1972.

Engels, Barbara. *Mothers and Daughters: Women of the Intelligentsia in Nineteenth-Century Russia*. Evanston: Northwestern UP, 2000.

Engels, Friedrich. *Socialism: Utopian and Scientific*. Trans. Paul Lafargue. Marx/Engels Internet Archive. 1993, 1999. 9 May 2002 <http://www.marxists.org/archive/marx/works/1880/soc-utop/>.

Evans, Mary. *Reflecting on* Anna Karenina. London: Routledge, 1989.

Evdokimova, Svetlana. "The Drawing and the Grease Spot: Creativity and Interpretation in *Anna Karenina*." *Tolstoy Studies Journal* 8 (1996): 33–45.

Feuer, Kathryn B. "Stiva." *Russian Literature and American Critics: In Honor of Deming B. Brown*. Ed. K. N. Brostrom. Ann Arbor: U of Michigan P, 1984. 347–56.

Fish, Stanley. *Surprised by Sin: The Reader in* Paradise Lost. London: Macmillan, 1967.

Freud, Sigmund. *The Interpretation of Dreams*. Trans. and ed. James Strachey. New York: Avon, 1998.

Freund, Elizabeth. *The Return of the Reader: Reader-Response Criticism*. London: Methuen, 1987.

Frieden, Ken. *Freud's Dream of Interpretation*. Albany: State U of New York P, 1990.

Frye, Northrop. *Anatomy of Criticism: Four Essays*. Princeton: Princeton UP, 1957.

Fulwiler, Toby. "Responding to Student Journals." *Writing and Response: Theory, Practice, and Research*. Ed. Chris M. Anson. Urbana: NCTE, 1989. 149–73.

Garnett, Edward. *Tolstoy, His Life and Writings*. Philadelphia: West, 1978.

Genatulin, Anatoly. "Rough Weather." *Glasnost: An Anthology of Russian Literature under Gorbachev*. Ed. Helena Goscilo. Ann Arbor: Ardis, 1990. 303–77.

Giannetti, Louis. *Understanding Movies*. 9th ed. Upper Saddle River: Prentice, 2002.

Gifford, Henry, ed. *Leo Tolstoy: A Critical Anthology*. Harmondsworth: Penguin, 1971.

————. "On Translating Tolstoy." M. Jones 17–37.

————. *Tolstoy*. Oxford: Oxford UP, 1983.

Ginzburg, Lydia. *On Psychological Prose*. Trans. and ed. Judson Rosengrant. Princeton: Princeton UP, 1988.

Gombrich, E. H. *Art and Illusion: A Study in the Psychology of Pictorial Representation*. Princeton: Princeton UP, 2000.

Gorky, Maxim. *Reminiscences of Leo Nikolaevich Tolstoy*. Trans. S. S. Koteliansky and Leonard Woolf. Folcroft: Folcroft Lib., 1977.

Gornaia, V. Z. *Mir chitaet* Annu Kareninu. Moscow: Kniga, 1979.

Goscilo, Helena, and Petre Petrov. Anna Karenina *on Page and Screen*. Studies in Slavic Cultures 2. Pittsburgh: Slavic Langs., Center for Russian and East European Studies, U of Pittsburgh, 2001.

Gosudarstvennaia Tret'iakovskaia Galereia: Albom reproduktsii. Moscow: Izobrazitel'noe iskusstvo, 1964, 1970.

Grenier, Svetlana. *Representing the Marginal Woman in Nineteenth-Century Russian Literature: Personalism, Feminism, and Polyphony*. Westport: Greenwood, 2001.

Gromeka, M. S. "Gromeka on Karenin, 'Russian Thought,' 1883, 1884." Knowles, *Tolstoy* 312–20.

Grossman, Joan Delaney. "Tolstoy's Portrait of Anna: Keystone in the Arch." *Criticism* 18 (1976): 1–14.

Gudzii, N. K. "Istoriia pisaniia i pechataniia *Anny Kareninoi*." Tolstoy, *Polnoe sobranie* 20: 577–645.

Gustafson, Richard F. *Leo Tolstoy, Resident and Stranger: A Study in Fiction and Theology*. Princeton: Princeton UP, 1986.

Gutkin, Irina. "The Dichotomy between Flesh and Spirit: Plato's *Symposium* in *Anna Karenina*." McLean, *In the Shade* 84–99.

Heldt, Barbara. "Tolstoy's Path to Feminism." *Terrible Perfection: Women and Russian Literature*. Bloomington: Indiana UP, 1987. 38–48.

Higonnet, Margaret. "Speaking Silences: Women's Suicides." *The Female Body in Western Culture: Contemporary Perspectives*. Ed. Susan Rubin Suleiman. Cambridge: Harvard UP, 1985. 68–83.

Hingley, Ronald. *Russian Writers and Society in the Nineteenth Century*. 2nd ed. London: Weidenfeld, 1977.

Hogan, Rebecca. "The Wisdom of Many, the Wit of One: The Narrative Function of the Proverb in Tolstoy's *Anna Karenina* and Trollope's *Orley Farm*." Diss. U of Colorado, Boulder, 1985.

Hoisington, Sona, ed. *A Plot of Her Own: The Female Protagonist in Russian Literature*. Evanston: Northwestern UP, 1995.

Hruska, Anne. "The Infected Family: Belonging and Estrangement in the Works of Leo Tolstoy." Diss. U of California, Berkeley, 2001.

Iser, Wolfgang. *The Act of Reading: A Theory of Aesthetic Response*. Baltimore: Johns Hopkins UP, 1978.

———. *The Implied Reader: Patterns of Communication in Prose Fiction from Bunyan to Beckett*. Baltimore: Johns Hopkins UP, 1974.

Jackson, Robert Louis. "Chance and Design in *Anna Karenina*." *The Disciplines of Criticism: Essays in Literary Theory, Interpretation, and History*. Ed. Peter Demetz, Thomas Greene, and Lowry Nelson, Jr. New Haven: Yale UP, 1968. 315–29.

———. "Father Sergius and the Paradox of the Fortunate Fall." *Russian Literature* 40 (1996): 463–80.

———. "On the Ambivalent Beginning of *Anna Karenina*." *Semantic Analysis of Literary Texts: To Honour Jan van der Eng on the Occasion of His Sixty-Fifth Birthday*. Ed. Eric de Haard et al. Amsterdam: Elsevier, 1990. 345–55.

Jahn, Gary R. "The Image of the Railroad in *Anna Karenina*." *Slavic and East European Journal* 25 (1981): 8–12.

James, Henry. *The Critical Muse: Selected Literary Criticism*. Ed. Roger Gard. New York: Penguin, 1987.

Janik, Allan, and Stephen Toulmin. *Wittgenstein's Vienna*. New York: Simon, 1973.

Jones, Malcolm V., ed. *New Essays on Tolstoy*. Cambridge: Cambridge UP, 1978.

Jones, Malcolm V., and Robin Feuer Miller, eds. *Cambridge Companion to the Classic Russian Novel*. New York: Cambridge UP, 1998.

Jones, W. Gareth. "George Eliot's *Adam Bede* and Tolstoy's Conception of *Anna Karenina*." W. Jones, *Tolstoi* 79–92.

———, ed. *Tolstoi and Britain*. Oxford: Berg, 1995.

Katkov, M. N. "Chto sluchilos' po smerti Anny Kareninoi." *Russkii vestnik* 7 (1877): 448–62.

Keillor, Garrison. "*Anna Karenina*: The Sequel." *Harper's Magazine* July 1993: 34.

Kermode, Frank. *The Sense of an Ending*. New York: Oxford UP, 1966.

Klimov, Alexis. "Is It 'Lévin' or 'Lëvin'?" *Tolstoy Studies Journal* 11 (1999): 108–11.

Knapp, Liza. "The Estates of Pokrovskoe and Vozdvizhenskoe: Tolstoy's Labyrinth of Linkings in *Anna Karenina*." *Tolstoy Studies Journal* 8 (1995-96): 81–98.

———. "'Tue-la! Tue-le!' Death Sentences, Words, and Inner Monologue in Tolstoy's *Anna Karenina* and 'Three More Deaths.'" *Tolstoy Studies Journal* 11 (1999): 1–19.

Knowles, A. V. "Russian Views of *Anna Karenina*, 1875–1878." *Slavic and East European Journal* 22 (1978): 301–12.

———, ed. *Tolstoy: The Critical Heritage*. London: Routledge, 1978.

Kovarsky, Gina. "Mimesis and Moral Education in *Anna Karenina*." *Tolstoy Studies Journal* 8 (1995-96): 61–80.

Krieger, Murray. *Ekphrasis: The Illusion of the Natural Sign*. Baltimore: Johns Hopkins UP, 1992.

Kujundžić, Dragan. "Pardoning Woman in *Anna Karenina*." *Tolstoy Studies Journal* 6 (1993): 65–85.

Lawrence, D. H. "The Novel." *"Study of Thomas Hardy" and Other Essays*. Ed. Bruce Steele. Cambridge: Cambridge UP, 1985. 170–90.

———. *Phoenix: The Posthumous Papers of D. H. Lawrence*. Ed. and introd. Edward D. McDonald. New York: Viking, 1936.

LeBlanc, Ronald. "Levin Visits Anna: The Iconology of Harlotry." *Tolstoy Studies Journal* 3 (1990): 1–20.

Lock, Charles. "Double Voicing, Sharing Words: Bakhtin's Dialogism and the History of the Theory of Free Indirect Discourse." *The Novelness of Bakhtin: Perspectives and Possibilities*. Ed. Jorgen Bruhn and Jan Lundquist. Copenhagen: Museum Tusculanum, 2001. 71–87.

Lotman, Iurii. "O siuzhetnom prostranstve russkogo romana XIX stoletiia." *Trudy po znakovym sistemam* 20 (1987): 102–14.

Maegd-Soëp, Carolina de. *The Emancipation of Women in Russian Literature and Society: A Contribution to the Knowledge of the Russian Society during the 1860s*. Ghent: Ghent UP, 1978.

Maguire, Robert A., ed. *Gogol from the Twentieth Century: Eleven Essays*. Princeton: Princeton UP, 1974.

———. "The Legacy of Criticism." Maguire, *Gogol* 3–54.

———. *Red Virgin Soil: Soviet Literature in the 1920s*. Princeton: Princeton UP, 1968.

Makoveeva, Irina. "Cinematic Adaptations of *Anna Karenina*." *Studies in Slavic Cultures* 2 (2001): 110–33.

Mandelbaum, Maurice. *History, Man, and Reason: A Study in Nineteenth-Century Thought*. Baltimore: Johns Hopkins UP, 1971.

Mandelker, Amy. *Framing* Anna Karenina: *Tolstoy, the Woman Question, and the Victorian Novel*. Columbus: Ohio State UP, 1993.

———. "Illustrate and Condemn: The Phenomenology of Vision in *Anna Karenina*." *Tolstoy Studies Journal* 8 (1996): 46–60.

Marx, Karl, and Frederick Engels. *The Communist Manifesto*. Trans. Samuel Moore. New York: Intl., 1948.

Matich, Olga. "A Typology of Fallen Women in Nineteenth-Century Russian Literature." *American Contributions to the Ninth International Congress of Slavists: Volume 2: Literature, Poetics, History*. Ed. Paul Debreczeny. Columbus: Slavica, 1983. 325–43.

Maude, Aylmer. *Leo Tolstoy*. New York: Haskell, 1975.

Mayakovsky, V. V. "Khoroshee otnoshenie k loshadiam." *Sochineniia v trekh tomakh*. Vol. 1. Moscow: Khudozhestvennaia literatura, 1965. 139–40.

McDermid, Jane. "The Influence of Western Ideas on the Development of the Woman Question in Nineteenth-Century Russian Thought." *Irish Slavonic Studies* 9 (1988): 2–36.

McLean, Hugh, ed. *In the Shade of the Giant: Essays on Tolstoy*. California Slavic Studies 13. Berkeley: U of California P, 1989.

———. "Truth in Dying." McLean, *In the Shade* 130–57.

———. "Which English *Anna*?" *Tolstoy Studies Journal* 13 (2001): 38–48.

Melzer, Arthur. *The Natural Goodness of Man: On the System of Rousseau's Thought*. Chicago: U of Chicago P, 1990.

Merezhkovskii, D. S. *L. Tolstoi i Dostoevskii*. 2 vols. 3rd ed. Saint Petersburg: Pirozhkova, 1902–03. Ed. E. A. Andrushchenko. Moscow: Nauka, 2000.

Meyer, Priscilla. "*Anna Karenina*: Tolstoy's Polemic with *Madame Bovary*." *Russian Review* 54 (1995): 243–59.

Mikhailova, Vera. *Russkie zakony o zhenshchinakh*. Moscow, 1913.

Mill, John Stuart. *The Subjection of Women*. On Liberty *and* The Subjection of Women. Introd. Jane O'Grady. Wordsworth Classics of World Lit. Ware, Eng.: Wordsworth, 1996.

Miller, D. A. *Narrative and Its Discontents: Problems of Closure in the Traditional Novel*. Princeton: Princeton UP, 1981.

Mirsky, D. S. *A History of Russian Literature, from Its Beginnings to 1900*. Ed. Francis J. Whitfield. New York: Vintage, 1958.

Modzalevsky, B. L., ed. *Perepiska L. N. Tolstogo s N. N. Strakhovym, 1870–1894*. Saint Petersburg: Obshchestvo Tolstovskogo Muzeia, 1914.

Monaco, James. *How to Read a Film: Movies, Media, Multimedia: Language, History, Theory*. 3rd ed. New York: Oxford UP, 2000.

Morson, Gary Saul. "Anna Karenina's Omens." Tolstoy, Anna Karenina 831–43.

———. "Brooding Stiva: The Masterpiece Theatre *Anna Karenina.*" *Tolstoy Studies Journal* 13 (2001): 49–58.

———. *Hidden in Plain View: Narrative and Creative Potentials in* War and Peace. Stanford: Stanford UP, 1987.

———. *Narrative and Freedom: The Shadows of Time*. New Haven: Yale UP, 1994.

———. "Prosaics in *Anna Karenina.*" *Tolstoy Studies Journal* 1 (1988): 1–12.

———. "The Reader as Voyeur: Tolstoi and the Poetics of Didactic Fiction." *Canadian-American Slavic Studies* 12 (1978): 465–80.

Morson, Gary Saul, and Caryl Emerson. *Mikhail Bakhtin: Creation of a Prosaics*. Stanford: Stanford UP, 1990.

Moser, Charles A. *Esthetics as Nightmare: Russian Literary Theory, 1855–1870*. Princeton: Princeton UP, 1989.

Nabokov, Vladimir. *Lectures on Russian Literature*. San Diego: Harcourt, 1981.

Nekrasov, N. A. "Zheleznaia doroga." *Sobranie sochinenii v vos′mi tomakh*. Vol. 2. Moscow: Khudozhestvennaia literatura, 1965. 118–23.

Nelles, William. "Myth and Symbol in *Madame Bovary.*" *Approaches to Teaching Flaubert's* Madame Bovary. Ed. Laurence M. Porter and Eugene F. Gray. New York: MLA, 1995. 55–60.

Orwin, Donna Tussing, ed. *Cambridge Critical Companion to Tolstoy*. Cambridge: Cambridge UP, 2002.

———. *Tolstoy's Art and Thought, 1847–1880*. Princeton: Princeton UP, 1993.

Osborne, Suzanne. "*Effi Briest* and *Anna Karenina.*" *Tolstoy Studies Journal* 5 (1992): 67–77.

Passage, Charles. *Character Names in Dostoevsky's Fiction*. Ann Arbor: Ardis, 1982.

Pavlovskis-Petit, Zoja. "*Anna Karenina.*" *Encyclopedia of Literary Translation into English*. Vol. 2. Ed. Olive Classe. London: Fitzroy, 2000. 1405–07.

Perry, Donna M. "Making Journal Writing Matter." *Teaching Writing: Pedagogy, Gender, and Equity*. Ed. Cynthia L. Caywood and Gillian R. Overing. Albany: State U of New York P, 1987. 151–56.

Pipes, Richard. *Russia under the Old Regime*. New York: Scribner's, 1974.

Plato. *Cratylus, Parmenides, Greater Hippias, Lesser Hippias*. Trans. N. N. Fowler. Loeb Classical Lib. 167. Cambridge: Harvard UP, 1977.

———. *Lysis, Symposium, Gorgias*. Trans. W. R. Lamb. Loeb Classical Lib. 166. Cambridge: Harvard UP, 1925.

———. *Republic*. Trans. Desmond Lee. 2nd ed. Rev. London: Penguin, 1987.

Prince, Gerald. *A Dictionary of Narratology*. Lincoln: U of Nebraska P, 1987.

Propp, Vladimir Ia. *Istoricheskie korni volshebnoi skazki*. Leningrad: Leningradskii U, 1946.

Pursglove, Michael. "The Smiles of Anna Karenina." *Slavic and East European Journal* 17 (1973): 42–48.

Pushkin, Aleksandr. *Eugene Onegin: A Novel in Verse.* 4 vols. Trans. Vladimir Nabokov. Princeton: Princeton UP, 1975.

———. "Mednyi vsadnik." *Polnoe sobranie sochinenii v desiati tomakh.* 4th ed. Vol. 4. Leningrad: Nauka, 1977. 273–88.

Remizov, Vitalii. " 'Ia esm', i ia liubiu': Lev Tolstoi za chteniem 'Brat'ev Karamazovykh.' " *L. N. Tolstoi: Dialogi vo vremeni.* Tula: Tulskogo gosudarstvennogo pedagogi-cheskogo universiteta im. L. N. Tolstogo, 1998. 83–94.

Rogers, Philip. "A Tolstoyan Reading of *David Copperfield.*" *Comparative Literature* 42 (1990): 1–28.

Roosevelt, Priscilla. *Life on the Russian Country Estate: A Social and Cultural History.* With photographs by William Brumfield. New Haven: Yale UP, 1995.

Rose, Phyllis. *Parallel Lives: Five Victorian Marriages.* New York: Random, 1984.

Rosenblatt, Louise M. *Literature as Exploration.* 3rd ed. New York: Noble, 1976.

Rosenthal, Bernice Glatzer. "Merezhkovskii's Readings of Tolstoi: Their Contemporary Relevance." *Russian Thought after Communism: The Recovery of a Philosophical Heritage.* Ed. James P. Scanlan. Armonk: Sharpe, 1994. 121–46.

Rousseau, Jean-Jacques. *The Confessions of Jean-Jacques Rousseau.* New York: Modern Lib., n.d.

———. *A Discourse on a Subject Proposed by the Academy of Dijon: What Is the Origin of Inequality among Men, and Is It Authorised by Natural Law?* Trans. G. D. H. Cole. Ed. John Roland. Constitution Soc. 15 Aug. 2002 <http://www.constitution .org/jjr/ineq.htm>.

———. *Discourse on the Sciences and Arts (First Discourse) and Polemics.* Ed. Roger D. Masters and Christopher Kelly. Hanover: UP of New England, 1992. Vol. 2 of *The Collected Works of Rousseau.*

———. *Emile; or, On Education.* Trans. Allan Bloom. New York: Basic, 1979.

———. *La nouvelle Héloïse.* Paris: Garnier, 1967.

Rozanov, V. V. *Semeinyi vopros v Rossii.* 2 vols. Saint Petersburg: n.p., 1903.

Schor, Naomi. "For a Restricted Thematics: Writing, Speech, and Difference in *Madame Bovary.*" *Breaking the Chain: Women, Theory, and French Fiction.* New York: Columbia UP, 1985. 3–28.

Schultze, Sydney. *The Structure of* Anna Karenina. Ann Arbor: Ardis, 1982.

Segal, Naomi. *The Adulteress's Child: Authorship and Desire in the Nineteenth-Century Novel.* Cambridge: Polity, 1992.

Seifrid, Thomas. "Gazing on Life's Page: Perspectival Vision in Tolstoy." *PMLA* 113 (1998): 436–48.

Selivanova, N. N. *Russia's Women.* New York: Dutton, 1923.

Shashkov, S. "Literaturnyi trud v Rossii (istoricheskii ocherk)." *Delo* 8 (1876): 3–48.

Sheldon, Richard. "Problems in the English Translations of *Anna Karenina.*" *Essays in the Art and Theory of Translation.* Ed. Lenore A. Grenoble and John M. Kopper. Lewiston: Mellen, 1997. 231–61.

Shestov, Lev. "The Good in the Teaching of Tolstoy and Nietzsche: Philosophy and Preaching." Trans. Bernard Martin. *Dostoevsky, Tolstoy, and Nietzsche.* Introd. Martin. Athens: Ohio UP, 1969. 11–140.

Shklovsky, Viktor. "Art as Technique." *Russian Formalist Criticism: Four Essays*. Trans. and ed. Lee T. Lemon and Marion J. Reis. Lincoln: U of Nebraska P, 1965. 3–24.

———. *Lev Tolstoy*. Trans. Olga Shartse. Moscow: Progress, 1978.

———. *O teorii prozy*. Moscow: Federatsiia, 1929.

Silbajoris, Rimvydas. *Tolstoy's Aesthetics and His Art*. Columbus: Slavica, 1991.

Simmons, Ernest J. *Leo Tolstoy*. New York: Vintage, 1960.

Sloane, David. "Pushkin's Legacy in *Anna Karenina*." *Tolstoy Studies Journal* 4 (1991): 1–23.

Smith, Barbara H. *Poetic Closure*. Chicago: U of Chicago P, 1968.

Steiner, George. *Tolstoy or Dostoevsky: An Essay in the Old Criticism*. 2nd ed. New Haven: Yale UP, 1996.

Stenbock-Fermor, Elisabeth. *The Architecture of* Anna Karenina: *A History of Its Writing, Structure, and Message*. Lisse: de Ridder, 1975.

Stern, J. P. M. "*Effi Briest; Madame Bovary; Anna Karenina*." Gifford, *Leo Tolstoy* 281–87.

Stites, Richard. *The Women's Liberation Movement in Russia: Feminism, Nihilism, and Bolshevism, 1860–1930*. Princeton: Princeton UP, 1978.

Suleiman, Susan R., and Inge Crosman, eds. *The Reader in the Text: Essays on Audience and Interpretation*. Princeton: Princeton UP, 1980.

Tanner, Tony. *Adultery in the Novel: Contract and Transgression*. Baltimore: Johns Hopkins UP, 1979.

Terras, Victor. *Belinskij and Russian Literary Criticism: The Heritage of Organic Aesthetics*. Madison: U of Wisconsin P, 1974.

———, ed. *Handbook of Russian Literature*. New Haven: Yale UP, 1985.

———. *A History of Russian Literature*. New Haven: Yale UP, 1991.

Thorlby, Anthony. *Leo Tolstoy*: Anna Karenina. Cambridge: Cambridge UP, 1997.

Todd, William M. *Fiction and Society in the Age of Pushkin: Ideology, Institution, and Narrative*. Cambridge: Harvard UP, 1986.

———. "Reading *Anna* in Parts." *Tolstoy Studies Journal* 8 (1995–96): 125–28.

———. "The Responsibilities of (Co-)Authorship: Notes on Revising the Serialized Version of *Anna Karenina*." Allen and Morson 162–69.

Tolstaia, S. A. *The Diaries of Sofia Tolstaya*. Ed. O. A. Golinenko et al. Trans. Cathy Porter. London: Cape, 1985.

Tolstoy, Leo. *Anna Karenina*. Trans. Joel Carmichael. New York: Bantam, 1981.

———. *Anna Karenina*. Trans. and introd. Rosemary Edmonds. Penguin Classic. New York: Penguin, 1997.

———. *Anna Karenina*. Trans. Constance Garnett. Rev. Leonard J. Kent and Nina Berberova. New York: Modern Lib., 2000.

———. *Anna Karenina*. Trans. Richard Pevear and Larissa Volokhonsky. New York: Penguin, 2001.

———. *Anna Karenina*. Ed. V. A. Zhdanov and E. E. Zaidenshnur. Moscow: Nauka, 1970.

———. Anna Karenina: *The Maude Translation*. Trans. Louise Maude and Aylmer Maude. Rev. and ed. George Gibian. 2nd ed. Norton Critical Ed. New York: Norton, 1995.

―――. *Childhood, Boyhood, Youth.* Trans. Rosemary Edmonds. London: Penguin, 1964.

―――. *"A Confession," "The Gospel in Brief," and "What I Believe."* Trans. Aylmer Maude. World's Classics 229. London: Oxford UP, 1967.

―――. *Great Short Works.* Introd. John Bayley. New York: Harper, 1967.

―――. *"On Life" and Essays on Religion.* Oxford: Oxford UP, 1934.

―――. *Polnoe sobranie sochinenii.* Ed. V. G. Chertkov et al. 90 vols. Moscow: Khudozhestvennaia literatura, 1928–58.

―――. *Strider: The Story of a Horse.* Trans. Louise Maude and Aylmer Maude. Tolstoy Lib. 4 Sept. 2002 <http://www.geocities.com/cmcarpenter28/Works/strider.txt>.

―――. *Tolstoy's Diaries.* Ed. and trans. R. F. Christian. 2 vols. London: Harper, 1994.

―――. *Tolstoy's Letters.* Ed. and trans. R. F. Christian. 2 vols. New York: Scribner, 1978.

―――. War and Peace: *The Maude Translation: Backgrounds and Sources, Essays in Criticism.* Ed. George Gibian. New York: Norton, 1966.

―――. *What Is Art?* Trans. Aylmer Maude. Indianapolis: Bobbs, 1960.

Tompkins, Jane P., ed. *Reader-Response Criticism: From Formalism to Structuralism.* Baltimore: Johns Hopkins UP, 1980.

Torgovnick, Marianna. *Closure in the Novel.* Princeton: Princeton UP, 1981.

Turgenev, Ivan. *Asya.* Ed. Lydia Savitzkaya. Lincolnwood: Natl. Textbook, 1988.

Turner, C. J. G. "Divorce and *Anna Karenina.*" *Forum for Modern Language Studies* 23.2 (1987): 97–116.

―――. *A Karenina Companion.* Waterloo, ON: Wilfrid Laurier UP, 1993.

―――. "The Maude Translation of *Anna Karenina*: Some Observations." *Russian Literature Journal* 168–70 (1997): 233–54.

"Twit." *The New Shorter Oxford English Dictionary.* 2 vols. 4th ed. Ed. Lesley Brown. 1993.

Uspensky, Boris. *A Poetics of Composition: The Structure of the Artistic Text and Typology of a Compositional Form.* Trans. Valentina Zavarina and Susan Wittig. Berkeley: U of California P, 1973.

Wagner, William G. *Marriage, Property, and Law in Late Imperial Russia.* Oxford: Clarendon, 1994.

Wasiolek, Edward, ed. *Critical Essays on Tolstoy.* Boston: Hall, 1986.

―――. *Tolstoy's Major Fiction.* Chicago: U of Chicago P, 1978.

West, Robin. *Narrative, Authority, and Law.* Ed. Michael Ryan, Martha Minnow, and Austin Sarat. Ann Arbor: U of Michigan P, 1993.

Whitcomb, Curt. "Treacherous 'Charm' in *Anna Karenina.*" *Slavic and East European Journal* 39 (1995): 214–26.

Wilson, A. N. *Tolstoy: A Biography.* New York: Norton, 1988.

Wittgenstein, Ludwig. *Tractatus Logico-Philosophicus.* Trans. D. F. Pears and B. F. McGuinness. London: Routledge, 1974.

Yermakov, Ivan. "The Nose." Maguire, *Gogol* 155–98.

Zenkovskii [Zenkovsky], V. V. "Problema bessmertiia u L. N. Tolstogo." *O religii L'va Tolstogo: Sbornik statei*. 1912. Paris: YMCA, 1978. 27–58.

Zhdanov, V. A. *Tvorcheskaia istoriia "Anny Kareninoi": Materialy i nabliudeniia*. Moscow: Sovetskii pisatel', 1957.

Zytaruk, George J. "D. H. Lawrence's *The Rainbow* and Leo Tolstoy's *Anna Karenina*: An Instance of Literary 'Clinamen.'" W. Jones, *Tolstoi* 225–38.

INDEX

Modern Language Association of America

Approaches to Teaching World Literature

Joseph Gibaldi, series editor

Achebe's Things Fall Apart. Ed. Bernth Lindfors. 1991.
Arthurian Tradition. Ed. Maureen Fries and Jeanie Watson. 1992.
Atwood's The Handmaid's Tale *and Other Works*. Ed. Sharon R. Wilson,
    Thomas B. Friedman, and Shannon Hengen. 1996.
Austen's Pride and Prejudice. Ed. Marcia McClintock Folsom. 1993.
Balzac's Old Goriot. Ed. Michal Peled Ginsburg. 2000.
Baudelaire's Flowers of Evil. Ed. Laurence M. Porter. 2000.
Beckett's Waiting for Godot. Ed. June Schlueter and Enoch Brater. 1991.
Beowulf. Ed. Jess B. Bessinger, Jr., and Robert F. Yeager. 1984.
Blake's Songs of Innocence and of Experience. Ed. Robert F. Gleckner and
    Mark L. Greenberg. 1989.
Boccaccio's Decameron. Ed. James H. McGregor. 2000.
British Women Poets of the Romantic Period. Ed. Stephen C. Behrendt and
    Harriet Kramer Linkin. 1997.
Brontë's Jane Eyre. Ed. Diane Long Hoeveler and Beth Lau. 1993.
Byron's Poetry. Ed. Frederick W. Shilstone. 1991.
Camus's The Plague. Ed. Steven G. Kellman. 1985.
Cather's My Ántonia. Ed. Susan J. Rosowski. 1989.
Cervantes' Don Quixote. Ed. Richard Bjornson. 1984.
Chaucer's Canterbury Tales. Ed. Joseph Gibaldi. 1980.
Chopin's The Awakening. Ed. Bernard Koloski. 1988.
Coleridge's Poetry and Prose. Ed. Richard E. Matlak. 1991.
Conrad's "Heart of Darkness" *and* "The Secret Sharer." Ed. Hunt Hawkins and
    Brian W. Shaffer. 2002.
Dante's Divine Comedy. Ed. Carole Slade. 1982.
Dickens' David Copperfield. Ed. Richard J. Dunn. 1984.
Dickinson's Poetry. Ed. Robin Riley Fast and Christine Mack Gordon. 1989.
Narrative of the Life of Frederick Douglass. Ed. James C. Hall. 1999.
Eliot's Middlemarch. Ed. Kathleen Blake. 1990.
Eliot's Poetry and Plays. Ed. Jewel Spears Brooker. 1988.
Shorter Elizabethan Poetry. Ed. Patrick Cheney and Anne Lake Prescott. 2000.
Ellison's Invisible Man. Ed. Susan Resneck Parr and Pancho Savery. 1989.
English Renaissance Drama. Ed. Karen Bamford and Alexander Leggatt. 2002.
Dramas of Euripides. Ed. Robin Mitchell-Boyask. 2002.
Faulkner's The Sound and the Fury. Ed. Stephen Hahn and Arthur F. Kinney. 1996.
Flaubert's Madame Bovary. Ed. Laurence M. Porter and Eugene F. Gray. 1995.
García Márquez's One Hundred Years of Solitude. Ed. María Elena de Valdés and
    Mario J. Valdés. 1990.

Gilman's "The Yellow Wall-Paper" and Herland. Ed. Denise D. Knight and
    Cynthia J. Davis
Goethe's Faust. Ed. Douglas J. McMillan. 1987.
Hebrew Bible as Literature in Translation. Ed. Barry N. Olshen and
    Yael S. Feldman. 1989.
Homer's Iliad *and* Odyssey. Ed. Kostas Myrsiades. 1987.
Ibsen's A Doll House. Ed. Yvonne Shafer. 1985.
Works of Samuel Johnson. Ed. David R. Anderson and Gwin J. Kolb. 1993.
Joyce's Ulysses. Ed. Kathleen McCormick and Erwin R. Steinberg. 1993.
Kafka's Short Fiction. Ed. Richard T. Gray. 1995.
Keats's Poetry. Ed. Walter H. Evert and Jack W. Rhodes. 1991.
Kingston's The Woman Warrior. Ed. Shirley Geok-lin Lim. 1991.
Lafayette's The Princess of Clèves. Ed. Faith E. Beasley and Katharine Ann
    Jensen. 1998.
Works of D. H. Lawrence. Ed. M. Elizabeth Sargent and Garry Watson. 2001.
Lessing's The Golden Notebook. Ed. Carey Kaplan and Ellen Cronan Rose. 1989.
Mann's Death in Venice *and Other Short Fiction.* Ed. Jeffrey B. Berlin. 1992.
Medieval English Drama. Ed. Richard K. Emmerson. 1990.
Melville's Moby-Dick. Ed. Martin Bickman. 1985.
Metaphysical Poets. Ed. Sidney Gottlieb. 1990.
Miller's Death of a Salesman. Ed. Matthew C. Roudané. 1995.
Milton's Paradise Lost. Ed. Galbraith M. Crump. 1986.
Molière's Tartuffe *and Other Plays.* Ed. James F. Gaines and
    Michael S. Koppisch. 1995.
Momaday's The Way to Rainy Mountain. Ed. Kenneth M. Roemer. 1988.
Montaigne's Essays. Ed. Patrick Henry. 1994.
Novels of Toni Morrison. Ed. Nellie Y. McKay and Kathryn Earle. 1997.
Murasaki Shikibu's The Tale of Genji. Ed. Edward Kamens. 1993.
Pope's Poetry. Ed. Wallace Jackson and R. Paul Yoder. 1993.
Shakespeare's Hamlet. Ed. Bernice W. Kliman. 2001.
Shakespeare's King Lear. Ed. Robert II. Ray. 1986.
Shakespeare's Romeo and Juliet. Ed. Maurice Hunt. 2000.
Shakespeare's The Tempest *and Other Late Romances.* Ed. Maurice Hunt. 1992.
Shelley's Frankenstein. Ed. Stephen C. Behrendt. 1990.
Shelley's Poetry. Ed. Spencer Hall. 1990.
Sir Gawain and the Green Knight. Ed. Miriam Youngerman Miller and
    Jane Chance. 1986.
Spenser's Faerie Queene. Ed. David Lee Miller and Alexander Dunlop. 1994.
Stendhal's The Red and the Black. Ed. Dean de la Motte and Stirling Haig. 1999.
Sterne's Tristram Shandy. Ed. Melvyn New. 1989.
Stowe's Uncle Tom's Cabin. Ed. Elizabeth Ammons and Susan Belasco. 2000.
Swift's Gulliver's Travels. Ed. Edward J. Rielly. 1988.
Thoreau's Walden *and Other Works.* Ed. Richard J. Schneider. 1996.

Tolstoy's Anna Karenina. Ed. Liza Knapp and Amy Mandelker. 2003.
Vergil's Aeneid. Ed. William S. Anderson and Lorina N. Quartarone. 2002.
Voltaire's Candide. Ed. Renée Waldinger. 1987.
Whitman's Leaves of Grass. Ed. Donald D. Kummings. 1990.
Woolf's To the Lighthouse. Ed. Beth Rigel Daugherty and Mary Beth Pringle. 2001.
Wordsworth's Poetry. Ed. Spencer Hall, with Jonathan Ramsey. 1986.
Wright's Native Son. Ed. James A. Miller. 1997.